Lockdown High

Lockdown High

When the Schoolhouse Becomes a Jailhouse

Annette Fuentes

VERSO

London • New York

This edition first published by Verso 2011
© Annette Fuentes 2011

The moral rights of the author have been asserted

1 3 5 7 9 10 8 6 4 2

Verso
UK: 6 Meard Street, London W1F 0EG
US: 20 Jay Street, Suite 1010, Brooklyn, NY 11201
www.versobooks.com

Verso is the imprint of New Left Books

ISBN-13: 978-1-84467-681-1

British Library Cataloguing in Publication Data
A catalogue record for this book is available from the British Library

Library of Congress Cataloging-in-Publication Data
A catalog record for this book is available from the Library of Congress

Typeset in Minon by Hewer Text UK Ltd, Edinburgh
Printed in the US by Quad/Graphics

CONTENTS

INTRODUCTION

Biko Edwards was an eleventh grader at Tilden High School in Brooklyn back in January 2007, and he made a little decision one day that had big consequences. He stayed after class to talk to his math teacher one morning and was a little late walking to chemistry class. The school's assistant principal for security, Val Lewis, blocked his way and ordered him to a detention room for being late. Edwards tried to explain why he was late and why he didn't want to miss chemistry, but Lewis would have none of it. "I turned and went the opposite way, trying to walk to my class," Edwards said, "and he called an officer to arrest me." A school cop arrived on the scene. "Officer Rivera pulled me and slammed my head on a column in the middle of the doorway. I got a little dizzy. Then he sprayed me with Mace and called for backup," Edwards said, recounting his story three months later. Seven officers took the seventeen-year-old boy to jail, where he stayed for twenty-four hours and was booked on five charges. The school suspended him for four days. "Instead of going to class, I end up in jail," he reflected.

The affluent Lower Merion School District in a Philadelphia suburb is known for its abundant student resources and high test scores. So when the district gave laptop computers to each of its 1,800 high schoolers as part of its technology initiative, everyone was pleased. But in November 2009, Harriton High student Blake J. Robbins was reprimanded by his assistant principal for "improper behavior in his home." The Robbins family and the school community soon learned that the laptops' webcams were secretly programmed to transmit what students or anyone else near the laptops were doing—at school or at home. The family filed a class-action lawsuit against the school board and district superintendent, claiming violations of the Fourth Amendment, as well as illegal wiretapping and surveillance. In May 2010, a Philadelphia judge banned the district from such cybermonitoring. The district acknowledged it had snapped 56,000 screen shots from the laptops of forty students, an effort it said was meant to track missing laptops.

In Harrold, Texas, a sleepy farm town where the total student population for all grades is about one hundred and the crime rate is zero, the local school board decided in August 2008 that their teachers could come to school armed. Harrold's two dozen teachers now have the right to bear concealed handguns, an idea radical even in a state known for its embrace of gun rights. Although the new rule got no public vetting and parents were mostly in the dark about its passage, Superintendent David Thweatt said, "Country people are take-care-of-yourself people. They are not under the illusion that the police are there to protect them." Not all parents share Thweatt's attitude, though, or are reassured that teachers who chose to start the new school year with a bang, so to speak, took a forty-hour training class. The school board had considered other options, such as Mace, armed guards, and Tasers, as a precaution against another Columbine, although the town's schools had no history of violence.

The Mobile, Alabama, district attorney had a brainstorm: Why not create a computer database of public school students most likely to end up in prison? Why wait until after the kids get in trouble, when he could profile them before and treat them accordingly? In no time, the DA had fingered more than nine hundred students as potential criminals based on the number of days they were absent or times they were suspended—a small fraction of them had been suspended for having drugs or guns. The DA boasted to the press, "I can tell you by name, address, and phone number the names of the future criminals of this county—before they are in the juvenile justice system and before they are in the criminal justice system." Rationalizing his scheme, he insisted that the point was to connect the youth and their parents with social services to keep them on the straight and narrow. But he also admitted he would use the information to investigate crimes—committed by parents, too.

Savana Redding was an honor student in the eighth grade at Safford Middle School in Safford, Arizona, in October 2003. One day, she was pulled from a class because a classmate had told an assistant principal that Redding, then thirteen, had ibuprofen, a pain medication often used for menstrual cramps but among drugs the school had banned under its zero tolerance rules. What followed was a search by the male administrator and a female nurse who demanded that Redding pull open her bra and underwear to prove she had no hidden pills. No pills were found, but Redding's family filed a suit claiming the search violated her constitutional rights. In June 2009, the US Supreme Court ruled in her favor by eight to one.

Every day in communities across the United States, children and adolescents spend the majority of their waking hours in schools that increasingly have come to resemble places of detention more than places of learning. From metal detectors to drug tests, from increased policing to all-seeing electronic surveillance, the public schools of the twenty-first century reflect a society that has become fixated on crime, security, and violence. Although the fear of crime and—since September 11, 2001—of terrorist acts is a fairly widespread malaise, the preoccupation with security and violence are particularly acute when it comes to children and teenagers.

In a strange paradox that is so American, children are considered both potential victims, vulnerable to dangers from every corner, and perpetrators of great violence and mayhem, demanding strict, preventive discipline. It's been said that one of the best measures of a society's development is the way it treats its children. By that measure, the United States has a long way to go, and at least part of the problem is that we are ambivalent about our kids. In 1997, at the height of a growing collective anxiety about young people and violence, the research and education group Public Agenda undertook to study the public's views of children and adolescents. Public Agenda's starting point was that "something is wrong" with America's kids, identifying such problems as poverty, rising drug use, and teen suicide, and violence in public schools. Its report, "Kids These Days: What Americans Really Think About the Next Generation," portrayed an American public that was critical of, even hostile to younger people—as if they were immigrants from another country invading and destroying true American values. Kids today are rude, irresponsible, and wild, according to two thirds of the survey group, and have a crisis of morals and values. Even young children received scathing criticism as obnoxious and spoiled and materialistic, and lacking respect for their elders. Perhaps the most depressing finding was that nearly 60 percent of the survey pool said that when the younger generation grows up, it will not make the world a better place, and might even make it worse.

In the late 1990s, my work as a journalist started pulling me toward reporting on education, youth, and juvenile justice. The kinds of widespread attitudes on display in the Public Agenda report were dramatically at odds with both my own interactions and experiences with children and teenagers living in New York City and with the true data on youth achievement and crime. I began noticing with greater frequency stories from newspapers all over the country that to my mind seemed freakish. A five-year-old being arrested for bringing a butter knife to school. A teenage girl suspended for bringing Midol to school for her menstrual cramps. A kindergartner suspended for having herbal cough drops that school administrators feared had illegal substances in them. Six-year-olds strip-searched in a classroom when a few dollars went missing from the teacher's desk. These were the kinds of stories that in another time would have been relegated to the section on "bizarre news," the infrequent and titillating man-bites-dog stories.

But I noticed that these stories were no longer rare, and the reactions to them were not shock and dismay but more likely affirmative and approving from people who reflected the attitudes captured in the Public Agenda report. At the time, state and federal lawmakers were in a frenzy about juvenile crime and were revising statutes to allow prosecutors to try juveniles as adults for certain felonies. Taken together the cultural, social, and political currents were running against youth, especially poor and minority kids in urban areas, who were perceived as the greatest threat. But after the Columbine High School tragedy in 1999, all youth came to be seen as "public enemy number one," and the criminalizing trends in juvenile justice that were swirling in the 1990s were by then flooding into public schools. Ironically, as the public's preoccupation swelled, the real trajectory of school violence and juvenile crime began to subside after reaching a peak in the early 1990s.

After reporting and writing about the criminalizing trends affecting our children and youth, with zero tolerance discipline as a main focus, I realized that the phenomenon was too extensive to be captured in a few articles. There was the need for a book to dissect the many and varied ways that children were being hurt and the way that the very foundation of our public school system was being undermined by what I came to view as a "lockdown" approach to security and safety. While it was evident that schools must grapple with issues of violence and safety, it also became clear as I conducted my research that the public's perception of school violence and youth behavior was seriously out of whack with reality. A school shooting like that at Columbine was tragic but extremely rare, and students were and remain safer at school than in their own homes and communities. For example, accidental gun deaths in their homes and neighborhoods claim between one hundred and two hundred young people nineteen years and younger every year. Hysteria, not clear-eyed analysis, has colored the public's understanding and, regrettably, tainted media coverage of school violence. The climate of fear has created ripe conditions for imposing unprecedented restrictions on young people's rights, dignity, and educational freedoms. Zero tolerance has triggered a process that pushes the most vulnerable and academically needy students out of the classroom and into harm's way—what many now call the school-to-prison pipeline. Failing schools breed failing students and place them at risk of falling into the juvenile justice system, especially as policing and the practices of that system increasingly make their way into the schoolhouse. Indeed, it is that two-way flow between the schoolhouse and the jailhouse that I try to expose with reporting and research that shows how the philosophy and practices of the criminal justice system seep into and undermine the very foundations of our public school system. I also highlight the entrenched interests—political and economic—that together have promoted and profited from the transformation of our schools into prisonlike institutions where children are treated like suspects. These interests have clout and will pose a challenge to those seeking change.

But there is hope and a growing movement to end the zero tolerance, lockdown approach to public school safety. This book also profiles the students, educators, psychologists, legal advocates, and community organizers who envision a different way to provide safe and secure schools, a way that restores public schools to their principal function as places of learning where mistakes and misbehavior are opportunities to teach, and the disciplinary process is integral to education, not an impediment to it.

1 A BRIEF HISTORY OF SCHOOL VIOLENCE

The next Friday, Danny again had a long list of offenses chalked up against him, whispering and giggling, mainly; and after school he was dragged into the outside hall to be beaten into another week of physical misery. This time the teacher had her own switches . . . and she wore out three of these on him. As she reached for the fourth, the boy stepped back and pulled his knife from his pocket.

"If you hit me again—I'll cut you to pieces," he shouted, opening the long blade and squaring himself for a finish fight.

For an instant the teacher stood dumbfounded. She raised her whip and took a step forward, but insanely angry as she was, she saw something in the boy's eyes that fortunately arrested her step . . . after a moment's hesitation, she backed into the school room and closed the door.

—From the memoir *Sod and Stubble: The Story of a Kansas Homestead*
by John Isle

Long before the term *school violence* entered popular parlance, before metal detectors became fixtures at the schoolhouse door, before the Lockdown High approach to school safety gained currency, conflict and violence of one sort or another were part of this country's education system. Prone as we are to nostalgia about our history, schools of the past are imagined as Norman Rockwell havens of quaint custom and benign behavior, in vivid contrast to the perception of today's schools as drug- and weapon-riddled hellholes where teachers daily risk their necks and worthy children can't get an education.

But for as long as there have been public schools—district schools or the common schools of early American educational history—there has been chaos and control, crime and punishment in the classroom as teacher and student have waged their power struggles and defined their roles. The rhythm of switch and ferule—even the cat-o'-nine-tails—provided the meter by which the early schoolmaster or -mistress imparted the three Rs and obedience to misbehaving youngsters. Challenging the master's supremacy was likewise common practice among older students like Danny who dared to teach the teachers a lesson about the limits of their authority. The jackknife, found in the pockets of many a farm boy, was as common in some schoolhouses, no doubt, as McGuffey's Readers.

The dialectic of dissent and discipline in classrooms has always existed because the schoolhouse, while a safer haven for children than most places, has never been immune to the turmoil and changes swirling outside its doors. But more than that, the genesis of the public school system was as a solution to the upheavals that characterized the late eighteenth and early nineteenth centuries. The industrializing nation witnessed growing social tumult and economic quakes as factory supplanted farm and rural areas hemorrhaged population to incipient urban enclaves. The order and authority that once derived from strong family and community networks frayed. Schools would be institutions of control and socialization, turning a potentially disruptive population into productive, law-abiding citizens.

Efforts at the state and local levels to create common schools were propelled as much by fears of social disorder and burgeoning crime as by high-minded ideals about forging an educated citizenry. This was especially true in cities of the northeast, where immigrants from Ireland and Germany streamed during the mid-1800s, joining displaced farm families and youths. Education reformers of the time, such as Horace Mann, were clear in their philosophy. At an 1842 convention of school superintendents in Utica, New York, which Mann attended, the prominent civic leader Rev. Alonzo Potter stated his philosophy for supporting public schools: "*Resolved,* That the best police for our cities, the lowest insurance of our houses, the firmest security for our banks, the most effective means of preventing pauperism, vice and crime, and the only sure defense of our country, are our common schools." Asked to respond to Potter's proposal, Mann gave it his stamp of approval.[1]

Given this background, it makes sense that the first compulsory-education law, passed in Massachusetts in 1852, involved reform schools—precursors to juvenile jails, in a sense. Aimed at youth who were not in school or gainfully employed, whom the law defined as truants, it permitted the police to scoop them up from the hurly-burly of Boston street life and its temptations of vice and crime. Almost an early version of current day racial profiling in law enforcement, this law targeted Irish children, who, along with their mostly impoverished families, were seen as contributing to social disorder and crime. According to one report on truants in 1853, 559 foreign-born youth were sent to reform schools for truancy, while 98 Americans were.[2]

The late nineteenth century brought promotion of compulsory-education laws for all children and youth by the same civic-minded reformers and educators, with the same rationale of securing social order. As one Chicago Board of Education member stated the issue in 1868: "We should rightfully have the power to arrest all these little beggars, loafers, and vagabonds that infest our city, take them from the streets and place them in schools where they are compelled to receive education and learn moral principles. . . . We certainly should not permit a reckless and indifferent part of our population to rear their children in ignorance to become a criminal and lawless class within our community."[3]

SCHOOLHOUSE RULES

The one-room schoolhouse that characterized most district schools around the country in the 1800s was distant from the reality of truant Irish youth on Boston or New York streets. But whether in a Midwestern log schoolhouse or in a brick city schoolhouse, student misbehavior and teacher discipline were an ever-present feature of education. By today's standards, methods of discipline could border on outright torture, and some incidents of student defiance would land such a perpetrator in police custody were he or she in a modern classroom. Imagine the outcome for a student in a contemporary classroom pulling a knife on a teacher as Danny did in that Kansas schoolroom! He would be arrested by school police, suspended for weapons possession, and face criminal prosecution.

Rural students attended school for several months during the winter, when their labors weren't needed at the family farm, and sometimes for a period during the summer. Depending on the population, forty or more students might be crammed into the room and supervised by one teacher, male or female, who might not be much older than the oldest students. For children and adolescents used to physical activity and the relative freedom of farm life, the constraints of the classroom and its requisite obedience could be as challenging as learning their letters. Sitting rod-straight on hard plank benches, paying rapt attention to their lessons, students had to battle natural instincts to fidget and play or risk the wrath of the schoolmaster.[4]

Rules of conduct could be straightjacket strict, transgressions almost impossible for youngsters to avoid. As the forerunners to current zero tolerance school discipline codes, the school rules of yesteryear were equally harsh and at odds with youthful natures. Schoolmasters often posted lists of infractions and the punishments they would elicit. In Stokes County, North Carolina, in 1848, one school's rules listed forty-seven prohibitions, including "Boys & Girls Playing Together," punishable with four lashes; "Telling Tales Out of School," eight lashes; "Telling Lyes (*sic*)," seven lashes; "For Misbehaving to Girls," ten lashes; and "Making Swings & Swinging on Them," seven lashes. Playing cards, gambling or betting, nicknaming other students, and fighting or quarreling were also prohibited and would draw whippings.[5]

The deterrent effect of such disciplinary codes was questionable, and many accounts from early school days tell of brutal punishments freely administered. In an 1833 memoir, Warren Burton recalled his education in a Massachusetts schoolhouse in the early 1800s with less than fondness for Mehitabel Holt, his teacher for the third summer of instruction.

> She kept order, for her punishments were horrible, especially to us little ones. She dungeoned us in that windowless closet just for a whisper. She tied us to her chair post for an hour because sportive nature tempted our fingers and toes into something like play. If we were restless on our seats, wearied of our posture, fretted by the heat, or sick of the unintelligible lesson, a twist of the ear or a snap on the head, from her thimbled finger, reminded us that sitting perfectly still, was the most important virtue of a little boy in school.

But Holt's methods paled in comparison with those of "the *particular* master," Burton's teacher for his fifth winter school session.

> The first morning of school he read us a long list of the regulations to be observed in school, and out. . . . Half the time was spent calling up scholars for little misdemeanors, trying to make them confess their faults, and promise stricter obedience or in devising punishments and inflicting them. Some were ferruled on the hand, some were whipped with a rod

on the back, some were compelled to hold out at arm's length, the largest book that could be found, or a great leaden inkstand, till muscle and nerve, bone and marrow were tortured with the continued exertion . . . Another mode of punishment, the anti-whispering process, was setting the jaws at painful distance apart, by inserting a chip, perpendicularly between the teeth . . ." Burton noted that the particular master's punishments were not unusual because "the prevailing opinion among both teachers and parents [was] that boys and girls *would* play and be mischievous at any rate, and that consequently masters *must* punish them in some way or other.[6]

In another bloodcurdling account, a writer in a teacher's monthly tells of his experience in a school held in the basement of a Gothic church in 1829.

Before there was any Society for the Prevention of Cruelty to Animals, it was my misfortune to be a school-boy in the city of New York. I mention this last benevolent institution, since if there then had been such a thing, there also might have been some society, or some law, for the prevention of cruelty to school-boys.

The schoolmaster delegated instruction to an older boy known as the "Dictator" but reserved the dispensing of punishment for himself.

On the wall, behind the master, in full view of the whole school, to keep the scholars in perpetual remembrance, hung a cat-o'-nine-tails of enormous size. The handle had the dimensions of a farmer's flail. The lashes were of corresponding length and as thick as your finger; it took both hands to wield it. This was taken down to be used on extra occasions only; but a single-handed one was in constant service. . . . In addition to these, erected on the platform to the right of the master, was another apparatus of the system, called "The Iron Bar." This was a rail of iron, about three feet long and about an inch square at its transverse section . . . The offending boy was made to mount upon it with his bare feet. He was allowed no means of balancing himself . . . If he fell off, or let one foot touch the platform, the master, sitting within striking distance would lash him on again with a savage stroke of the "Cat."

Like Warren Burton, this writer forgave the schoolmaster's classroom cruelties: "[He] acted in accordance with the opinions and desires of those to whom he was immediately accountable. He no doubt thought he was doing his duty." But as to the effectiveness of the methods, the writer was dubious and suggested that the harsh school environment had only prepared some of his classmates for more of the same as adults: "And the hundred and fifty scholars, where are they? I have never heard that any one of them rose above the common walks of life. Many grew up to be hard cases. Having graduated at the severest of penitentiaries, they found no terror in the idea of State-prison."[7]

By the late nineteenth century, draconian punishment by school-masters was no longer unquestioningly accepted in an atmosphere of educational reform. Educators debated the limits of school discipline in their journals, and the courts joined the fray by considering the legal limits of a teacher's physical authority. By 1865, for example, courts in Vermont and Massachusetts had found permissible the use of the ferule, while Indiana's Supreme Court had outlawed it. An article in the *American Educational Monthly* published that year noted that "Discipline, school discipline, government, —the words are heard at every gathering of teachers and school commissioners from Maine to Mexico . . ." The shifting standards meant that "From some schools the rod is banished, while in others it is considered that the sparing of the rod is the spoiling of the child, and a contempt of the Holy Writ . . ."

REBELLIONS AND SHOWDOWNS

In a time when police officers patrol public schools and effect arrests for pushing and shoving—now defined as disorderly conduct—it's astounding to learn just how disorderly students could be back in the supposedly bucolic days of the one-room schoolhouse. Yet student-teacher confrontations over authority and punishments were not only common, but almost a tradition. The practice of "turning the teacher out" was a test of strength and wills in which older, usually male students tried to boot the teacher out of the classroom. There were rarely serious repercussions, and certainly no arrests. Loulie Ayer Beall wrote of a memorable incident from her school days in Webster County, Nebraska, in 1880, when students ganged up on a "stern and dictatorial" teacher who was whacking a classmate with an eighteen-inch ruler.

[T]he boy positively refused to obey, saying, "I won't do it!" before an assembly of forty pupils. Quickly the teacher snatched up the long black ruler and stalked to the boy's desk, declaring, "We'll see about that!" A hush pervaded the room; all eyes were turned in the direction of the scene about to be enacted. A calloused hand was outstretched before the teacher-dictator . . . the strokes numbered five. "Now will you go?" "Never" was the only word spoken. Again the ruler was raised . . . a dozen boys sprang from their seats as if by signal, seized the uplifted arm, wrested the ruler from the master's hand, and thrust the hated ruler into the stove. . . . The larger boys caught up the teacher and carried him out of doors, rolled him over and over in the snow, and admonished him to "study his lesson" for the rest of the afternoon.

Beall noted that school was held as usual the next day, with no mention of the incident, and "little comment was made concerning it in the neighborhood."[8]

There was almost an expectation that students, especially boys, would challenge the schoolmaster as something of a rite of passage. In his recollection of school days in 1815 in "the wilds of Clearfield County, Pennsylvania," I. L. Kephart wrote of "barring out the teacher" six days before Christmas to persuade him to buy holiday treats for the students. Barricading the door of the log cabin schoolhouse, armed with wooden slabs, Kephart and his classmates repelled the master when he returned from his lunchtime.

The conditions of surrender were presented to him. He read them, indignantly pronounced them outrageous . . . and declared he was coming in if he had to pull the house down . . . the master started for his boarding-place, and soon returned with an ax on his shoulder. We knew this meant business, and the excitement from within was rapidly rising to a white heat. Some were crying, some were alternately pleading and demanding that the door be opened, while the more courageous were loudly asserting their determination to keep him out at all hazards. . . . At this juncture, the teacher vigorously assaulted the door, pounding it with the ax until he split it in several places. This availing him nothing, he climbed the roof and commenced tearing away the clapboards . . . we sent the end of the slab through the roof with such force that, striking him in the breast, we sent him clear over the eaves to the ground. This caused a shout of triumph to ascend from below which was almost deafening. True, he might have been killed by the fall, but that was a secondary consideration for us.

The student takeover ended after several days and, as in Beall's account, there were no consequences for their rebellion. The schoolmaster was "in a jolly good humor, and everything proceeded as if there had been no 'barring out.' " He even bought them ten pounds of loaf sugar at the term's end.[9]

THE BATH SCHOOL DISASTER

No history, brief or otherwise, of school violence would be complete without the tale of the Bath, Michigan, school tragedy. Most people consider the Columbine High School incident of 1999 to be the worst-ever example of school violence, with its total of fifteen deaths. But the 1927 Bath incident, in which forty-four died, had the highest human toll and perhaps most diabolical plot. The former school board member and farmer Andrew Kehoe dynamited the district school, killing thirty-eight pupils. Kehoe, who'd spent months plotting, was angry about soaring school taxes and the impending foreclosure on his farm. He aimed, according to newspaper accounts, to destroy the whole school and kill all 260 students. Kehoe dynamited his own car, with himself in it, as the school burned, but not before murdering his wife and setting his farm ablaze. The terrible scale of Kehoe's destruction and its aftermath are recounted in minute detail in an eyewitness account titled *The Bath School Disaster*, self-published by the Bath resident Monty J. Ellsworth. If ever an incident deserved the categorization of "school violence," the Bath Disaster does.

While school violence is usually associated with actions carried out by students against other students and teachers within the school-house—the Columbine scenario—it encompasses a wider array of actions and perpetrators. The outside intruder, like Kehoe, who targets students, teachers or other school staff, is also part of the phenomenon. In September 2006, a drifter entered a Colorado high school and held six female students hostage, finally killing himself and one girl. Five days later, in early October, an apparently mentally unbalanced man, not unlike Andrew Kehoe, walked into a one-room Amish schoolhouse in Lancaster, Pennsylvania, and shot to death five girls and then himself. Charles Roberts, age thirty-two, was a dairy truck driver with no connection to the school, no criminal record, and no apparent reason for wanting to harm the children. These incidents generated headline coverage and much speculation about the attackers' motivations—never explained—and fears that they were the start of a murderous trend of intruder school violence. No such trend was initiated, and, thankfully, criminologists and school safety experts were loath to forecast any surge in intruder crimes.

JUVENILE DELINQUENTS IN A BLACKBOARD JUNGLE

Post–World War II saw another period of upheavals and shifts in the country's economic and social order. A mass migration from the south brought new populations of blacks to the northern cities, Puerto Ricans began a major migration to the mainland, and returning veterans came home to a different world. Women who had filled the factory jobs vacated by GI Joe were booted back to the domestic sphere. Cities were bulging and the suburbs were about to become the next latest thing in residential development. An old problem with a new urgency called juvenile delinquency was emerging to the alarm of psychologists and sociologists, and to the vexation of parents and schools. The 1950s, for all its veneer of nuclear family normalcy, was also a time of youth gangs in urban areas and of the alienated youth immortalized by James Dean in *Rebel Without a Cause*. Delinquency was blamed for rising crime rates in New York and other cities by "youthful offenders." New York's police commissioner reported a 32 percent increase from 1955 to 1956 in arrests of youths under age sixteen, and the FBI estimated similar national trends.[10]

Researchers of this era cranked out volumes on the causes and characteristics of delinquency, calling it "one of the most critical problems confronting the American people." Social disorganization was to blame, declared the psychologist Martin Neumeyer. "Maladjustments seem to be the inevitable consequences of rapid and unequal changes in the social order. Juveniles, in particular, seem to be affected in an unusual way by these rapidly changing conditions."[11] Viewed as part mental illness and part social disease, delinquency was blamed on such factors as broken homes, poverty, "cultural differences," and even comic books, television, and movies. The missing mother and father were to blame, according to the psychologist Richard McCann: Delinquent children "have been crippled by an inadequate concept of themselves, a distorted self-image. In many cases it has been caused by a lack of stable, meaningful relationships and a consequent deficiency of love."[12]

A landmark 1950 study by Sheldon and Eleanor Glueck compared five hundred delinquent and nondelinquent children. Delinquents, they found, were more likely to repeat grades and drop out of school, and typically did not get along well with their schoolmates. They "misbehaved more extensively than did non-delinquents."[13] The Gluecks' portrait of young delinquents was brought to life vividly in the 1953 novel *The Blackboard Jungle*, by Evan Hunter, a pulp novelist of minor talent and florid prose. The jungle is North Manual Trades High School in New York City, and the inhabitants are poor white, black, and Puerto Rican boys relegated to a vocational school. The ostensible hero is a Navy veteran, Richard Dadier, who becomes an English teacher after returning from the war and learns his tough-guy demeanor and earnest desire to teach are no match for his unruly students: "A last-period class is always a restless one, and when a boy is thinking about the money he can be out earning, it can become a torture, even if the English teacher is the best English teacher in the world—which Rick was not . . . Nor can you push around a nineteen-year-old boy when he sometimes outweighs you and outmuscles you and outreaches you."

Dadier's idealism clashes with the veteran teacher Solly's view of the students and vocational education: "This is the garbage can of the educational system. Every vocational school in the city. You put them all together and you got one big, fat, overflowing garbage can. And you want to know what our job is? Our job is to sit on the lid of the garbage can and see that none of the filth overflows into the streets." And much like new teachers of the common schools who faced disciplinary challenges, Dadier experiences a more modern version of "turning out the teacher," when a group of students ambush him outside school. "They gave it to him until they felt they'd squashed his scrotum flat, and then they gave it to him equally around the head. He stopped struggling at last, and they grabbed his briefcase and dumped everything into the gutter, tearing the papers and the notebook, and then ripping the stitching on the bag . . .

The kid with the knife in his hands got ideas, but the sport was over now, and when the sport is over you get the hell out of the neighborhood before the cops show on the scene."

Disciplinary policies at North Manual were explained to Dadier by the administrator Max Schaefer: "Clobber the bastards," he said. "It's the only thing that works. What do you think happens at home when they open their yaps? Pow, right on the noggin. That's the only language they understand."

Although Dadier believes he is above physical discipline, he is tempted because "despite any edicts about corporal punishment, there were a good many vocational school kids who got clobbered every day, and when the heavy hand of someone like Captain Max Schaefer clobbers, the clobberee knows he's been clobbered, but good. Clobbering, then, was one accepted means of establishing discipline in a trade school."

Hunter's novel is cartoonlike in its caricature of the teenagers in North Manual. But *The Blackboard Jungle* was accurate in reflecting the stereotypes and class biases of the time that fed white, middle-class America's fears of urban youth and a growing youth culture, which would burst out of conformity in another decade.

ENTER "SCHOOL VIOLENCE"

It's impossible to understand the history of public schools and of school violence without situating them in the larger picture of the nation's history and the prevailing economic, political, and social currents that shaped it. The fear of social disorder and swelling immigrant populations that gripped the middle class of the nineteenth century motivated reformers such as Horace Mann to champion public schools. In successive generations, educational debates would mirror contemporary concerns about workforce preparation and the need for vocational schools, and about racial segregation in schools. In the mid-to-late 1960s, the irresistible forces acting on public schools were varied and potent. Social protest movements, including those focused on war, civil rights, student rights, and black, Puerto Rican, and Chicano nationalism, were in play. At the same time, in urban areas especially, increasing residential racial segregation and economic hardship for the poor fueled crime and violence. Race riots exploded in Watts, a Los Angeles neighborhood, and in New

York City, in 1966 and a year later in Newark and Detroit. Schools were, not surprisingly, one institution where these combustible trends reached their flashpoint.

It was during this period, in fact, that the words *school* and *violence* were first joined in news reporting. The stories had nothing to do with the Columbine-type incident that's come to define the term. Instead, they described a nation whose public schools, especially in cities, were gripped by racial turmoil and the property crimes that were a side effect of it. Perhaps the first news media reference to "school violence" appeared in a *Los Angeles Times* op ed published in April 1968, which criticized Mayor Richard J. Daley of Chicago for his reaction to riots sparked by the assassination of Rev. Martin Luther King, Jr. Rioters set swaths of Chicago ablaze, eleven people were killed, and eleven thousand city police, seven thousand National Guard soldiers, and five hundred federal troops were called in. Daley later ordered police to shoot to kill arsonists and shoot to maim looters—even children among them could be gassed, Daley ordered. The writer noted that in Chicago's "West Side ghetto," which was predominantly black, "the level of school violence, always high, was rising dangerously."[14]

In New York City, racial tensions prompted similar student clashes and reporting on "school violence." In March 1969, the *New York Times* debuted the term *school violence* in an article on Mayor John Lindsay's reactions to escalating "school disorders" and parent protests at public schools around the city. Lindsay, considered a political liberal, faced racial conflict flaring out of control: black parents in two Harlem elementary schools began a boycott to demand appointment of a black school supervisor; black and Puerto Rican students "rampaged" through Eastern District High School in Brooklyn in protest against a white Jewish administrator accused of "harassing" them; and the United Federation of Teachers, a predominantly white union, protested against the protestors. Lindsay anticipated a greater police presence in the schools to address the crisis, the *Times* reported. The student and parent protests, while violent and disruptive, were an urgent response to rapidly segregating New York City public schools and their deteriorating physical conditions. Eastern District, the article noted, was 65 percent Puerto Rican and 25 percent black and bursting at its ancient seams with 3,080 students crammed into a building meant for 1,900.[15]

Eight months later, the *Times* ran an article about the continuing "racial unrest and disorders" in the city's schools. The superintendent had launched an "inquiry" intended to improve race relations between black and white students and "eradicate racial tension and hostility in the school neighborhoods." The article detailed violent incidents at Wingate High in Brooklyn: a fifteen-year-old white student was slashed but uninjured, Molotov cocktails were planted in a gym locker, black students set off fire bombs in the cafeteria, and white students were beaten outside the school. Wingate, once "a model of integration," the superintendent stated, became 70 percent black after rezoning sent black students from overcrowded schools in the Bedford-Stuyvesant and Brownsville neighborhoods. "We've got to get back to the goal of integration," the superintendent said. "It would be a shame to turn this into a segregated school."[16]

Washington, D.C.'s public schools likewise were gripped by racial turmoil and violence. In January 1969, the *Washington Post* reported the fatal shooting of an assistant principal at Cardozo High School by three teens who robbed the school's safe.[17] In the fall, fights broke out between black and white students at several high schools in Prince George's County, Maryland. In January 1970, the *Post* reported on the first death of a student in the D.C. schools, in an accidental shooting that occurred when two fifteen-year-olds at Hine Junior High were looking at a gun during lunchtime. The article noted that the two deaths were not connected, but called both "part of a pattern of violence that is afflicting many schools in Washington and other big cities." A week later, the *Post* reported that racial fights had broken out at DuVal High after "racial tensions had been building for days," and police arrested twenty-two students. The same day, the D.C. school administration announced the appointment of a new, full-time director of school safety. A day later, police were brought into the city's public schools for the first time in their history, a move denounced by the teachers' union president, who said, "You cannot dispense education under armed guard."[18]

School violence broke into the national news as an issue bedeviling the entire country when the media publicized a report on school violence from the U.S. Senate Subcommittee to Investigate Juvenile Delinquency. The committee's report, which was the first national study to name and examine school violence, surveyed 110 school districts around the country and found "sharp increases in specific categories of crime and violence." The Dodd report, named for Senator Thomas J. Dodd of Connecticut, the committee's chair, found that the number of homicides in those schools had increased from fifteen in 1964 to twenty-six in 1968. (Those figures are staggeringly high considering that they come from a fraction of all school districts; in 1999, the year of Columbine, the *national* total of school-related homicides was *thirty-six*.) A *Times* article about the Dodd report also stated that more schools were hiring private guards because of "such incidents, coupled with student disruptions and evidence of racial polarization at some schools." The causes of school violence, the report claimed, were the same as those causing violence in general society: poverty, physical deterioration of housing and surroundings, racial and ethnic concentration, and high unemployment and high population density, among other factors.[19] A *Post* article stated that the Dodd report "said it was a myth that most of the violence was racially directed," because most incidents "involved violence by whites against whites or Negroes against Negroes."[20]

The fact that a Senate study framed school violence primarily as crimes against property and persons, distinct from racial clashes and political protests, indicates how fearful government was of the era's volatility. Fear of popular uprisings, especially among youth, wasn't paranoia; it was logical. The confluence of black activism, campus protests, antiwar demonstrations, and urban riots shook the government to its core. But some observers saw the connections, if through a jaundiced, conservative lens. The *Washington Post* columnists Rowland Evans and Robert Novak wrote, a week before the Dodd report was released, that public high schools were becoming a "battleground" of racial turmoil. "No single high school disturbance has the magnitude of a Berkeley rebellion or a Watts riot to stir national imagination," they said, but schools were becoming "the most violence-prone and divisive battleground of American society" as a "spontaneous reflection of national racial tensions and black militancy." The duo listed a half-dozen incidents of "Negro students" assaulting white students, calling them examples of "a national blackboard jungle dominated by racial hatred." The problem, Evans and Novak said, was not the influence of the Black Panthers or Students for a Democratic Society or any extremist groups. No, it was "the militancy now instilled in black youths," which unless controlled would steel "middle-class white determination against racially integrated schools, North and South."[21]

Their analysis was skewed by bias, but the columnists were right about high schools: they were hotbeds of all kinds of activity, not simply the racial clashes Evans and Novak singled out. A study released around the same time as the Dodd report by the National School Public Relations Association, titled "High School Student Unrest," found that "59 percent of high schools and 56 percent of junior highs had experienced some form of protest by January of last year."[22] These public school protests did indeed mirror the college protests rocking campuses from Berkeley to Kent State to Columbia. In many cities and suburbs, high school students brought the spirit of protest inside the schoolhouse over the issues that were relevant to their lives and in ways that befitted their experience and circumstances. They walked out of classes as part of the nationally planned war moratorium of 1972. They protested dress codes as restrictions on their freedom of expression. Black students demanded black administrators and the inclusion of black history in their curricula. They staged walkouts when Reverend King was assassinated in 1968. In cities such as Washington, D.C., New York, and Chicago, where poverty and segregation fostered racial unrest, school violence and disruptions were also manifested as crimes against property and people. Alienation from schools that didn't speak to their experiences could spark a walkout or just plain vandalism. All of it, though, was a sign of the turbulent times.

In the early 1970s, racial segregation in the public schools was addressed in a series of U.S. Supreme Court rulings that built on the historic 1954 *Brown v. Board of Education* decision. Interestingly, desegregation and the busing plans that often accompanied it did not produce a new round of school violence among black and white students. The Boston example of pitched battles between white residents opposed to busing and proponents of integration was the exception, not the rule. In his 1978 study of busing, Gary Orfield noted that "while the fear of violence often plays a large role in local debates over desegregation plans, a recent Justice Department report indicates that desegregation seldom produces increases in school violence and even lowers the level when a local plan specifically addresses the problem. . . . The Detroit school system had fewer racial incidents than before . . . students usually adjusted rapidly to desegregated schools, particularly at the elementary level. Most of the violence was among adults outside the school and it diminished after the transition."[23]

As the activism of the 1960s and early '70s receded, different currents outside the schoolhouse came flowing through its doors: the economic downturn of the mid-1970s brought with it a bubble in violent and property crimes. Schools were now permanently fixed on the radar of government officials and bureaucrats as one locus of crime trends worthy of study. So, in 1978, Secretary of Health, Education and Welfare Joseph Califano released findings of a three-year study of school crime. And like so many government-financed studies of school violence to come, Califano's report offered an odd mix of scary statistics and sobering perspective. Teenagers ran a greater risk of being robbed, assaulted, or otherwise becoming victims of violence at school than at any other time, the report stated. Yet Califano also offered that while the problem of school crime "remains extremely serious," the study found vandalism and violence little changed from 1971 to 1976, with some improvement in urban areas. The HEW study also found, not surprisingly, that in communities where violence and crime were high, schools also had higher rates of violence and crime—and that held true in urban, rural and suburban areas.[24] Despite the nuanced findings and clear connections between what occurred outside and inside the schoolhouse, the HEW report reflected an emerging consensus among policy makers: school violence was a growing social ill, distinct from crime in general, and that youth engaged in it were a breed apart. But the statistical jump in assaults and robberies was more a blip than a tsunami, and a relative increase could not reverse the fact that the overwhelming majority of students then, as now, were safe in school and faced a greater likelihood of harm at home or in their communities.

SUPERPREDATORS AND STUDENTS GONE WILD

The decade of the 1980s ushered in an entirely new era, as conservatism began its ascension to power in government and out. Ronald Reagan began his two-term presidency and initiated radical changes in social and economic policy. A crack-cocaine epidemic infected many cities around the country with an accompanying spike in violent crime through the early 1990s. Between 1984 and 1993, arrest rates for homicides more than doubled; aggravated assault arrests in 1992 were nearly double the 1980 rate.[25] The Reagan Administration made crime and drugs among its chief domestic and foreign policy issues, and school violence was part of the agenda.

In 1984, Attorney General Edwin Meese created the National School Safety Center to reduce crime and violence and improve discipline and attendance at schools. It was the first of what would be many public and private centers created around the country to address, study, prevent, and fix the problem—the seed of an embryonic school-violence industry, so to speak. The center was born in controversy, however, when Justice Department insiders leaked information to journalists that cast Meese's actions in a different light. In a classic example of pork barrel spending, the $3.9 million grant went to George Nicholson, a close friend of the attorney general, to establish the center at Pepperdine University, which had received private donations from both Meese and Reagan that year.[26] Nothing came of the revelations and the NSSC exists today as a sort of clearinghouse.

Reagan also launched the War on Drugs, heralded with the Drug-Free America Act of 1986. With it came the "zero tolerance" approach to sentencing offenders of drug-related crimes. That year, Congress passed the Drug-Free Schools and Communities Act, a program within the Department of Education that has funneled roughly half a million dollars a year to states and localities to reduce drug use. Given the federal drumbeat and frightening statistics, it's not surprising that the national preoccupation became violent crime, especially drug-related violent crime and the escalation of gun violence associated with drug trafficking. Here's a measure of how dramatically crime came to dominate the public psyche: In 1982, 3 percent of adults surveyed in a national poll named crime and violence as the country's main problems. By 1994, more than 50 percent did, and violence was named as the chief problem of public schools.[27] As shown by the statistics on reported incidents of violence and crime discussed below, the public fears of school violence and youth were disproportionate to any actual rise in the problem.

The Reagan years laid the foundation for the Lockdown High model. But it was during the Clinton administration, ironically, that the bricks and mortar of the school-as-prison theory and practice were applied to the problems of discipline and safety. Ironic both because Clinton was considered a liberal and because the actual incidence of school violence, as well as youth crime in general, was beginning to crest in 1992—the year he took office. By then, though, the criminal justice system was on growth hormones, revved up by draconian laws from Congress and state legislatures that were filling the nation's ever-growing prison system, mostly with offenders of drug-related crimes. Young offenders, especially, came into the crosshairs of legislators and prosecutors who were egged on by the widely quoted criminologists James Q. Wilson, John DiIulio, and James Alan Fox. Wilson used dubious population projections to forewarn of a "cloud that the winds will soon bring over us," tens of thousands of juvenile thieves, muggers, and killers. DiIulio pumped up the hysteria with his own predictions of a new breed of young criminal, whom he dubbed the "superpredator." And Fox jumped on the fearmongering bandwagon with warnings of a "blood bath" of juvenile crime.[28] Their concern was focused on a particular portion of the juvenile population—black and Latino males in urban settings—and their language revealed their not-so-subtle biases. The political response to the hype was not to prevent the supposed future crime wave. It was to crack down on youth. Between 1992 and 1995, forty-one states passed laws making it easier to prosecute juveniles in adult criminal court. (Today, all fifty states have such laws.) In more than half of the states, children younger than fourteen can be tried as adults for some crimes, and thirteen states have no minimum age for transferring a youth to adult court.

School violence, especially in urban areas, assumed a prominent place in the national fixation on juvenile crime. A 1993 *New York Times* article about New York City noted the "spread of guns and youth violence into schools." The article mentioned a parent boycott to protest hallway violence in Eastern District High School—the same Brooklyn school that twenty-four years earlier was the site of protests by black and Puerto Rican students against perceived racism.[29] Over just one generation, the nature of school violence had morphed to reflect a different society outside the schoolhouse doors. The social protest and racial and ethnic rights movements of the 1960s and '70s had faded. The crack-fueled drug wars of many urban areas sent violence and guns coursing through neighborhoods. Schools in those neighborhoods were not insulated from the dangers, and any news reports of crime in schools contributed to the public's perception that young people and schools were dangerous—especially in cities. But there were no statistics at the time to prove it.

This time, the official response at every level—from school boards to state legislatures on up to the White House and Congress—matched the widespread fear of youth violence. In 1994, President Clinton took Reagan's Drug Free Schools Act and went it one better, creating the Safe and Drug Free Schools and Communities Act, adding violence-prevention funding to the agenda of the legislation. The same year, he signed the Gun Free Schools Act, which required states to enact their own zero tolerance laws for weapons possession by students, which would be punishable by mandatory expulsion. Clinton followed the law with a presidential directive that encouraged school districts to adopt policies requiring school uniforms for students as a way to reduce violence and promote discipline, and ordered the Department of Education (DOE) to distribute a uniforms manual. Clinton also initiated an annual report on school safety produced jointly by the DOE and the Department of Justice, called "Indicators of School Crime and Safety." It was the first effort to collect data from schools nationally in order to track the actual incidence of crimes and violence. It has been published since 1998, with data on victimizations of students and teachers, discipline, and police actions, and its release usually prompts the news media to report key findings. Under Clinton, an entire multiagency, legislatively driven school violence and safety bureaucracy was elaborated with its requisite millions in annual public funding.

The White House set an agenda that reinforced and inflated the view that schools and students were out of control, as a political response to the public clamor about a perceived problem. At the local school district level, administrators and school boards responded to parent and teacher fears of violence and disruption, whether real or imagined. A 1995 survey by the American Federation of Teachers of school districts in two hundred of the largest U.S. cities indicated not only an entrenched and widespread fear of student violence, but also an embrace of a penal-system approach to the problem: 95 percent of respondents employed security personnel; 59 percent had metal detectors; and 53 percent had installed security cameras.

JOHNNY GOT A GUN

This fear and loathing of student violence and disorderly schools could have come to a low simmer, ultimately evaporating, just as school crime and violence itself had been diminishing. After all, the downward trend was unmistakable for anyone who payed attention to those annual reports on school crime and safety. Mirroring the same decline in crime experienced in the general population, youth crime overall began to plummet after its apex in 1993. For youth homicides, the numbers are dramatic: from 1993 to 1998, juvenile homicide arrests dropped by 56 percent, reaching their lowest rate since the FBI began recording this statistic in 1964.[30] School crime echoed this trend: Between 1992 and 1998, the rate of nonfatal violent crimes for students ages twelve to eighteen dropped from 48 per 1,000 students, to 43 per 1,000.[31] From 1995 to 1999, the percentage of students in that age group who reported being victims of theft or violent crime decreased from 10 percent to 8 percent, a trend most prominent among middle-school students, who are often characterized as the most difficult. Over that same time span, students were feeling safer, with 5 percent in 1999 saying they avoided one or more places in their school, compared to 9 percent in 1995.[32] Even these small numbers suggest that the public's view of schools as dangerous was out of proportion to the reality for 90 percent of students during those years with higher rates of reported incidents.

As for violent deaths at schools—the boogeyman of the school-violence nightmare—there simply is no real trend at all. In the 1992–1993 school year (the first year such data were collected) there were fifty-seven "school-associated deaths," and that included thirty-four students killed by other students and six student suicides; the rest were teachers and other school employees. The total dipped over the next few years, and then reached fifty-seven again in 1997–1998. The 1998–1999 school year, the year of Columbine, would have had the lowest number of school deaths on record—twenty-five—but for the fifteen deaths in that tragic incident. According to the National Center for Education Statistics, the DOE agency that copublishes the annual school crime and safety report, "Between July 1, 1992, and June 30, 1999, no consistent pattern of increase or decrease was observed in the number of homicides at school." Indeed, each year's report typically begins with a summary noting that students are safer at school than away from school. The 2000 report noted that students were less than half as likely to be victims of a violent crime at school than elsewhere. And the trend continued: in the 2003–2004 school year, young people were more than *50 times* more likely to be murdered, and almost *150 times* more likely to commit suicide, away from school. Schools, it seems, are a much safer haven than children's homes and communities, and much safer than prevailing perceptions suggest.[33]

So why didn't school violence simply fade from the radar of legislators and the public? How could the reality of more than 50 million school kids be so completely at odds with public perception? The answer involves the combustible mix of race, geography, guns, and the news media, which in the late 1990s brought public fears to a boiling point. Falling rates of all categories of school crime and violence were simply drowned by the tsunami of news reporting on a series of shocking—and unquestionably rare—multiple school shootings in America's rural and suburban redoubts. From 1997 to 1998, a string of incidents in which students fatally shot other students and teachers made headline news nationally. Coming in close succession over a seven-month period, each event inflated the growing public panic a bit more, until school violence was diagnosed as epidemic.

- On October 1, 1997, Luke Woodham, sixteen, of Pearl, Mississippi, stabbed his mother to death and then went to Pearl High School, where he shot and killed two students and wounded seven others with a rifle.
- On December 1, 1997, Michael Carneal, fourteen, took a .22-caliber handgun to Heath High School in West Paducah, Kentucky, where he killed three students and wounded five who were part of a morning prayer group in the school lobby.
- On March 24, 1998, Mitchell Johnson, thirteen, and Andrew Golden, eleven, waited outside Westside Middle School in Jonesboro, Arkansas, with rifles, and killed four fellow students and one teacher after they exited the building for a fire alarm; Golden had pulled the alarm, and the boys retrieved the guns, which had been taken from his grandfather's cabinet and hidden in nearby bushes.

- On May 21, 1998, Kipland Kinkle, fifteen, shot and killed his parents in Springfield, Oregon, and then went to Thurston High School, where he shot and killed two students and wounded twenty-one others.

The characteristics of the shooters and where they lived were key in pumping up the fears of school violence. All the shooters were white males living in rural and suburban communities. These were not John DiIulio's Latino and black superpredators, living in urban centers. Those youths were "gangstas" and "thugs" who were expected to be violent and kill one another, in the view of many Americans. But how could such horrible things happen in Pearl or Jonesboro, asked a chorus of commentators. If it could happen there, then it could happen here in our community, came the answer. A poll conducted after the Jonesboro incident for NBC News and the *Wall Street Journal* found that 71 percent of those surveyed believed it likely or very likely a school shooting could happen in their community.[34] "I am struggling to make sense of the senseless, and to understand what could drive a teenager to commit such a terrible act," said President Bill Clinton in a radio address after the Oregon shooting. Of course, school shootings were nothing new—recall that Washington, D.C., saw its first back in 1970. And during 1997–1998, there were other school shootings around the country. But the quick succession of these incidents, the greater number of wounded and fatalities, and the intense news media coverage of them combined to create the perception of epidemic school violence despite a very different reality.

When less than a year after the Springfield incident, another even more shocking school shooting occurred, it cemented public fears and misconceptions about school violence beyond the reach of reason. On April 20, 1999, eighteen-year-old Eric Harris and Dylan Klebold, seventeen, conducted an assault on Columbine High School in Jefferson County, Colorado, a white, suburban, affluent enclave. Using semiautomatic guns procured at a Denver gun market and homemade explosive devices, they killed twelve students, one teacher, and then themselves within a half-hour. The death toll of fifteen, counting Harris and Klebold, was the highest of any school shooting. The news media, primed to cover Columbine because of the earlier string of incidents, mined every possible angle to create a dramatic parable of saints and sinners, good and evil. Every angle except two crucial ones: that school shootings were even rarer than ever, *despite* the brutal events at Columbine, and that it was easy access to automatic firearms that had given Harris and Klebold the ability to kill so many people so quickly. Even with Columbine's terrible death toll, that school year had fewer student-on-student homicides than in 1992–1993.

In the wake of these incidents, elected officials scrambled to react with programs and policies to further penalize youthful offenders and to ratchet up zero tolerance disciplinary codes at the school level. Senators Orrin Hatch of Nevada and Jeff Sessions of Alabama introduced the Juvenile Crime Bill, designed to toughen sentencing of juvenile offenders, including elimination of the long-standing practice of separating incarcerated juveniles and adults. President Clinton held a conference on school violence, called for spending $60 million to hire thousands of police officers for schools, and announced a $12 million program called SERV—School Emergency Response to Violence—to help schools and communities cope with violent deaths. Clinton also asked Congress to pass legislation that would prohibit the sale of guns to violent juvenile offenders for life, a measure akin to closing the barn door after the cows have gone. This new breed of school shooter was more akin to a terrorist, the feds determined, and school violence should be elevated to the status of a national security threat. So post-Columbine, the Secret Service's Threat Assessment Center was enlisted to study school shootings, producing the "Safe School Initiative" in 2002, which profiled the shooters—all males—who had carefully, not impulsively, planned their attacks, and who had easy access to guns (two thirds had taken guns from their homes or a relative's). The two-year study also found that most shooters had exhibited behavior before their attacks that signaled their need for help, and bullying was a motivator in a number of incidents. The report concluded that there was no profile of a school shooter and that *some* attacks are preventable.

Each year since Columbine, the incidence of school crime and violence, including shooting deaths, has continued its downward trend, in lockstep with declining crime rates in society overall. Still, there have been several other high-profile incidents. On March 21, 2005, sixteen-year-old

Jeff Weise, a Chippewa teen in Red Lake, Wisconsin, shot and killed nine people, including students at his school and relatives, and then committed suicide, using a gun he'd taken from home. News coverage invoked the specter of Columbine and quoted hand-wringing parents and school administrators worried about copycat shootings. The National Rifle Association offered its solution: let teachers have guns. In fall of 2006, the two previously cited incidents in Colorado and then Pennsylvania involving adult men invading schools and taking students hostage again invoked fears of Columbines erupting around the country. President George W. Bush responded like his predecessor did. He held a conference on school violence, even though neither incident was initiated by students. Pennsylvania legislators responded by revisiting a gun-control bill that had just been defeated.

President Bush continued the trajectory initiated by Bill Clinton of legislating punitive approaches to school security. His No Child Left Behind (NCLB) Act of 2001 continued the Safe and Drug Free Schools and Communities program. One new provision required state and local education agencies to identify "persistently dangerous" schools, as defined by their own standards. Such schools risked losing funding and students. But early reports on this requirement showed state standards and definitions of violence varying wildly, with some schools reporting every push and shove, while others ignored serious incidents to avoid penalties. The provision also provided grants for drug prevention education, drug testing, purchase of metal detectors, and security guards. Funding was also available for conflict resolution and peer mediation education, but overall funding levels dropped after 2003—except for drug testing in schools. For a Republican administration that made accountability a cornerstone of its education policy, the Bush White House was no different from its predecessor in doling out funds without requiring measurable results from millions spent on drug abuse or safe schools efforts.

The only attempts to evaluate the Safe and Drug Free Schools program, which is now more than twenty years old, were undertaken during the Clinton years, and findings were dismal. A review by the criminal justice professor Lawrence W. Sherman for the Brookings Institute in 2000 called the program "symbolic pork" that Congress supports in order to show concern for a problem that constituents are worried about, regardless of effectiveness. "Since 1986, this program has given more than $6 billion to some fifteen thousand local school districts and fifty state governors to spend largely at their own discretion," Sherman wrote. "No evidence shows that this half-billion-dollar-per-year program has made schools any safer or more drug-free. . . . Both the Office of Management and Budget and the Congressional Budget Office have tried to kill this program. Yet both Republican and Democratic presidents have joined with opposition parties in Congress to keep the program alive."[35] The public's willingness to swallow symbolic pork instead of clamoring for meatier programs is evident in a lengthy investigative article published by the *Los Angeles Times* on the Safe and Drug Free Schools program, perhaps the only such journalistic examination by a national newspaper. Published after a year of high-profile school shootings in Oregon and Kentucky, the article found "gaping holes in government attempts to ensure safe schools," formed by often bizarre expenditures of safe-schools funds. "In Richmond, Virginia, where a ninth grader shot and wounded a basketball coach and a teacher's aide two days before school let out in June, state education officials spent $16,000 to publish a drug-free party guide that recommends staging activities such as Jell-O wrestling and pageants "where guys dress up in women's wear," wrote the reporter, Ralph Frammolino. He also found that "taxpayer dollars paid for motivational speakers, puppet shows, tickets to Disneyland, resort weekends and a $6,500 toy police car. Federal funds also are routinely spent on dunking booths, lifeguards and entertainers, including magicians, clowns and a Southern beauty queen, who serenades students with pop hits." In one of his most disturbing discoveries, he wrote that months before the middle school shooting in Jonesboro, Arkansas, by two adolescent boys, local officials used some of the safe-schools funding to hire a magician to perform in the school.[36]

School violence as now understood and experienced is not a new phenomenon, but part of a continuum that stretches back in time. The particular safety and discipline challenges schools and students face have shifted as conditions outside the schoolhouse have changed. Guns are the most threatening part of the equation, and as long as children and teens have ready access to them, lethal violence will always be with us, in schools and out. While the vast majority of public schools continue to be safe—safer than students' own homes or neighborhoods in many cases—addressing disruptive behavior and safety issues will always be part of the educational process. The question is how those issues are approached, and at the end of the twentieth century, the answer was the criminal justice model that has so dramatically shaped society. It's small wonder. When prisons are built faster than new schools as a solution to social and economic problems, a penal approach to school violence of any magnitude appears as the logical fix even if there is little evidence that it works to make schools and students safer. Parents, educators, and communities that should have known better were willing to follow in lockstep as politicians and so-called experts began the crackdown on students. Every choice to adopt another punitive measure—policing, surveillance, metal detectors, zero tolerance rules—has turned students into suspects, and moved the schoolhouse further down the slippery slope to the jailhouse.

2 WE ARE COLUMBINE

Guns are not to blame, and the ready availability of them is not to blame . . . It's in the minds of the children . . . I'm not a psychologist.
  —J. D. Tanner, owner of the Denver gun show where Dylan Klebold and Eric Harris obtained their guns, two weeks after the Columbine incident

When someone says, "Well, if this law had been in effect, would it have prevented what happened? We will never know. I believe there is a chance if that law was in effect and Robyn Anderson [who bought guns for Harris and Klebold] couldn't get the guns so easily, that she would have said, "No, I can't do this." They [Harris and Klebold] would have gone to somebody else. Sure. But maybe that next person would have said, "Whoa, what's going on here. I better talk to somebody about this."
  —Tom Mauser, a gun control activist whose son, Daniel, was killed in Columbine High School, on a state law to require background checks for sales at gun shows.

The Columbine Memorial is carved into a knoll in Clement Park, a vast tract of emerald lawns, sports fields, and playgrounds on Pierce Street, abutting Columbine High School. Past the baseball field and picnic areas, the memorial is hidden from view until you are right at its entrance. A few discreet signs around the park direct visitors to the red rock and granite environmental design, with its inner "ring of remembrance" and outer "ring of healing." The inner ring offers individual biographies of the twelve students and one teacher killed that day, spelled out on the top surface of a granite wall. On the ground, a looped ribbon and the words "Never Forgotten," the motto of those touched by the tragedy, are worked into a stone paving design. Etched onto dark tablets on the red wall of the outer ring are quotes from unnamed students, teachers, and community members, as well as one from Bill Clinton, who was president when the assault occurred. One unattributed quote asks rhetorically, yet provocatively, "It brought the nation to its knees but now that we've gotten back up how have things changed; what have we learned?" I visited Columbine High School and the surrounding community in May 2008, nine years after the iconic incident of school violence. Had anything changed, and were lessons learned by students, teachers, parents, and administrators? Despite the motto's sentiments, many would prefer to forget the events of April 20, 1999, and the dubious notoriety it conferred on their hometown. "There's an element in the community that is ashamed of what happened," says Tom Mauser, whose son, Daniel, was fifteen when he was killed. "They want Columbine to be this place of healing, but it's this place that had this terrible tragedy."

Although Columbine High's postal address is Littleton, the area is actually an unincorporated part of Jefferson County and the suburban sprawl that radiates out from Denver twelve miles to the north. It is an area of upper-middle-class affluence and homogeneity, with a population that is about 90 percent white. Christian evangelical churches are abundant and the politics are decidedly Republican. Former farmlands have been gobbled up by cookie-cutter strip malls and McMansion developments with names like the Hamlet at Columbine and Columbine Knolls. Many declare at their entrances, "A covenant protected community," referring to the standards for residents' property maintenance—even what colors houses may be painted—in the name of maintaining homogeneity and property values for all. The snow-frosted Rocky Mountains rise up rugged and wild in the near distance, an incongruous backdrop to the manicured landscapes below them. Conformity, not notoriety, is what people who live in the Columbine Valley expect. When Eric Harris and Dylan Klebold committed their terrible assault, they not only destroyed lives, they put their community on the map, held it up for public dissection and disapproval, and breached a tacit covenant on conventionality that residents take as an article of faith.

It would be difficult to overstate the impact the Columbine attack has had on popular attitudes about youth violence and school safety, and on policing and security policies in public schools. It wasn't the first public school shooting with multiple victims. There was a string of them from 1997 to 1998, including the incidents in Springfield, Oregon, and Jonesboro, Arkansas. But the toll at Columbine High—fifteen dead, including the two attackers, and twenty-four wounded—was the highest, and the teens' weaponry was unprecedented. Columbine, as the incident is now known, is the yardstick by which all school shootings will be measured. Ironically, the tragedy occurred as rates of school violence in general and shootings in particular were declining. However, statistical realities were easily swamped by widespread public fears of school and youth violence. Polls taken after the well-publicized 1998 elementary school shooting in Jonesboro, for example, found that 71 percent of respondents expected a school shooting in their community; a poll conducted two days after Columbine found 80 percent expected more school shootings. Reporting on school shootings and Columbine in particular played no small role in bringing school violence into communities and homes around the country with coverage that created an echo chamber for simmering public panic about schools. For the news media, Columbine was a terrible tragedy but a great story. It garnered the most public interest of any story that year, with one survey finding that 68 percent of Americans followed it closely.[1] Top newspaper and broadcast executives named Columbine the year's second most important story, right after President Bill Clinton's impeachment.[2]

Healing hasn't come for all in Columbine. Some still puzzle about why the two boys became killers, and the need to assign responsibility persists. There is no redemption for Harris and Klebold, even in this strongly religious community. They are reviled. Their parents still live there and are no better than pariahs, having paid out $1.6 million to settle thirty-seven wrongful death and injury lawsuits brought by the families of victims. Depositions given in those suits by Wayne and Katherine Harris and Thom and Susan Klebold were sealed by the court. But a legal tug-of-war to open them up to parents of victims and researchers who believe they will answer lingering questions continued into the next decade. Lawsuits filed by victims' families that blamed Principal Frank DeAngelis, teachers, and the Jefferson County sheriff and deputies for not preventing the tragedy were all dismissed; as public employees, school officials and sheriffs were judged legally immune from such charges. A lawsuit filed by the family of Dave Sanders, the teacher who was killed, against the distributors of violent video games, including Doom, blamed them for Harris and Klebold's rampage. That suit was dismissed.

Harris and Klebold were widely known to be disturbed. Their downward spiral took more than a year and was marked by a burglary arrest, involvement in the juvenile justice system, flagrant gun and explosives purchases, and their use in company with friends. Harris's web threats against another student caused his parents to go to the Jefferson County sheriff. Columbine High School's disciplinary dean, Peter Horvath, knew about their arrests and school discipline problems, and declared that Harris "was on the edge of losing control" before April 20. Teachers in the boys' psychology and creative writing classes read their essays about their guns, anger, hatred, and intent to kill or injure Columbine students and others. A video production teacher viewed a project the boys filmed, enacting revenge shootings on other Columbine students with fake guns; another video the teacher saw showed Harris and Klebold shooting real guns. Apparently, none of these educators shared information or concerns with school administrators, leaving Principal DeAngelis strangely detached from the goings-on in his building. Wayne Harris reportedly found and confiscated a loaded pipe bomb in Eric's room but allowed him to keep other explosives-related supplies. Susan and Thom Klebold maintained silence for ten years until Susan wrote an essay for O magazine's October 13, 2009, issue, publicly offering the first explanation for their inaction, and it amounted to ignorance: "We didn't know that he and Eric had assembled an arsenal of explosives and guns. We believed his participation in the massacre was accidental or that he had been coerced. We believed that he did not intend to hurt anyone. One friend was sure that Dylan had been tricked at the last minute into using live ammunition. None of us could accept that he was capable of doing what he did."

Down the line, the adults in the assailants' lives failed to connect the many dots and respond to the warning signs. From their parents to the school principal and teachers to sheriff's deputies to friends who shared their fascination with guns, no one paid needed attention until Harris and Klebold couldn't be ignored.

Do the parents and teachers and administrators at Columbine pay attention now? Well, a decade later, the issue of bullying and intolerance among students, spotlighted by the incident, has not been programmatically addressed at Columbine High School. And just as important, the gun culture that provided Harris and Klebold easy access to firearms has been a taboo topic for most everyone—except for one parent-crusader. Tom Mauser alone seems to get it: as disturbed as Harris and Klebold were, without guns, Columbine could never have occurred.

TEENS AS TERRORISTS

The events of April 20, 1999, have been recounted in news accounts, books, even film, making many basic details familiar: eighteen-year-old Eric Harris and Dylan Klebold, seventeen, carried out a well-planned assault on their high school armed with a TEC-DC9 semiautomatic handgun, a rifle, two sawed-off shotguns, knives, and dozens of home-made explosive devices in order to kill as many students as possible, and then themselves. In Harris's home, they videotaped their arsenal of weapons, vented their anger and hatred for other students, and mocked their parents, police, and teachers. They shot and killed one teacher and twelve students, some at point-blank range, most of them in the school library, wounded twenty-four others, and then committed suicide. Dave Sanders bled to death before SWAT teams got to him three hours after he was shot. Law enforcement officers thought the shooters were still active as the explosive devices continued to go off. But the boys had killed themselves forty-seven minutes after their attack began.

With the eyes of the nation on Colorado, Governor Bill Owens declared, "Our innocence is lost today." Owens, a Republican, had been supporting a bill before the statehouse to make it easier to carry concealed weapons. Ironically, the bill was scheduled for debate on April 20, but legislators postponed it after the school assault. Owens named the Columbine Review Commission nine months later to conduct a postmortem and offer recommendations for change. Its focus was on law enforcement's performance, the adequacy of school safety protocols, the emergency medical response, and how well victims and families were assisted. The blue-ribbon panel, which included the Denver district attorney, Bill Ritter (later governor), delivered a hard-nosed critique of the police response and of the Jefferson County Sheriff's lack of cooperation with the commission. For law enforce-ment, Columbine was a debacle, a crisis in which they appeared impotent while a school full of students and faculty waited for rescue. Deputy Neil Gardner, Columbine's school resource officer, exchanged fire with Harris in the first moments of the attack but missed him and did not pursue the teen into the school. Gardner and five other deputies were untrained in the kind of rescue procedures required. Denver and Jefferson County SWAT teams arrived but delayed entry for hours into those areas of the school where Dave Sanders and injured students were waiting. Radios of the different police units operated on different frequencies, making communication among teams impossible. Police had no plans of the school building and were hampered by smoke-filled hallways. As the report stated: "It is fair to observe that neither law enforcement command personnel nor school administrators were well prepared to counter the violence that erupted at Columbine High School . . ." The commission's first recommendation among a dozen cut to the chase: "Law enforcement and training should emphasize that the highest priority of law enforcement officers, after arriving at the scene of a crisis, is to stop any ongoing assault."

Columbine was a human tragedy in a small Colorado town. But for school districts around the country it was a nightmare of what-ifs. For law enforcement it was a humiliation in which two disturbed teenagers with four guns and homemade bombs stymied the professionals. The reaction to Columbine by both sectors was dramatic and severe. Strict zero tolerance policies were ratcheted up tighter, security hardware piled on, and policing became more militaristic, viewing students as potential enemies. Law enforcement devised the "active shooter" drill, in which officers practice responding to an incident of multiple suspects who are armed and shooting, as a response to Columbine-type attacks, and it is now a popular training method offered by NASRO (the National Assoiation of School Resource Officers), as well as local school police units. Lockdown drills became the new duck-and-cover drills practiced by earlier generations of Cold War–era children instructed to hide under their desks in case of a nuclear attack by the Soviet Union. The new threat was not foreign, though. It was the alienated boy next door, and many states decided to treat him as a terrorist. State legislatures and school districts around the country embraced laws to treat Columbine-like threats, even student essays with dark subject matter, as terroristic and potentially criminal. Better to err on the side of being overzealous, was the consensus. A *New York Times* article published five months after the Columbine attack described the radical change in treatment students faced:

In the months since Columbine, authorities' rules for what is, and is not, acceptable behavior for teenagers have been drastically rewritten. Hoping to prevent another tragedy, parents, teachers, police officers, and the courts are trying to attack violence at its roots. Instead of waiting for another disturbed student to gun down his or her classmates, they have widened the radar scope for acts that could be signs of potential trouble.

The result: Teenagers are being interrogated, suspended, reprimanded, and even arrested—not for committing actual crimes, but for what they say in class, write on tests, post on the Internet, or e-mail to a friend, as well as what they wear and even how they do their hair. Taken together, civil-liberties advocates say, these policies amount to the biggest crackdown on teen rights in recent history.

"It all seems driven by post-Columbine hysteria and misinformation about safety," says Ann Beeson, an attorney with the American Civil Liberties Union (ACLU). "Students have always been irreverent, but we shouldn't punish them for that behavior."[3]

More than a decade later, the post-Columbine hysteria has not evaporated. It's been integrated into the lockdown philosophy of school safety and youth discipline. Students making threats of violence—real or make-believe—are subjected to swift and harsh prosecution, even if no crime has occurred. Witness seventeen-year-old Jeremie Dalin from Fox River Grove, Illinois, who was convicted in June 2008 for making a "false terrorist threat." Dalin, a senior at Barrington High School, posted a message on a website about Japanese anime, warning of an attack on Halloween at Adlai E. Stevenson High School. There are four schools in the country with that name and Dalin didn't specify which. The FBI traced the posting to Dalin's house hours after a student at a school named Stevenson High in a nearby town saw it on the website and reported it. Although Dalin had second thoughts and removed the posting and the FBI ruled it a prank, the teen was arrested and prosecuted. Odder still, Dennis Oh, the teen who reported Dalin's prank, was arrested and charged with obstructing a peace officer because he posted the phony threat on another website. Dalin faced up to fifteen years in prison.

Since the September 11, 2001, terror attacks, school administrators and law enforcement officials have been even more emboldened to apply the terrorist label to students with the usual behavioral problems, as well as more serious ones. Looked at another way, the lockdown approach to school security, which views students as potential terrorists and schools as likely targets requiring heavy policing and surveillance, was in many ways the paradigm for the national security crackdown that swept the country after September 2001. Columbine, a rare act of violence at one school, became the excuse for implementing costly new security systems and disciplinary codes that curtailed students' rights to free speech, due process, and privacy. Likewise, the September 11 attacks, horrifying but rare acts of foreign terrorism on U.S. soil, have been used to justify retrenchments in civil liberties and widening surveillance by the government. In both incidents, authorities declared that "everything has changed" to justify extraordinary measures supposed to make us all safer, but which provided little evidence of that outcome. The Columbine scenario is terrifying, but the odds of it occurring in your hometown are about one in two million.[4] Still, many people believe it can happen anytime, anywhere.

ARE WE ALL COLUMBINE?

Columbine provoked not only a crackdown on students but a spate of philosophizing on the causes of youth violence. President Bill Clinton, the figurative patriarch of the national family, said "perhaps we'll never fully understand it," and opined, "St. Paul reminds us that we all see things in life darkly . . . We do know that we must do more to reach out to our children and teach them to express their anger . . . with words, not weapons." The Littleton district attorney called for "a national soul-searching mission to stop the culture of violence," which he blamed on "a society with too little respect for life . . . schools with too few rules . . . movies with too many murders and . . . video games that glorify too much gore and mayhem." Experts proffered their two cents on what motivated Harris and Klebold, with psychologists blaming depression, isolation, and aggression and others dragging out the usual suspects: youth culture and its violent, nihilistic bent. News coverage segued from reporting on the particulars of Columbine, its victims, and the assailants to articles depicting an epidemic of hand-wringing among students, teachers, and parents who wondered: Could it happen here?

Columbine High School's principal, Frank DeAngelis, would tell them unhesitatingly yes. "If you had asked me April 15 of '99, 'Could a

Columbine shooting occur?' I would say, there's no way, not in this community," DeAngelis says during an interview in his office in May 2008. "I can't tell you the number of people who e-mailed me, or called me, or that I run into who said, 'Your school is just like our school, your community is just like our community.' And for anyone to state it could never happen is an inaccurate statement." DeAngelis is compact, a Joe Pesci lookalike who has spent three decades at Columbine High, more than a dozen as principal. "If you look at school shootings, there is not a profile. They have occurred in rural communities, they've occurred in a suburban area, upper-middle-class, middle-class communities. They've occurred throughout. To say they only occur in inner cities, or they only occur in large high schools—there's not one set profile." DeAngelis calls what happened during his tenure a "wake-up call" to communities around the nation, even the world, and says he still doesn't understand why Harris and Klebold did what they did. "That's what is scary. That's why people are afraid. If you could pinpoint it, then there's a chance you could stop school shootings from occurring," he says. "If you could state the reason—it was video games or it was the music. But you can't! There are millions and millions of kids who played the game Doom, which Harris and Klebold played. Or millions of kids who listened to Marilyn Manson. Why did Klebold and Harris go off and these other kids didn't?"

DeAngelis has a vested interest in claiming that what happened in his school could happen anywhere, and that Harris and Klebold behaved like millions of other teens. After all, he was a defendant in lawsuits that held him partly responsible for what occurred; his defense has been that he was clueless about two students in his charge or of the pecking order in his school. But facts indicate that a Columbine does not and will not happen just anywhere. There is less mystery and more clear information about where such incidents occur and who the likely perpetrators are than is generally acknowledged. Columbine-style violence has specific race, sex, and class characteristics, which are usually ignored or glossed over. The majority of school-shooting incidents with multiple victims have been committed by white, male teenagers and they have occurred in rural or suburban settings.[5] There has never been a Columbine in a public city school. Yes, gun violence occurs in public city schools, but the school shootings that have grabbed headlines, what the sociologist Mike Males calls "rage killings," have common characteristics: "All involved males, none poor, nearly all white, nearly all wielding guns (or more rarely, bombs), nearly all motivated by generalized rage." These middle-class or affluent boys are motivated by rejection by girlfriends or school suspensions, Males found, and are not drug or alcohol users. They usually spend months or years planning their assaults and often amass arsenals of weapons.[6] One reason that Columbine was spread across headlines and TV newscasts was that it shocked a nation that believed communities like the Denver suburb were supposed to be safe from extreme violence. Those sentiments were on display in news articles that quoted stunned Columbine residents saying, "This can't be happening at our school," and "I just can't believe it is happening at my school." Implicit is the idea that it would be believable and even expected for a shooting incident to occur at some schools. Which schools is made explicit in one *New York Times* article published two days after the incident, quoting one student's mother: "As for safety, Mrs. Staley said she had never worried about violence at the school. 'It's a big deal when someone throws eggs at your house on Halloween,' she said. Metal detectors? No one even thought about installing them at Columbine, she said. They were for urban schools."[7]

If Columbine was a big story because it wasn't supposed to happen in an affluent, white, suburban school, violence in urban schools with Latino or black victims and perpetrators isn't news at all. In his analysis of school killings and news coverage of them, Males found that race and class played a role in what rated attention. Less than two months after Columbine, two Latina teenagers were shot to death outside their Southern California high school, rating a brief article inside the paper. Similarly, when a thirteen-year-old Latino boy shot and killed a thirteen-year-old Latina girl in a New Mexico middle school, it made no headlines. Yet a March 2001 shooting of two teens by another student— all three white—at a high school in Santee, California, was a national story. If high death tolls determined newsworthiness, several ignored school shootings had as many or more victims as well-publicized incidents in Springfield, Oregon, and Pearl, Mississippi, among others, Males noted. Why, then, did the media, as well as politicians, treat the white, suburban student shootings as more alarming than those involving minority students at urban schools? "To ask the question is to answer it: in the crass logic of reporters and editors, things like that are 'supposed to happen' to darker skinned youth," Males argues.[8]

The alarms sounded over teen terrorists at school reached far beyond suburban Denver to Washington, D.C., where elected officials had to respond to their fretting constituents. What Harris and Klebold had done was seen as a threat to national security, demanding an investigation worthy of a terrorist attack. In June 1999, the U.S. Secret Service teamed up with the Department of Education to study "targeted violence in schools." The Safe School Initiative, as it was called, examined thirty-seven previous incidents of violence at schools between 1974 and 2000 to understand the behavior and planning of students involved. The goal was to identify risk factors and threats in order to prevent future Columbine-type events. The Secret Service applied the same framework it had developed for an earlier study of assassination attempts against public officials.[9] After three years, the joint task force issued a report, which offered few surprises and little solace to those in the Columbine community like DeAngelis who believe that the attack was unforeseeable. Among the key findings were:

- Incidents of targeted violence at school are rarely sudden, impulsive acts.
- Prior to most incidents, other people knew about the attacker's idea and/or plan to attack.
- Most attackers engaged in some behavior, prior to the incident, that caused concern or indicated a need for help.
- Most attackers were known to have difficulty coping with significant losses or personal failures. Many had considered or attempted suicide.
- Many attackers felt bullied, persecuted, or injured by others prior to the attack.
- Most attackers had access to and had used weapons prior to the attack.

The report, while culling these commonalities, asserted that there was no one useful profile of a school shooter, making prevention a highly individualized challenge for school districts. In a follow-up report, the Safe School Initiative provided a detailed guide to threat assessment that, surprisingly, called it just "one component" in a wider strategy to reduce school violence. The best prevention strategies, the guide asserts, "create cultures and climates of safety, respect, and emotional support within educational institutions ... environments [that] emphasize " 'emotional intelligence,' as well as educational or intellectual pursuits." But a public panicked about crazed student terrorists would not be mollified by recommendations to bolster "emotional support" and "emotional intelligence" at school. No, if anything students had been coddled too much, for too long. Bring on the metal detectors and zero tolerance rules.

JOHNNY GOT HIS GUNS

The tidy single-family homes that dot the streets in the area surrounding Columbine High School are like so many pixels forming a familiar picture of American suburbia, with shiny new minivans in driveways and tow-headed toddlers in strollers. Like folks in communities around the country, residents in this corner of Jefferson County enjoy the popular cultural tradition known as garage sales. Driving to an interview with Principal Frank DeAngelis one morning, I saw hand-drawn flyers advertising garage sales taped to utility poles, beckoning me to a closer intimacy with Columbine residents. What better way to explore a community than to mingle with neighbors perusing one another's household clutter? Spotting a bold black arrow at an upcoming corner, I took a right turn, passing an entry sign: COLUMBINE WEST, A COVENANT PROTECTED COMMUNITY. A few more flyers led me to a cul-de-sac where the sale was under way, with kitchen utensils and pillows, excess clothing and kids' toys displayed on the driveway. The home owner chatted with another woman inside the open garage as I rummaged around. Here was something odd, I thought, as I reached for what looked like a wide, tan leather belt. It was an old ammo belt and its small loops were holding about four spent shell casings and what appeared to be half a dozen three-inch copper-tipped rifle rounds. Having shopped at hundreds of garage sales over the years, this certainly was a first. I held it up to the owner, showing surprise about finding live ammunition plopped next to her old kitchen curtains. Nonchalantly she said, "Oh, I guess I should take those out." She didn't, and I departed. Welcome to Colorado, where gun culture is a vibrant element of its identity as part of the Wild West.

*   *   *

In the days, weeks, months, and years since April 20, 1999, the Columbine attack has been dissected and researched from just about every possible angle—except for one. It is the elephant in the room, the topic that at most gets minor mention and even less serious scrutiny. Simply put, without easy access to guns, Harris and Klebold never could have killed so many people. School shootings cannot happen without guns. Period. In fall 1998, Harris and Klebold were only seventeen years old, so they brought a friend, Robyn Anderson, eighteen, to the Tanner Gun Show, Denver's largest and oldest gun mart, where she purchased two shotguns and a 9mm carbine rifle from the dealers Ronald Hartmann and James Royce Washington with her friends' money. She broke no law in handing over the guns to Harris and Klebold, because it wasn't technically a sale. Anderson, who was sued by victims and their families and settled by paying $300,000 for her role, reportedly said she was comfortable going to the Tanner show because she knew the transaction would not be documented. At that time, Colorado law permitted gun dealers who were not federally licensed to sell long arms to anyone eighteen and older without conducting the background check required by federal law. The boys also bought a TEC-DC9 semiautomatic handgun from Mark Manes, an acquaintance of Phillip Duran, who worked with Harris and Klebold at a pizzeria. That handgun also originated at the Tanner show. Manes's sale to the boys, however, was illegal, and he was convicted on felony charges of selling a handgun to a minor and sentenced to six years in prison. Duran, who steered the boys to Manes, was convicted of related charges and sentenced to four and a half years. Manes and Duran were also sued by victims' families and settled for $720,000 and $250,000 respectively. Victims sued the dealers Hartmann and Washington and the gun show's owner, J. D. Tanner, but they avoided liability. In Colorado as in many states, gun-rights sentiment is strong and gun-control supporters are marginally less reviled than sex predators. Weeks after Columbine, it was business as usual as J. D. Tanner held his gun show—although he did cancel one scheduled for the weekend after the attack. Tanner's thirty-year-old show, held monthly at Denver's Merchandise Mart, faced no public protests or disruptions. Tanner told a reporter he couldn't explain Columbine. "Guns are not to blame, and the ready availability of them is not to blame," he said. "It's in the minds of the children . . . I'm not a psychologist." His dealers, however, were reportedly upset that state legislators were entertaining gun-control measures as a consequence of the school tragedy.[10]

Principal Frank DeAngelis might reasonably be expected to have strong feelings about gun control. But he doesn't. "Robyn Anderson, she was eighteen and she actually went down to a gun show and purchased the guns," DeAngelis says. "And so those laws were in place, so you question some of those laws. If there would have been tougher laws—she wouldn't get the guns. But some of these others they purchased were purchased illegally from someone else in the community, and that's where there's a question of guns laws. If Klebold and Harris wanted to get guns—and I truly believe this—whether you talk about Washington, D.C., and things, if kids want guns they're gonna get guns. It's not the law-abiding citizens. Criminals are gonna get the guns." The flaw in this reasoning is that Harris and Klebold were not "criminals," even if they'd burglarized a van. They were emotionally disturbed teenagers, not gun-toting drug dealers, and there is a vast difference. It may be true that in our gun-infested culture, criminals will always get guns. It's also true that gun-control laws make it more difficult for everyone to get guns. The Brady Law requires federally licensed gun dealers to document purchases by conducting background checks on buyers, a significant hurdle for anyone—not just criminals—who does not want to leave a legal paper trail. The law's loophole permits dealers who are not federally licensed to forgo the process. For Tom Mauser, gun-control laws are speed bumps on the way to dangerous gun use. "In terms of, could they have gotten [guns] somewhere else? The fact is they didn't," he says. "It's the law of odds. How many obstacles are you going to put there? We had a very easy way for someone to buy guns without any records. And that's what they used. That's the point. They could so easily get them at the gun show." For Principal DeAngelis, a neutral stance on guns might be part of surviving what could have been a career-ending disaster.

"I think that Frank says, 'Well, there's different points of view,' because he has to. Anybody who's in a public position has to be so concerned about how they address the gun issue because the gun lobby is so powerful in this country, and they punish people who step out of line," says Mauser. "So, if Frank DeAngelis suddenly became a gun-control advocate, I think his job would be at risk. Seriously. How dare you? This isn't about guns, and you shouldn't be going there." We met for breakfast at

La Peep, a diner-style restaurant not far from the high school, which was crammed with Saturday morning patrons. Mauser is a Pittsburgh native who made his way to Colorado long ago, married Linda, and raised Daniel and his younger sister. A year after Daniel's death, they adopted a baby girl from China. Tom works for the state Department of Transportation, where he developed a stand-up persona for all the public presentations he does related to his job. Sort of a wry, Bob Neuhart–style humor with a quirky slide show. "It's all about timing," he explains. "You say something about how important safety is, and then click on a picture of a highway worker in a full suit of armor, with the cones next to him and holding a 'slow' sign. Things like that." After Daniel's death, Tom found a new public persona, speaking out about guns, and he wasn't kidding around anymore. He'd supported gun control before Columbine, and that year for the first time he'd become active. He wrote letters to his state legislator opposing pro-gun measures, like the concealed weapons bill, in the statehouse. Then came what he calls "an omen." Shortly before the attack, Daniel was doing research on gun laws for his debate team and talked to Tom about the loophole in the Brady Law—the very one that Harris and Klebold exploited to obtain guns from the gun show. For a grieving father, Daniel's senseless death was a call to arms for full-throttle activism on gun control.

"What really primed me was the fact that those laws were being promoted," he says. "On the day of Columbine, the governor of Colorado came to the school and I confronted him. I said, 'Hey, Governor, here you were promoting these gun laws.' He said, 'This isn't the appropriate time for this.' He didn't know I was a victim at that point. But in particular, I was watching a little of the news coverage of Columbine afterwards. I was hearing some of the things that were said, and it was just flabbergasting. 'If teachers had been armed, this wouldn't have happened.'" Then, ten days later, Tom's friend Margie called to say the National Rifle Association was coming to Denver for its national convention. The gun lobby shortened its convention to a one-day event for board business and a few other festivities, eliminating the massive gun show that was the popular draw. But a lot of people, including Denver's mayor, thought it shouldn't happen in light of Columbine. Did Tom want to go and speak? Linda was supportive but concerned because it was so soon after the tragedy. It would be Tom's first time publicly talking about his son's death and his first public speaking experience outside of work. "When I spoke that day to the crowd, I said, 'I'm not arguing like many of you that they shouldn't be here," he says. "My message was why did they feel the need to cut back on any of it? If they didn't feel any responsibility for what happened at Columbine, why should they cut the convention at all? I don't believe they did it out of respect. They did it to save themselves because it would have been extremely embarrassing to have that gun show, that bravado and all those assault weapons, those gun clips. They knew damn well the media would have been there focusing on it."

Unfortunately, media attention to the issue of guns in school shootings has been sporadic and shallow. Lurid descriptions of the Columbine aftermath and photos of Harris and Klebold dead in the school library, guns nearby, reflect the sensationalized coverage that drove so much news of the tragedy. Several articles did little more than mention the Colorado pro-gun laws being considered and the topic of gun availability in general. A deeper look provides a perspective on school shootings and violence that makes guns more integral to the discussion. First is the question of where the guns come from. Although Harris and Klebold got their firearms directly and indirectly through a poorly regulated marketplace, the single most common source of guns used by students in a school shooting is their home. The second-greatest source is from a relative or friend. The 1998 Jonesboro incident is a good example: two boys, aged eleven and thirteen, shot and killed four students and a teacher at their middle school with rifles they took from a grandfather's gun cabinet. An analysis by the Centers for Disease Control and Prevention of all the gun-related deaths at schools between 1992 and 1999 found that 123 students used 128 guns to commit violence at school, with 48 of those guns taken from home and 30 from a friend or relative. And not all the gun violence at school is homicidal. While 85 students shot and killed others, 33 used a gun to commit suicide. Five students, including Harris and Klebold, committed homicide and then suicide.[11]

Suicide is virtually absent from discussions of school violence, and that couldn't be clearer than with Columbine. Harris and Klebold were suicidal teens whose anger and depression was directed at their school, classmates, and the world—and themselves. Columbine wasn't simply a horrendous school shooting. It was a multiple homicide-suicide, a not uncommon form of rage killing by adults. But to consider the suicides of Harris and Klebold requires granting them some humanity, acknowledging that despair drove them to end their lives before they'd even really begun. It is easier, perhaps, to think of them as evil and lacking in any humanity. And it is easier to ignore the issue of suicide, especially among young people. In Colorado in 1999, the suicide rate was 14.4 per 100,000 people, compared to a national rate of 10.6. Colorado's suicide rate is among the highest in the country, and Jefferson County is one of four Denver-area counties with the highest number of suicide deaths. Guns are used in 52 percent of all suicides.[12] Nationally, suicide is among the top three causes of death for those aged thirteen to nineteen, claiming about four lives every day—or 1,460 lives every year. For added perspective on the real scope of school deaths, consider this: nationally during the 2006–2007 school year, there were three student suicides on school grounds, compared to two student-on-student shooting fatalities and two stabbing deaths, according to the National Center for School Safety.

Temporarily chastened by the national spotlight on Columbine, the Colorado legislature tabled two gun-rights bills, but they were revived the next session. In 2000, Tom Mauser took a one-year leave from his state job to work as a full-time lobbyist for SAFE (Sane Alternatives to the Firearms Epidemic) Colorado, where he fought against the pro-gun bills and for a law to close the gun-show loophole in the Brady Law. But legislators were weak-kneed and the NRA's clout was strong, and tougher control measures foundered. So SAFE Colorado took a new tack, to put before voters in the November 2000 election a ballot initiative to close the loophole. It was an overwhelming success despite the NRA's well-funded campaign to defeat Amendment 22, as it was known, which passed with 70 percent of the votes. "When someone says, 'Well, if this law had been in effect, would it have prevented what happened?' We will never know," Mauser says. "I believe there is a chance if that law was in effect and Robyn Anderson couldn't get the guns so easily, that she would have said, 'No, I can't do this.' They [Harris and Klebold] would have gone to somebody else. Sure. But maybe that next person would have said, 'Whoa, what's going on here. I better talk to somebody about this.'"

Mauser still speaks out on gun control and lobbies for safer gun laws as president of Colorado Cease Fire. Their push now is for a CAP law—child access prevention—to hold adult gun owners responsible if children shoot others or themselves with their firearms. "I've seen too many cases where kids have gotten access to guns, especially in accidental shooting cases—not so much school shootings—and the parents don't get charged," Mauser says. "A gun under the mattress, a gun in the nightstand, and the parent says, 'I told him to get it.' We're charging a child for God's sake, and we don't charge the parent." Mauser's group made suicide prevention a big focus of the bill in 2008, and hoped to find allies among groups doing such work. Instead, they waded into taboo territory. "Nobody wants to talk about suicide. In fact, it was very difficult for us in working the bill and trying to get the suicide prevention people with us," he says. "Some of the leaders of the suicide prevention movement are people who indeed lost their children to suicide. And in a few of those cases, how do you think they committed suicide? And then when you go to those people and say, 'We'd like your support for a bill that does this,' they say, 'You're gonna punish people who lost their child?'" The bill actually would give prosecutors discretion in filing charges against an adult, which would only be a misdemeanor. Pretty mild. But it would also require gun shops and gun show dealers to post signs and hand out flyers stating that the law holds adults responsible for keeping guns away from children. And those simple measures are anathema to the NRA and its more extreme offshoots.

The gun lobby's power is occasionally exposed in surprising ways and places. After two tragic incidents in fall 2006—at an Amish schoolhouse in Pennsylvania and a Bailey, Colorado, high school—a coalition of educators, school psychologists, and health professionals came together and issued a statement on school violence. In both incidents, adult male intruders took students hostage and then shot and killed students and themselves. The coalition, called the National Consortium of School Violence Prevention Researchers and Practitioners, was concerned that the hysterical overreaction to the incidents would simply continue the harsh and ineffective approaches to school safety anointed in the wake of Columbine. The statement noted that schools are safer places for children than their homes or communities, where more violence occurs. In one brief paragraph, it takes direct aim at the role of guns:

Finally, it is also important to acknowledge that access to guns plays an important role in many acts of serious violence in the United States. Although guns are never the simple cause of a violent act, the availability of lethal weapons to youth and to emotionally disturbed or antisocial adults poses a serious public health problem that cannot be overlooked. Our political leaders need to find a reasonable and constitutional way to limit the widespread availability of guns to persons who are unwilling or unable to use them in a responsible, lawful manner.

Hardly a radical manifesto, the statement was endorsed by more than a hundred leading researchers and educators, as well as two dozen national professional organizations. Among them were the American Academy of Pediatrics, the National Education Association, the National Association of School Psychologists, and the American Psychological Association. But one organization with a natural interest in school safety—the American Federation of Teachers—declined to sign the statement because it was afraid of controversy with the pro-gun lobby. "We lost the AFT over the last paragraph on guns," says Matthew J. Mayer, a Rutgers University professor and a founder of the coalition. "Once you raise the issue of gun control you create a dynamic where some people feel there is no discussion. It's like taking on the NRA lobbying machine."

COLUMBINE: HIGH SCHOOL OR FORTRESS?

The Columbine attack unleashed a national frenzy of security equipment purchases, with metal detectors a popular choice. Closed campuses to restrict student movement, pumped-up school policing, and zero tolerance policies that criminalized a range of typical teen behaviors were also part of the equation. Educators were suddenly discussing bullying and programs to address its negative influence on the learning environment. Given that the Columbine tragedy was the impetus behind these changes, I was curious about how that infamous symbol of school violence had responded to concerns about security and a climate that fostered bullying of less popular students. Most people think the place must be a fortress with state-of-the-art antibullying programs and conflict resolution training. And they'd be wrong. Columbine High School has no metal detectors. Zero. There are a few more surveillance cameras, but there had been some in place before April 20, 1999. School resource officers? Still one SRO, same as before. Three new positions were added—campus supervisors, unarmed middle-aged men who walk around the campus. All but two entry doors are locked now, but the campus is not closed and students come and go freely during lunch-time and breaks.

On the Friday afternoon I visited Columbine High, school was over and clusters of students lingered outside the main entrance and inside the lobby. I walked through the unlocked front doors, which displayed a sign stating that the school was "protected by V-Soft," a computer soft-ware program that scans visitor IDs to detect registered sex offenders. Another sign instructs all visitors to stop at the main office. There was no adult presence at the entrance, and no one questioned me as I walked in. The office was bustling with students, teachers, and staff preparing for the next day's fifth annual Community Day, an event created to "give back to the community" that had rallied to help the school post–April 20, 1999. Over several e-mails and phone calls with his secretary, Principal DeAngelis had agreed to grant me a one-hour interview after school hours to discuss safety and security at Columbine, a large, two-story, multiwing campus with about 1,700 students. Businesslike but cordial, he ushered me into his office and talked about April 20 and school security as if he'd done it a hundred times before. He has. What did he do to create a sense of safety in the building after the tragedy? "I think we have surveillance camera systems second to none that we can access via our Blackberries," he explains. "Campus supervisors can be anywhere in the building and can have access to what's happening throughout the school. We have keyless entries. We have two entrances into the building that are open during the day. The one you just walked in and the one downstairs, and we have staff members monitoring them. All the other doors, when we're locked down, are keyless entries. So if a key was to be lost—if this card was to be lost [holding a card on a lanyard around his neck]—it's all tied into a computer system, so we can deacti-vate it. I'm the only that has twenty-four/seven access, along with our custodial person. Every period of the day we have adult supervision. So there are teachers during their planning periods that either monitor the doors downstairs or walk the halls upstairs."

Jefferson County School District, of which Columbine is part, created threat-assessment teams that in each school began to identify students who posed potential risks. DeAngelis says he has used the process several times successfully, starting with his school social worker and moving up to the district level if action is warranted. Columbine devised an emergency response plan, and each semester it practices evacuations and lockdowns, he says, "and we talk to teachers about assignments, and are there red flags." People always ask him why there are no metal detectors, DeAngelis says, and he poses his own question. "Would metal detectors have stopped Klebold and Harris? They would not. When they came on campus, we had a Jefferson [County] police officer who was armed. He exchanged gunfire. They drove into the parking lot. They're not gonna stop at the metal detector and go through. They came in blasting," he says. "A lot of times metal detectors are false security, and the presence of that security system, or the metal detector—is it really gonna stop another school shooting? Not necessarily. And then you look at the practicality of it. A month after the shooting at Columbine, President Clinton came to Dakota Ridge High School to address us, and all because of security reasons, all the people had to go through metal detectors. And it was an hour. Do we do that every day with students and make them go through metal detectors? It's still a place to educate students, and do students, and do parents, want a fortress?"

The Columbine community considered that question, and so did the Columbine Review Commission. It rejected the high-tech fortress approach to making Colorado schools safer, noting the limitations of metal detectors and other hardware: "Although security devices can effectively deter certain forms of school crimes, including theft, graffiti and gang violence, they have not yet proven to be cost effective in preventing major school violence like that experienced by Columbine High School. Therefore, the Commission does not recommend the universal installation of metal detectors, video surveillance cameras and other security equipment as a means of forestalling violence generally; for the present, such devices can serve only to offer transient solutions to specific problems at individual schools."[13]

The commission also offered prescriptions for addressing conditions in a school that could foster a Columbine-type incident. One called for changing what it termed the "code of silence" in student culture to encourage reporting potential threats from classmates. Another recommendation homed in on bullying, which the commission stated was either a huge problem at Columbine or not very significant, based on contradictory testimony it heard from parents, students, and Principal DeAngelis. Acknowledging that bullying was a "risk factor" for school violence, the commission urged every Colorado school to adopt proven antibullying programs. Under Principal DeAngelis, the student-informer model found traction while bullying prevention hasn't. At Columbine, students are educated that it's "safe to tell" on one another, DeAngelis says, and to that end he has an anonymous tip box. "I can't tell you the number of tips I get in my office about 'You may want to check so-and-so, he may have drugs,' or 'You may want to check so-and-so, who may have a weapon.' That's what the key is," he says. "It's very difficult for these kids to narc or rat on someone but at least give them the skills to put an anonymous tip in my tip box." DeAngelis had no statistics on the number of tips that were substantiated, but Columbine High's state profile indicates a school most administrators would consider trouble-free. For the 2005–2006 school year, fifteen drug-related incidents, eleven alcohol incidents, and one dangerous weapon (unspecified) were reported. No assaults or fights were reported, but there were ninety-eight other violations of the code of conduct, and a total of five expulsions—this from a population of 1,677 teenagers.[14]

On bullying, DeAngelis has not heeded the recommendations on prevention, and he seems to have conflicting ideas about the subject. For the official record, the principal has stated that he doesn't consider it was or is an issue in his school, which was a necessary defense against those who alleged he ignored the school's social hierarchy and its casualties. He testified to the commission that "bullying was not a problem at Columbine High School," and that the school had acted firmly when any incident occurred. Others disagree. The commission interviewed forty-eight Columbine parents and students who said "bullying was rampant and the school's administration did little to control it," that "a significant amount of bullying had occurred (especially from athletes)," and that students were reluctant to report it for fear of retribution. These witnesses described a school where "school rules were inconsistently enforced, so that some groups of students were given more lenient treatment than others."[15] A decade later, DeAngelis's perspective on bullying at his school has not changed, although he now suggests that it was really

Harris and Klebold who were the bullies. "I'm not denying that there was bullying taking place in the school, but I knew Klebold and Harris somewhat, and those two were very intimidating. I mean, Klebold was a kid who was six-three, six-four," the principal says. "They played mind games. They actually were intimidating people. And it was more of a verbal-type harassment of bullying." Yet, at another point in the interview, DeAngelis does suggest that the teen killers could have been affected by bullying they endured before they arrived at his school, and that bullying prevention might be useful. "The question I have and no one can answer: What caused so much hate in the heart of Klebold and Harris?" he asks. "What caused so much hate in their heart that they were willing to kill classmates or teachers? Where did it start? Did it start in elementary school? If it was bullying, are there programs you can use? Antibullying programs." Asked if he has implemented any bullying education programs, DeAngelis said there is a Big Brother, Big Sister–type program called Links, which matches seniors and juniors with first-year students. All in all, DeAngelis believes the climate of his school has changed since the terrible tragedy: "Yes. I truly believe that the kids are more accepting. I think we're a stronger community than what we were in April prior to the tragedy."

In a great irony of the Columbine tragedy, the school that is synonymous with school violence has opted not to turn itself into a fortress, rejecting metal detectors and an increased police presence. Meanwhile, the rest of the country has embraced just such measures, supposedly to prevent another Columbine.

3 CRIME AND PUNISHMENT: THE ZERO TOLERANCE EPIDEMIC

We face two major issues: how to fund our schools and how to govern them. . . . Texas must . . . have safe classrooms. We must adopt one policy for those who terrorize teachers or disrupt classrooms—zero tolerance. School districts must be encouraged, not mandated, to start "Tough Love Academies." These alternative schools would be staffed by a different type of teacher, perhaps retired Marine drill sergeants, who understand that discipline and love go hand in hand. . . . If we are going to save a generation of young people, our children must know they will face bad consequences for bad behavior.
—From Governor George W. Bush's first Texas state of the state address

There is a belief that zero tolerance is a critical and important measure for preserving safe learning climates and that we have to remove a certain proportion of students to do so. But even if we say these are bad kids, the data we're talking about says zero tolerance doesn't make a difference. It is not teaching kids what they need to succeed and is putting them in jeopardy. What if we are creating the conditions for placing higher proportions of students at risk for jail?
—Russell Skiba, Indiana University's Center for Safe and Responsive Schools

Creola Cotton says her zero tolerance nightmare started with a game of foot tag played by two eleven-year-old kids—her daughter, Shaquanda, and a friend at their middle school in Paris, Texas. "One of the teachers saw them and thought they were fighting each other," she says. The principal punished the other student, Brenda Cherry's son Rico Lewis, writing him up for the infraction and giving him on-campus suspension. Cherry went to the school and complained about his treatment, so administrators cleared her boy and wrote up Shaquanda instead. Then things got worse for both children—and their mothers. "After I filed a complaint, my son started getting written up for silly things," Cherry says, "and they never had a problem with him before, either." Cotton, who had moved to Paris from Oklahoma a few years earlier to be near family, began to notice a different "mentality" in Paris toward African-American children.

"It didn't take long for me to realize something was wrong. Whenever our kids did something that white kids would do, they would turn it into a crime," she says. "When two or three black kids were standing together after school, the principal called them a gang. I could see there were so many more African-American kids in detention hall. It made me wonder."

Brenda Cherry and Creola Cotton came together in 2003 as concerned parents and supportive friends to challenge the Paris Independent School District. It wasn't just their kids, but other black students, some of them with learning disabilities, who were facing harsh disciplinary treatment for minor misbehaving or for doing nothing at all. In September 2003, Cherry filed a complaint with the federal Office of Civil Rights at the Department of Education, alleging racial discrimination in Paris schools' disciplinary practices. Hers was the first of twelve complaints filed over the next four years by parents, including Creola Cotton. There was the eight-year-old boy with ADHD who was written up for rolling his eyes at a teacher in the cafeteria. After his mother filed a complaint, Cherry says, the administration retaliated by keeping a log on his every action and movement. And there was the eleven-year-old boy who got into a scuffle with his friend after school on the playground. "The principal went outside, threw down one boy, and kicked him in ribs. He put the boy in a headlock, dragged him into the school, and called the school police," Cherry says. "When his mother came, the principal hit the boy in his groin area in front of her." The boy was arrested and put in a detention school sixty miles away. Cherry didn't know his mother, but she knew it was time to act. "We decided to have a protest the next morning in front of the school," she says, "and that's what we did." Instead of addressing the parents' concerns, Paris school officials targeted the activists' children for more disciplinary harassment. Cherry and Cotton acted as advocates, going to school to talk to the principal, so their kids faced retaliation. "My son started getting written up every day for not having his shirt tucked in. He started to get depressed. I thought they were fixing to do something to him," Cherry says. One teacher claimed her son gave him the finger, which was contradicted by other students present at the time. She took her son out of school and began to homeschool him. "I told Creola to take Shaquanda out, but she didn't want to leave her friends. She liked being in school," Cherry says. It was a fateful decision that would change Shaquanda's life—and not for the better.

In fall 2005, Shaquanda was fourteen and a ninth grader at Paris High School. She'd been diagnosed with attention deficit hyperactivity disorder before her family moved from Oklahoma and was taking medication for that as well as for a stomach ulcer. One morning, she woke with a stomachache, but they were out of her ulcer medication, so her mother told her to go to school early to see the nurse for Prevacid and her ADHD meds. But a male teacher stopped her inside the school and pushed her toward the door to leave, saying she could not enter early. As Shaquanda was about to exit, she saw two white students enter and turned to ask a female teacher's aide why she couldn't also couldn't go in. What happened next was debated by both sides. The school district claimed Shaquanda pushed the woman and caused her injury, although there was no medical evidence to support that. Shaquanda claimed the woman pushed her first and she reacted in kind. No one debates the result: the school police arrested Shaquanda, and she was charged in March 2006, convicted of assault, and sentenced to seven years in a juvenile detention center run by the Texas Youth Commission. It was only when the *Chicago Tribune* reporter Howard Witt wrote about her story, and the Paris school district's disciplinary practices and the widespread abuses in the TYC facility, that Shaquanda was finally freed.[1] She spent a year in prison and finished her education with homeschooling. In July 2008, a soft-spoken Shaquanda spoke by phone about her plans to get a GED and attend community college and her goal of becoming a criminal-law attorney. "I want to help other kids," she says, "so they don't have to go through what I went through."[2]

Shaquanda Cotton's story provoked outrage when it made national headlines in March 2007, but outrageous discipline has become as much a part of public schooling as high-stakes testing. Blame it on zero tolerance policies enacted since the mid-1990s that treat student misbehavior and mischief as if they were criminal acts. Horseplay on the playground or a shove in the hallway is no longer just youthful shenanigans. In the zero tolerance view, such behavior is disorderly conduct and assault. Lesser infractions, like tardiness or speaking out in class, as well as innocuous acts such as bringing aspirin to school or violating dress codes, can trigger suspensions from class lasting up to ten days in many states, including Texas. Zero tolerance has also chilled students' First Amendment freedoms as irrational fears of school violence prompt teachers and principals to interpret harmless student writings or comments as terroristic threats. In-school suspensions send students to a detention room, while out-of-school suspensions have fueled the growth of alternative schools, some operated by private, for-profit companies without sound educational programs. Zero tolerance discipline has distinct demographics, too: it is used more often on boys and on African-American students than other groups, in lopsided proportions that seem to clearly point to racial discrimination. Special education students and those with learning disabilities, like Shaquanda Cotton, are also more likely to be singled out for punishment.

For longer than a decade now, education and youth advocates have been sounding the alarm about zero tolerance and its toll on students, especially those struggling to achieve. Excluding kids from school for two days or two months increases the odds of academic failure and dropping out. What's more, suspensions and academic failure are strong predictors of entry into the criminal justice system, especially for African-American males. It's a phenomenon that legal and education experts have dubbed the "school-to-prison pipeline." If yesteryear's prank got a slap on the wrist, today those wrists could be slapped with handcuffs. Russ Skiba, educational psychologist and a leading authority on race and disciplinary policies, says "hype" over school violence has encouraged the use of zero tolerance and school exclusions even though there is no evidence that they work. "There is a belief that zero tolerance is a critical and important measure for preserving safe learning climates and that we have to remove a certain proportion of students to do so," says Skiba, director of the Equity Project at Indiana University's Safe and Responsive Schools center. "But even if we say these are bad kids, the data we're talking about says zero tolerance doesn't make a difference. It is not teaching kids what they need to succeed and is putting them in jeopardy. What if we are creating the conditions for placing higher proportions of students at risk for jail?"

In 2000, the Advancement Project, a civil rights organization in Washington, D.C., and the Civil Rights Project, then based at Harvard, published a seminal assessment of the impact of zero tolerance in schools, and its conclusions were devastating: "Zero Tolerance has become a philosophy that has permeated our schools; it employs a brutally strict disciplinary model that embraces harsh punishment over education . . . children are not only being treated like criminals in school, but many are being shunted into the criminal justice system as schools have begun to rely heavily upon law enforcement officials to punish students."[3] "We are breeding a generation of children who think they are criminals for the way they are being treated in school," said Judith Browne-Dianis, co-director of the Advancement Project. "School used to be a refuge. Now it's a lockdown environment. We are bringing the practices of criminal justice into the schools."

FROM GUNS TO DRUGS TO . . . WEDGIES?

Zero tolerance entered the mainstream vernacular during the Reagan administration's War on Drugs back in the mid-1980s, when domestic drug trafficking and its related violence were ravaging urban areas while foreign trafficking by the Reagan-backed contras funded civil war in Nicaragua. The crackdown on the drug trade extended only as far as the U.S. borders, however, and entailed aggressive policing and prosecution and long sentences for even small amounts of illegal drugs. Reagan's education secretary William Bennett (who had also been the first drug czar) brought the War on Drugs and a zero tolerance mentality into public schools, and Congress backed him up. In 1986, it passed the Drug Free Schools Act to require that schools adopt strict rules against student possession of drugs and alcohol on campus. But it was during the Clinton administration that zero tolerance gained a more vigorous and dangerous foothold in the schools. In 1994, Congress enacted the Safe and Gun Free Schools Act as part of a comprehensive education bill. It mandated a one-year expulsion of students who bring a gun to school and provided funding to schools for antiviolence programs. It was a time of public hysteria about youth crime, hyped by pop criminologists such as James Q. Wilson, who predicted a violent juvenile crime wave, and John DiIulio, whose "superpredator" was a new, vicious young criminal—implicitly a black or Latino urban male. Racial coding and stereotypes infused such theories and fed the public's rampant fear of young minority males. The real dimensions of juvenile crime were far milder: a spike in violent offenses that began in the late 1980s, crested in the early 1990s, and has been falling ever since. When the Columbine school incident occurred in 1999, school violence, including homicides, was at its lowest point in a decade. But by then, fear of African-American and Latino "ghetto gangstas" had expanded to include youth of all demographics, whether they lived in affluent suburbs or poor inner cities. Columbine only accelerated the zero tolerance juggernaut already in motion.

Federal mandates for zero tolerance policies on guns and drugs at school were kid stuff compared to those that state and local school authorities cooked up. Egged on by a fearful populace, schools have devised disciplinary codes that extend prohibitions on weapons well beyond firearms to include such things as nail clippers or files, or kitchen knives innocently packed with school lunches. Drug prohibitions have ensnared over-the-counter pain medications, such as Midol or aspirin, even herbal cough drops. But it is the zero tolerance approach to student behavior that has caused the most far-reaching damage, unleashing an epidemic of suspensions or, as in Shaquanda Cotton's case, criminal prosecutions, that grows exponentially every year. Examples of zero tolerance run amok are a daily occurrence, but only the most bizarre seem to surface in the news:

- Four boys, twelve and thirteen, in a Wisconsin middle school are suspended for three days and issued police citations for disorderly conduct after yanking up a classmate's underwear, giving him a wedgie.
- A girl, twelve, is suspended and assigned to an alternative school for four months after writing "I love Alex" in blue marker on a gymnasium wall—a violation the Katy, Texas, school district rates in severity with assault, terrorist threats, and drug possession.
- A boy, sixteen, is expelled from his high school in a Chicago suburb for a notebook doodle that included his initials, a crown, and a spiderweb, which school officials said was a gang symbol. The boy had received fifty-four other citations for disturbing or cutting class, and his mother believed they simply wanted him out of the school.[4]

Although school administrators are bound to adhere to federal and state laws requiring suspension or expulsion for gun and drug violations, on student behavior they determine if a shove or a wedgie is an assault, or if talking out in class is insubordination. "The zeitgeist now is zero tolerance, so that sets the tone for how we're going to handle behavior issues in schools," says Linda M. Raffaele-Mendez, professor of school psychology at the University of South Florida. "Zero tolerance says you get the kid out when there is an infraction that meets one of these criteria." A study by Raffaele-Mendez of suspensions in Tampa public schools found that weapons and drug violations accounted for less than 1 percent of disciplinary actions while a huge amount were for disruptive behavior. "There is a sense among administrators that they want their school to be a certain way, and this kid is not like that, so I want him out," she says. "I don't think most administrators believe suspension will have any effect on a kid's behavior."

Zero tolerance policies have maintained a tenacity and intensity in schools that defies logic, given consistently falling rates of school violence and youth crime overall. One reason, according to many educators and legal advocates, is the obsessive focus on testing and standards encouraged by the No Child Left Behind Act of 2001. From classroom teachers to principals to district superintendents, the pressure to show "AYP"—adequate yearly progress—and avoid a succession of penalties is a powerful incentive to weed out the most difficult students, who are often underachievers. "The wave of school shootings fed concerns and states went wild with zero tolerance, giving principals total discretion to kick out any student they wanted," says Mark Soler, president of the Children's Law and Policy Center in Washington, D.C. "Now, zero tolerance is fed less by fear of crime and more by high-stakes testing. Principals want to get rid of kids they perceive as trouble." In Texas schools, which were the guinea pigs for NCLB-style education reform during George W. Bush's tenure as governor, zero tolerance plus high-stakes testing has added up to produce astronomical suspension rates and a system of alternative detention schools that warehouse poor, minority low achievers. "We've had testing in Texas much longer, before Bush [was governor], and I've seen over the years how life on campus revolves around testing," says Augustina Reyes, education professor at the University of Houston. Reyes researched Texas's zero tolerance practices and found, like Raffaele-Mendez, that mandatory suspensions were a tiny fraction and discretionary disciplinary actions were the lion's share, with such subjective violations as "serious and persistent misbehavior" common. "Teachers think, 'With bad kids in my class I'll have lower achievements on my tests. I'll use discretion and remove that student,'" she says. "If teachers are told, 'Your scores go down, you lose your job,' all of a sudden your values shift very quickly."

Texas, according to its own reported statistics, is a national leader in harsh school discipline and suspensions, but it isn't unique. Every year, millions of suspensions are disrupting the education of students, with many tens of thousands of children expelled or placed in lower-quality disciplinary schools. Getting an accurate national tally of disciplinary actions and the offenses that trigger them is difficult for several reasons. The federal Department of Education (DOE) requires states to collect data on student discipline, but that data is not compiled into a national total. And adding up state numbers is an apples-and-oranges proposition because states and localities create their own disciplinary codes. So what Texas calls "insubordination" or "terroristic threats" won't necessarily have a match in New York's statutes. Some states break down their disciplinary action data into more specific components, such as in-school or out-of-school suspensions, while others do not. Nonetheless, it's possible to get a bead on the magnitude of the suspension epidemic. The DOE's National Center for Education Statistics provides some trend data on school disciplinary policies and actions in its School Survey on Crime and Safety. The survey is a sampling of the nation's public schools, and school administrators can opt to participate or not. The 2003–2004 survey reported that 46 percent of schools took serious disciplinary action against students, and the total number of such actions was 655,700. Nearly three quarters of those actions were suspensions. About a fifth were for insubordination. The survey's definition of *insubordination* is something with which many parents of adolescents and teens are probably familiar: "deliberate and inexcusable defiance of or refusal to obey a school rule, authority, or a reasonable order. It includes but is not limited to direct defiance of school authority, failure to attend assigned detention or on-campus supervision, failure to respond to a call slip, and physical or verbal intimidation/abuse." In the 2007–2008 survey, the same percentage of schools reported taking a total of 767,900 disciplinary actions against students, with the same proportion for insubordination, and a slightly higher number of suspensions.

The School Survey on Crime and Safety vastly understates the suspension epidemic, however, for several reasons. First, it counts only out-of-school suspensions of five days or longer. States devise their own rules on suspensions—how long they last, if there is a cap on the total number of days a student may be suspended, and what activity a suspended student must perform for in-school punishments. In Texas, for example, in-school suspensions can mean long-term exile. Deborah Fowler, legal director of Texas Appleseed, a public interest law center in Austin, led a team of legal and educational experts researching the state's disciplinary practices and was shocked to see the "enormous number of students being referred to ISS [in-school suspensions] every year. We became very concerned about that. And there is no cap on the number of days the student can spend there. We've heard of kids sitting in ISS for thirty days," Fowler says. "And there doesn't have to be any instruction. They may be given work, maybe not."

Second, the survey samples fewer than three thousand schools nationwide, so its numbers are projections. Even a quick tally of suspensions reported by a handful of states with aggressive zero tolerance policies reveals that a more realistic national total of suspensions would number in the millions annually. Let's start with California: with 6.2 million students, it has the largest public school enrollment in the United States. It also has the second-highest number of suspensions of any state, with 783,000 in the 2008–2009 school year. Texas, with 4.7 million students, has a rate of disciplinary actions of all types that is certainly true to its boastful reputation for bigness. In 2009–2010, the Lone Star State's public schools ordered 1.6 million in-school suspensions, affecting 625,000 students. Out-of-school suspensions totaled 575,000. Given those numbers, it's clear that some students are getting multiple suspensions.

Now, look at the Sunshine State, where the climate for students is generally so sunny. Florida's K–12 enrollment was more than 3 million in the 2008–2009 school year, and it had 264,000 in-school plus 235,000 out-of-school suspensions. (Florida doesn't report the number of students suspended.) Nearby, Georgia's public schools have an astronomical rate of suspensions for their students, who numbered 1.75 million in 2005–2006. In-school suspensions were 505,000 and out-of-school suspensions 314,000 that year, and the brunt was borne by some 300,000 students facing multiple disciplinary actions.

Focusing in on the ballooning casualty rates from zero tolerance discipline, it's clear that punishment is being indiscriminately, almost compulsively applied for a laundry list of student infractions that in another era would have been handled in the principal's office. School disciplinary codes redefined ordinary student actions and behaviors as prohibited, and created catchall categories for violations that didn't seem to fit anywhere else. And it is those violations, not weapons possession or violent crimes, that account for the preponderance of student incidents leading to suspensions and other disciplinary actions. The University of Houston's Augustina Reyes, who also was a Houston school board member, discovered this disturbing trend when she first started looking at the Texas data from 1998 on. Suspensions were climbing despite harsher zero tolerance policies, and they weren't for mandatory reasons, such as gun possession or drugs. The overwhelming majority were so-called discretionary suspensions for disruptive or defiant behavior as defined by teachers or administrators. For out-of-school suspensions, arguably the most disruptive to a student's education, Reyes found that just under 5 percent were mandatory. The rest were ordered for discretionary reasons.[5] "After a while I thought I was going blind with the numbers," Reyes says. "When I saw ninety-five versus five I couldn't believe it. And some of those mandatory suspensions included students who were smoking cigarettes." That trend holds true in more recent Texas data, for 2009–2010: there were more than 2 million in- and out-of-school suspensions, and about 1.9 million were for what the system calls "violating local code of conduct," a discretionary suspension. As for guns on campus, that year there were eighty-four incidents of students having firearms in school leading to any suspension.

But Texas isn't an outlier. Pick any state and see a similar pattern of disciplinary suspensions for violating codes of conduct and misbehavior. Colorado, ground zero for Columbine-fed hysteria over school violence, had 106,000 suspensions involving 78,000 students in the 2006–2007 school year. That's out of a total student population of about 800,000 students. A whopping 80 percent of suspensions were for just three categories: "disobedient/defiant" and "detrimental" behavior and the amorphous "other code of conduct" violations. Mark Soler says schools simply no longer are prepared to deal with typical adolescent behavior. "It is the nature of adolescents to defy authority, to be immature to an extent. Their brains are not fully matured and kids can make bad choices," Soler says. "Defiance of authority is talking in class, talking back to teachers. It's irritating behavior. You can't have kids disrupting class all the time, but schools have abdicated responsibility for finding a middle ground." Eliminate suspensions for minor instances of bad behavior, Soler argues, and the epidemic would subside.

INTOLERANCE AND RACISM

There's another dimension to zero tolerance that makes the picture even more disturbing, if it weren't bad enough. All students are harmed by its intolerant, ineffective policies and the school environment it fosters. But African-American, and to a lesser extent Latino, students, particularly males, bear the disproportionate brunt of disciplinary actions. They face the greatest risks of being pushed into the school-to-prison pipeline, a reality underscored by the huge percentage of black and Latino males who have been incarcerated. Shaquanda Cotton, though female, is a poster child for inequities of zero tolerance discipline. The Paris school district's records reveal that black students were eight times more likely to be disciplined for "disruptive" and "disrespectful" behavior than white students, according to data provided by the Paris Board of Education to the federal Office of Civil Rights of the education department. In 2006, the OCR began a review of Paris schools' disciplinary policies, prompted by discrimination complaints filed by Brenda Cherry, Creola Cotton, and other African-American parents. It was the first such federal civil rights investigation into school disciplinary policies in the country. Shaquanda Cotton was fortunate to have escaped a fate shared by thousands of students pushed out of school.

Lockdown High as a feeder into the prison system is what concerned youth advocates have been documenting around the country. National 2000 statistics from the U.S. Department of Education give a glimpse of the glaring discipline disparity: African-American students were 17 percent of the entire public school population but accounted for 34 percent of all out-of-school suspensions and 30 percent of expulsions. White students, by contrast, were 62 percent of the student population but accounted for 48 percent of out-of-school suspensions and 49 percent of expulsions. In almost every state, suspension, expulsion, and incarceration rates were higher for African-Americans than for the general student population. Some state education departments have begun to acknowledge the race gap on disciplinary actions as problematic and requiring action. The Georgia Department of Education, for example, is required to conduct annual analyses of disciplinary data from its public schools, and the issue of racial and gender disparity is prominent in the disaggregated data, which looks at students as well as the administrators doing the disciplining. The 2005–2006 report found that from 2000 to 2005, black students were over-represented among students facing disciplinary actions. Despite being 39 percent of Georgia's public school students, black students accounted for 50 percent of those disciplined; for teacher removal from class, 74 percent. Further, 65 percent of all disciplinary cases were boys. The report called for further research "to determine if disparities in the discipline data can be attributed to differential treatment of the various racial subgroups."[6]

California's DOE has an informational page about zero tolerance on its website under the "School Environment" section that both describes the genesis of the policy and limns the problems with it. Going even further than the Georgia analysis, this narrative accurately calls zero tolerance a "catch-all solution [that] has educators going in a lot of different directions," and cites the Civil Rights Project's findings on the disproportionate impact on minority students. However, state education agencies exercise little oversight when it comes to the disciplinary policies and practices of local school authorities.

Indiana University's Russ Skiba notes that the racial disparity has been apparent for more than twenty-five years and zero tolerance policies have exacerbated it. A 2000 study of race and discipline co-authored by Skiba goes beyond the general consensus that minority students are overrepresented among those suspended and expelled, to explain why it occurs. The authors find that the discrepancy begins with teachers' reactions to student behavior. Teachers were referring African-American students to the principal's office for less serious and more subjective reasons, such as disrespect, excessive noise, threat, and loitering. White students were more likely to be cited for smoking, vandalism, obscene language, and leaving school without permission—all more objectively defined violations, Skiba and his colleagues found. While some would explain that the higher rates of discipline reflect higher rates of wrong-doing by African-American students, Skiba et al. cite research on the overrepresentation of blacks in the criminal justice system and on the decreased number of disciplinary actions against them in schools with greater numbers of black faculty. Taking income levels into account, too, they conclude that the discipline gap is "evidence of a pervasive and systematic bias that may very well be inherent in the use of exclusionary discipline." Call it a form of profiling in our classrooms.[7]

"If you parse out socioeconomic status in figuring out the racial disparity, the disparity still remains," Skiba says. "I'm beginning to think of this as an unplanned conspiracy. When there is racial disparity, it isn't because anyone is consciously saying, 'We are going to place a higher proportion of minority children in special education.' It is institutional behaviors perpetuated over time." Skiba and other researchers suggest that when teachers are inexperienced or come from racial and class backgrounds very different from the students they teach, "cultural discontinuities" can set up adversarial dynamics n the classroom. Poor classroom management skills and stereotypes of African-American youth, especially boys, as threatening can lead to authoritarian disciplining and overreliance on suspensions.[8]

Administrators' attitudes toward their students, in fact, can make the difference between schools in which students are on track and ones that are suspension-heavy. Linda Raffaele-Mendez's research looked at suspension rates at elementary, middle, and high schools, comparing schools with similar profiles. "We wanted to look at schools that were demographically similar but had different rates of suspension," she says, "and indeed we did find schools that matched. We found schools with the highest rates of suspensions were those with lots of minority kids, and those getting free and reduced-cost lunch," she says. "But we also interviewed administrators, and found interesting things. There were attitudinal differences. One of the administrators at a high-suspending school said, 'Well, we just have too many black students.'"

DOUBLE JEOPARDY

Daniel Brion was fourteen, an eighth grader with a bright mind, a diagnosis of ADHD (attention deficit hyperactivity disorder), and a typical adolescent's jubilation as summer approached in May 2003. Walking down the hall of his Lexington, Kentucky, school, Daniel remarked that he wished the school would burn down and take the principal with it. The principal had picked on Daniel for two years, making comments when the teen dyed his hair red and ignoring his complaints of bullying. Daniel's adolescent imaginings were absurdly typical. "For two years I had the crap beat out of me, pushed down the stairs," Daniel says, "and I went to the principal and he didn't do anything." Daniel's wishful words were overheard by a younger student and translated to said principal thus: Daniel had gasoline and was recruiting a gang to burn down the school. Without notifying Daniel or his parents, the principal launched a two-week investigation leading to an interrogation by the police in his office. "The whole thing is like Franz Kafka's *The Trial*," says Gail Brion, his mother. "They were ready to arrest him on charges of terrorist threats." After Daniel admitted to what he really said, the principal backed down, but Daniel felt the principal was out to get him and was afraid to return to school. "My son has an IEP [individual education plan]. He's a bright kid," says his mother, "but he needs focusing, and they never spoke to his teacher to discuss what happened."

Adding yet another wrinkle to the matrix of inequities in school discipline is the disparate impact it has on students with learning disabilities or behavioral disorders, whether mainstreamed or in special education classes. Black and Latino kids also tend to be overrepresented among these students, creating double jeopardy in conjunction with zero tolerance. The high rates of disciplinary actions for this population became difficult even for policy makers to ignore, so, in 1997, amendments to the Individuals with Disabilities Education Act (IDEA) mandated states to collect demographic data on students enrolled in special ed and their suspensions and expulsions. IDEA prohibits disciplining students for behavior related to their disability, and the revisions were intended to make monitoring easier. But the reality in public school districts is far from the letter of the law. Minority children in special ed are still targeted for disciplinary actions at rates much higher than other groups.

The University of South Florida's Linda Raffaele-Mendez, whose area of expertise includes students with learning and behavioral disorders, did a study in 2003 of students with special needs in Hillsborough public schools and found the pattern holds true. "We asked parents of special education kids if their kids had been suspended and twenty-five percent said they had," she says, "and of those, sixty-seven percent of parents thought their child's suspension was as direct result of something related to their disability." She also analyzed data from a longitudinal study of one cohort of Pinellas County schoolchildren, from second through twelfth grades, and discovered that double jeopardy in dramatic numbers. She found that suspensions rose sharply in middle school for black boys, 48 percent of whom were suspended at least once. In one year, 66 percent of black boys with disabilities were suspended at least once, and multiple times for many of them. "When kids are sent to special ed, the classes aren't much smaller than regular classes and often the teachers are on emergency certification. They aren't prepared to work with these kids. They are like babysitters. A lot of black parents I've spoken to see special ed as an inferior system, a way of segregating their kids."

In Texas, similar inequities surfaced in a yearlong study of disciplinary data released by Texas Appleseed in the fall of 2007. In addition to the lopsided statistics on punishments for black and Latino students, Texas Appleseed found that special education students were disproportionately in the zero tolerance crosshairs. Although they were 11 percent of all Texas public school students, special ed kids received 26 percent of out-of-school suspensions, 21 percent of in-school suspensions, and 22 percent of placements in a Disciplinary Alternative Education Program (DEAP) for the 2005–2006 school year.[9] "We have a lot of pressure on teachers right now because of accountability," says Deborah Fowler, the primary author of the study. "For teachers who have a student who is acting out and disruptive in class, it's easier to send him to ISS or DEAP rather than figure out what's wrong. The huge overrepresentation of special ed students is indicative of the problem, and it's not being addressed adequately."

In Kentucky, the crackdown on students sharpened after several notorious school shootings in the late 1990s, including one in Peducah, according to Jackie Town, director of case advocacy at Kentucky Youth Advocates. She assisted Gail Brion when Daniel was investigated. "There is an increase in the need for special ed services. It costs districts money and they are all hurting. Particularly here in Kentucky, we have lots of rural areas and many of these districts don't have resources to provide special ed kids what they need. Many of these families don't have resources. They may be families that don't have a lot of education and don't understand their rights," Town says. "Special ed kids cost school districts money and if they are not in your school they are not costing you money." Town recounts the case of an eight-year-old boy who was in a class for students with emotional behavior disorders with four other students. "The school built time-out boxes inside the classroom, seclusion rooms, and this child kept being placed in one," she says. "He understandably became very upset, and sometimes as they dragged him to the room he would become violent and hit or kick at the teacher." The boy was suspended over and over again and finally was charged with assault and taken to juvenile court. The advocates were able to convince the school to drop the charges and petitioned the Kentucky education department to eliminate the time-out boxes.

INTO THE PIPELINE

The architects of zero tolerance discipline argue that tough rules are needed to keep schools safe and orderly and point to the increasingly low rates of school violence as proof that it works. But that's tautological reasoning at its worst. If zero tolerance works, why are the suspensions and other disciplinary actions climbing? With data showing that students are being pushed out of school for nonviolent incidents, the emphasis should be on the effectiveness of teachers and administrators, not on students. A study led by Indiana University's Russ Skiba found that school principals' attitudes were a key determinant in the kinds of discipline dispensed and school environment created. They surveyed 325 principals regarding their attitudes toward zero tolerance, suspension and expulsion, and violence prevention strategies. Principals' attitudes and school disciplinary outcomes were correlated: rates of out-of-school suspension were lower, and the use of preventive measures more frequent, at schools whose principals believed that suspension and expulsion were unnecessary given a positive school climate.

The prospects for students who are suspended are often more suspensions in and out of school and ultimately placement in an alternative school for "problem" students. Those sent to detention schools typically are low-achieving and at high risk of academic failure. Marginalizing them in a detention school, where it is rare to find a rigorous remedial curriculum and highly qualified teachers, is to sentence them to becoming dropouts. And a drop-out sentence for many students is tantamount to greasing the skids for entry into the juvenile or adult criminal justice system. This is the simple chain of

events that comprise the school-to-prison pipeline, and it often is initiated very early in children's school careers, becoming a self-fulfilling
prophecy of failure as they get older. "Kids are on a path. If they are
suspended frequently at the end of elementary school, it's likely that will
continue in middle school. And when they get to high school, it's very
likely they will drop out," Linda Raffaele-Mendez says. She found a
connection between suspensions and dropouts for all students. In her
study of a Pinellas public school cohort across thirteen years, a third of
students disappeared between ninth and twelfth grades.

Suspensions and even expulsions are increasing for the very young,
not just middle school students, a trend advocates have noted in regions
around the country. A 2005 study from Yale's Child Study Center found
that prekindergarten students were being expelled at a rate three times
that of K–12 students. The researcher Walter Gilliam found the same
racial and gender gap: African-American children were twice as likely
to be expelled as white or Latino children, and boys were expelled at a
rate 4.5 times that of girls. He also found that teachers who had help in
classroom management from behavioral consultants expelled fewer
students.[10]

Exclusion from school, whether by expulsion in pre-K or suspension
later on, creates for many students a vicious circle of failure that becomes
more difficult to break as they get older. Once stigmatized as "trouble-
makers" by teachers, students will continue to be viewed that way as
they move up in grade. Raffaele-Mendez found that to be the case in her
study of Pinellas County students. "The thing most surprising to me was
teacher ratings of behavior. There was such consistency. Their ratings
were good predictors of who would be suspended. I thought it meaningful that even though three different teachers across time would identify
these kids as struggling, there was no intervention. As a kid moves on
from third to fourth grade, are those teachers communicating with each
other and with administrators?" Russ Skiba's research shows that
students suspended in elementary school are more likely to act out in
middle school, and with that comes an increased risk of dropping out.
This in turn creates a greater risk of them ending up in jail. Skiba looked
at zero tolerance policies in thirty-seven states, using data from 2000 to
gauge their relationship to achievement, behavior, and youth incarceration. Schools with high out-of-school suspension rates had lower

achievement in eighth-grade math, writing, and reading. And states with higher school-suspension rates were also more likely to have higher juvenile incarceration rates. "What do we expect? If one of the potent predictors of achievement is time spent learning, then suspension's affect on achievement is not surprising," he said.

To advance the school-to-prison-pipeline theory through careful documentation and analysis, Texas Appleseed began a three-part, three-year project to assess how the state's disciplinary policies and practices connect to student failure and, in turn, to high rates of incarceration. Some would find it fitting that Texas advocates take up such a challenge, given the state's history of pioneering the deadly duo of zero tolerance discipline and high-stakes testing in schools. Credit—or blame—George W. Bush, who as governor promoted a fear-based approach to safe schools that suited the times and his political mantra of "accountability." In his first state address as governor, Bush talked the talk of "tough love:"

> We face two major issues: how to fund our schools and how to govern them. . . . Texas must . . . have safe classrooms. We must adopt one policy for those who terrorize teachers or disrupt classrooms—zero tolerance. School districts must be encouraged, not mandated, to start "Tough Love Academies." These alternative schools would be staffed by a differ-ent type of teacher, perhaps retired Marine drill sergeants, who understand that discipline and love go hand in hand. . . . If we are going to save a generation of young people, our children must know they will face bad consequences for bad behavior.[11]

During Governor Bush's first year in office, the Texas legislature revised the state's education law to include Chapter 37, which for the first time codified zero tolerance in its state law. Chapter 37 listed student actions that mandated placement in alternative DAEP or juvenile justice programs and gave administrators broad discretion in judging behavior and dispensing punishments. But while holding students accountable, Chapter 37 doesn't hold the Texas Education Agency or local school districts accountable for the quality of the alternative programs that have flourished. Until 2007, DAEP and JJAEP schools had no mini-mum standards, and to date, the TEA is not mandated to oversee their operation. That's why the watchdogs of public interest are needed. "TEA really does not want to have any monitoring or oversight," says Texas Appleseed's Deborah Fowler. "It would be a burden. There would have to be additional funding. But it's got to be done."

The Texas Appleseed project is an extraordinary collaboration among children's advocates, educators, civil rights attorneys, criminal justice experts, and a cadre of forty corporate attorneys working pro bono under the direction of Vinson & Elkins, a Houston firm. "It's a surprising array of advocates," Fowler admits. "We're working with the Texas Public Policy Foundation, which is extremely conservative. They think zero tolerance discipline is bad economics because it pushes kids out of school, leads to drop out, and fiscally is a bad idea." The project's goal is to articulate the component parts of the pipeline, with its portal in elementary, middle, and high school, a connector leading into disciplinary schools or juvenile justice schools, and the final section, leading into the adult prison system. The first report, on suspensions and referrals to DAEP schools, was built with data provided by the Texas Education Agency, and interviews with teachers, principals, school police, and counselors conducted by the pro bono lawyers. To flesh out the picture, Texas Appleseed staff held focus groups with parents, students, teachers, and school board members for their opinions. Many echoed the same problems with zero tolerance discipline that critics have identified over the years: individual students merit case-by-case consideration, one-size-fits-all discipline doesn't work, and zero tolerance is a "knee-jerk" reaction often dispensed without consistency.[12]

The project's initial purpose was to look at the DAEP schools, Fowler says, but soon the staff saw the staggering number of students receiving suspensions for discretionary reasons and realized that this was feeding the pipeline. In addition to their analysis showing the disproportionate suspensions for special ed and African-American students described earlier, the first report describes a Texas disciplinary system that churns students out of regular classrooms into DAEP schools, often multiple times, where the alternative program continues the failure to educate. Even the youngest students were vulnerable to being sucked into the pipeline: several thousand pre-K through first grade children were sent to DAEP schools, in violation of state prohibitions on such placement of students under age six—unless they bring a gun to school. Two thirds of referrals to the disciplinary schools were at the discretion of the school district, not because of mandatory removals for serious offenses. And about 30 percent of students in DAEP schools were repeat placements. The end result? The drop-out rate for DAEP schools is on average *five times* the rate at regular public schools. The quality varied from district to district, Fowler notes, but there is no uniform standard. "If you look at the DAEP in Austin, you can see the principal has some vision for it. He has a sense of what he wants children to get out of it," she says. "If you go to the DAEP in Hays, they are nice people, but there is no sense of a program. The kids are getting packets of work and no real instruction. If we're going to have these programs, we have to make sure districts are educating students while they are there." Texas Appleseed's work is strong evidence for the connection between ineffective disciplinary policies and the high incarceration rates in Texas, home of the largest prison system in the country: a third of public school students drop out, a third of youths sent to juvenile jails are dropouts, and 80 percent of Texas prison inmates are dropouts.[13]

Zero tolerance discipline that feeds students into the maw of mediocre or worse public alternative schools is also channeling them into another sort of school. These alternative disciplinary schools form a shadow system, just off the radar of public scrutiny. They are operated by for-profit companies under contract to public school districts, and their record is often far worse. One such company has its roots in Texas and Bush Republican Party politics.

COMMUNITY EDUCATION PROFITEERS[14]

Morris Gandy's son was a problem student throughout elementary school, playing hooky and acting up. A few days after he began sixth grade in 2002 at Gillespie Middle School in Philadelphia, he was suspended. Gandy, a single parent, beseeched the principal, "What can you do for a problem child?" He got no help. Then a neighbor told him about Community Education Partners (CEP), an alternative school for kids like his son. So Gandy enrolled the boy, expecting that teachers there would know how to handle him. Instead, the situation went from bad to worse. "The teacher said my son shot him in the head with a rubber band," Gandy said. "I said, 'What are you going to do about it? This is supposed to be a school for troubled kids.'" His son told him that all they did was watch movies. He went truant. "They are supposed to be the experts on the kids outside the box. They are supposed to get them back inside the box," Gandy said. "They couldn't hold his interest." Morris Gandy is what you'd call a dissatisfied CEP customer; CEP, however, continues to prosper. The company, founded ten years ago in Houston, entered the private-school market at a time when Texas was a roiling caldron of Republican politics and Enron-style corporate dealing—and a laboratory for education reform. George W. Bush was governor, the mantra was accountability for public schools, and the tools were high-stakes testing and privatization. What emerged from the mix were the so-called Texas Miracle, which boosted student achievement; the former Houston schools superintendent Rod Paige as President Bush's education secretary; and ultimately Bush's No Child Left Behind (NCLB) law, authored by the Texas education player Sandy Kress. The Texas Miracle has since been debunked as so much manipulation of test scores and phony graduation rates. Paige, who rode to the White House on its falsehoods, is history. And Bush's NCLB is sagging under the weight of impossible test goals and unfunded mandates, with even some Republicans now criticizing it. But privatization in public education and the credo of accountability through testing still chug along. CEP is one beneficiary. Despite a tarnished history and no independent evidence that its student-customers fare better than in regular public schools, CEP uses political clout to carve a niche market serving students the public schools don't want, and it makes millions in the process. CEP's story is a primer on how the politics of education reform serve business interests. Its success represents the triumph of free-market ideology over sound pedagogy, and the fallacy of the accountability-through-testing approach to teaching. "It's fair to say they [CEP] have avoided true scrutiny," said Carl Shaw, a former Texas state official who evaluated CEP's program. "Their modus operandi is political, not educational and not scientific."

CEP contracts with public school districts in Houston, Atlanta, Philadelphia, Richmond, and Orlando, and in the Pinellas and Bay districts in Florida, to run alternative schools for students in grades six through twelve who've been suspended for behavioral problems. Most students sent to CEP also are academically failing, and the vast majority are African-American and Latino. CEP's contract requires that students spend 120–180 days in the program—far in excess of the typical ten-day suspensions public schools impose on misbehaving students. CEP's rationale is that it needs time to transform kids' behavior and academic performance, but the company also has an obvious financial incentive for a longer placement. CEP's per-student charge varies by district, but it's more than the districts spend per pupil on regular students. In Orlando CEP gets $8,865 per pupil, double the district's own cost. Philadelphia pays CEP about $13,000 per pupil—almost twice the district's $7,000 average cost. "We charge more. We're a premium product," said Randle Richardson, the CEO of CEP. "Anyone can warehouse a child." CEP renovates abandoned big-box stores or industrial spaces, creating sex-segregated "learning communities." The students can't mingle and are walked in groups to bathrooms at specific times. Lunch is provided in their classrooms. Students may not bring money to school and are screened as if going through airport security, shoes and coats off. Teachers take attendance with an electronic fingerprint scanner that transmits the information back to CEP headquarters for payment.

Some critics have called CEP schools "soft jails." CEP boasts that it employs "certified teachers and degreed individuals with experience in behavior management, counseling or social services." But CEP faces the same shortage of certified teachers the public schools do, and it pays lower salaries. In its early Houston days, says Marsha Sonnenberg, a Fort Worth educator who consulted for CEP, "they used some people from corrections and some they trained. Some had been from the streets themselves and rehabbed. Some were a little more like me." Richardson said CEP pays for teacher-certification training when needed, and that such classes are brought onsite for his Philadelphia staff. "Be Here, Behave and Be Learning," is CEP's motto, but it should include "Be Tested," because students spend much of their learning time at computers with Plato, a self-paced tutorial that tests and assesses achievement. CEP uses Plato data to prove its claims of student improvement, but assessment experts give Plato mixed reviews, and some who've worked with it say cheating is not difficult.

Richardson, who founded CEP with his college buddy Phil Baggett, CEP's vice chairman, says his inspiration came from his early years as a small-town lawyer taking fifty-dollar juvenile delinquency cases from the family court judge. Then Richardson ran the Tennessee Farmers Home Administration, making loans to low-income home owners. John

Danielson, who would become undersecretary of education to Paige, was also a founder. Initial investors included Bill McInnes, formerly of the Hospital Corporation of America, and Tom Beasley, founder of the Corrections Corporation of America, the private prison company. CEP's early investors put up $65 million; the company is now backed by Stephens, Inc., a Little Rock, Arkansas, investment bank, and the Texas Growth Fund, a private equity firm created by the Texas legislature with public employee pension funds. Richardson says CEP's annual revenues are $70 million. Richardson bristles at questions about Beasley's role, sensitive to critics who've likened CEP schools to juvenile jails. "We had discussions early on that we are not going to be correctional," he says. "Tom understood. He said, 'I'm an investor. You guys are here to run the company.'"

But like Beasley, Richardson saw a ripe business opportunity in privatizing a public service—one that, like prisons, deals with society's messy failures. CEP's first contract was to operate a juvenile detention alternative-education program for Harris County, Texas. Giving CEP entrée into the Texas education scene was George Scott, then president of the Tax Research Association, a nonprofit education-reform group in Houston, and now a senior writer for the online newspaper *Education News*. Scott, who was close to Paige when Paige was Houston schools superintendent, helped CEP score its first public school contract, with the Houston district. Scott said he told Paige, "Rod, this is it. This is privatized accountability at its best." Scott later became a CEP critic, though, charging that the company evaded real accountability for a program that was educationally flawed and a waste of taxpayer money. "I look back on my role with CEP, my dedication and commitment to accountability, and it is the greatest professional disgrace in my career," Scott said. "As long as the district and the vendor have influence over accountability measures, it is corrupt." Richardson says his background is in government, but it's his Republican Party credentials that pay off. Like Tom Beasley before him, Richardson was Tennessee's GOP chair—from 1992 to 1995—helping to lead Republicans "out of the wilderness and into control of statewide offices," according to one news account. Richardson soft-pedals his political ties, calling himself a "Howard Baker Republican" and insisting CEP is above the partisan fray. But CEP has thrived on the accumulated political juice, mostly

Republican-flavored, Richardson and his cohorts have squeezed since its founding. In Texas CEP executives cultivated powerful friends, hiring the Houston school board member Larry Marshall as a $6,000-a-month consultant and landing an endorsement from George Bush, Sr., at the opening of CEP's first Houston school. "They were putting together the juiciest political team," Scott said. "They had powerful people at their beck and call." Political pull helped CEP waltz into Florida. Richardson and Baggett contributed to Charlie Crist's successful 2000 run for state education commissioner and to Governor Jeb Bush's 2002 campaign. In 2001 CEP's Florida lobbyist Juhan Mixon helped write a provision in a state appropriations bill that earmarked $4.8 million for "Alternative Schools/Public Private Partnerships." It was "to serve a minimum of 500 or more disruptive and low performing students"—a description tailored to CEP. Mixon also lobbies for several Florida school districts, including Bay, which hired CEP.

In Philadelphia CEP found privatization high on the agendas of Governor Tom Ridge, a Republican, and state politicians. The state took control of the bankrupt Philadelphia school district in 2001, and state legislators made privatizing schools one of the conditions for the bail-out. CEP's chief political ally in the statehouse was John Perzel, the Republican Speaker, whose beefy visage graces the company's website along with his testimonial. Richardson, Baggett, and CEP execs have contributed more than $11,000 to Perzel's campaigns. CEP's five-year, $28-million-a-year contract with Philadelphia schools was renewed in May 2004 with no debate.

CEP is a product of the high-stakes testing and accountability approach to education reform, which aims to run public schools like businesses whose products are students. Yet holding CEP accountable has been a quixotic undertaking because of the fluidity of the student population, the malleability of statistics, and the company's political savvy. The few totally independent evaluations of CEP's effectiveness have rated it poorly. Several evaluations were paid for by CEP, like one in 1999 by Diane Ravitch, an appointee to the first President Bush's education department, whose glowing endorsement of CEP's Houston program appears on its website. Others were based on testing data completely controlled by CEP. Texas CEP's first brush with evaluation was a lesson in the pitfalls of accountability and the importance of data control. In 1997 the Texas state education commissioner, Mike Moses, hired Carl Shaw, former chair of the Texas Education Agency's (TEA) assessment committee and head of Houston's testing for years, to assess CEP's first contract, the juvenile detention program. Shaw found limited student progress after six months in CEP, and after a year, actual regression. "I could find no evidence that there was a strong-enough academic program in place to produce change," he said. "One report I wrote for [the Houston Independent School District] said few CEP students would be smart enough for prison education. It's shocking, and here's a company touted as a leader." Shaw said Randle Richardson was angry at his findings and his refusal to compromise his work. "The first reaction I had from Richardson was, 'I am more powerful than you,'" Shaw said. CEP executives turned to Scott, the taxpayers' group president, for backup. "They wanted support that his test had gone awry," Scott said. "I told them I was one hundred percent into Dr. Shaw's approach." Scott says discussions he and CEP had been having about a consultancy and shares of founders' stock broke down because he refused to repudiate Shaw. Richardson says CEP raised concerns about Shaw's tests having "both positive and negative aberrations," and that they couldn't be validated by the TEA. Richardson noted that his relationship with Scott soured after the problems with Shaw's testing emerged.

Next up was Dr. Tom Kellow, an evaluation specialist for Houston's schools. In 1999 Superintendent Paige asked Kellow to evaluate CEP—but he was forbidden to visit the school and could only use data CEP provided. Kellow learned that CEP's contract stated that it could be held accountable based only on its own in-house testing, not the statewide Texas Assessment of Academic Skills (TAAS). "What I found is what Carl Shaw found," Kellow said. "The longer [students] stayed, the worse their performance." Although under NCLB all schools must meet Adequate Yearly Progress (AYP) standards for specific percentages of students testing at grade level in math and reading, the TEA exempts CEP. For both 2003 and 2004, the AYP status of CEP's two Houston schools is listed as "Not Evaluated." CEP's school profiles on the Houston schools website also reveal that the company evades the accountability that public schools face: no TAAS scores are listed and no information is provided for either state or district accountability measures.

Houston continues to contract with CEP despite those early assessments, but Dallas's public school district was more discriminating. Dallas hired CEP in 1999, with a five-year, $10 million yearly contract. But after three years the district bowed out; its own evaluation of CEP in 2002 recommended ending the contract, stating that "the model of education provided by [CEP] was untenable from a pedagogical standpoint. The reliance on non-certified teachers for the bulk of the student-teacher interaction was useful for the company to save money, but was not a design in the best interest of the students. . . . Students who attended Community Education Partners did not do very well academically." CEP had refused to provide its budget data, the report noted, making it impossible to know just how it was spending the district's money.

Dallas's report and a series of critical articles about CEP in the *Houston Press*, an alternative newsweekly, helped New Orleans public schools decide against a contract with CEP, according to the former school board president Cheryl Mills. And in Columbus, Ohio, CEP faced organized resistance in the black community when it first approached the public school district in 1999. The company took school board members to Houston and lobbied local community leadership. Support didn't reach critical mass but CEP resurfaced in 2003 and hired a local black woman to organize trips to CEP's Philadelphia school. CEP might have gotten a contract in Columbus but for Bill Moss, a school board member and talk-radio host who crusaded against CEP and the plan for a detention school, which he considered racially discriminatory. "CEP is a phony alternative," Moss says. "The kids are stigmatized. They've already been deprived and mishandled in the school system. What you're creating is a pipeline to the prison system." Moss thinks the school district suspends black students for minor infractions as a way to get rid of students whose low test scores bring down their school's overall achievement levels. Other board members and the school superintendent pressured Moss to vote for a CEP contract, but his broadcasts critical of CEP and the school board stirred up too much opposition in Columbus's black community. Moss won that round but was voted off the school board in August 2003.

CEP marched into Atlanta in 2002 and got a five-year, $10-million-a-year contract to run an alternative school for up to one thousand students with no debate and minimal mention in *The Atlanta Journal-Constitution*. In a city where the dropout rate is about 50 percent and the stringent mandates of NCLB hang like the sword of Damocles over administrators' heads, CEP offered a way to sweep low achievers out of regular classrooms, where they bring achievement levels down, opines Dr. Irving Mitchell, who was principal of the CEP school. "It's simple mathematics," said Mitchell. "You contract those kids out and they're in a separate environment; they aren't counted in the total." CEP's Atlanta school was the target of community organizing in early 2005 after the *Atlanta Voice*, a black-oriented newspaper, ran a series exposing serious inadequacies there. The articles provided accounts from Mitchell and a former CEP teacher. The CEP school was surrounded by a tall fence and guarded by ten to fifteen off-duty police officers as well as four to five full-time security guards. Students were permitted no books, pencils, or money when they entered through metal detectors and a pat-down search. Attendance was taken with electronic fingerprint readers that transmitted the data to CEP's headquarters to insure payment from the school district. There were sets of books in classrooms, but students could not take them home. Their movements within the school building were controlled. "Classes were ninety minutes long, and when kids moved from class to class, it was in a circle pattern so there was little opportunity to make contact with each other. They were fed in the class-room, the food brought in," he said. Teacher turnover was huge, with few certified teachers in the classrooms, he said. CEP promised to have one certified teacher and one paraprofessional in each class of ten students, but on an average day there weren't enough teachers and classes would be doubled up.

Mitchell had been a public school principal for twenty years in Georgia, Ohio, Tennessee, and South Carolina before retiring. CEP recruited him to take over the Atlanta school. "I feel I'm a reformer and have been very successful in turning schools around," he says. "I wanted to increase support, bring probation officers in, bring in some of the postsecondary educators who were in charge of community schools and involve the community." But CEP nixed his plans. "It's a for-profit and the kids are their product. They look at bottom-line figures and we ofttimes know that's not in the best interest of kids," Mitchell said. "It became a dump for human waste. Accountability is with the Atlanta school board for disenfranchising these kids. There was a contract and expectations, and I feel they were not met. The statistics show they weren't met." The Atlanta schools deputy superintendent Kathy Augustine called Mitchell "disgruntled." She said she was unaware that students could not take books home, that there was no homework, or that there was a teacher shortage. "I think we're improving," Augustine said. "It's a developing relationship. Finding leadership is key to that." She said she had no evidence that CEP was not living up to its contract. Told that CEP's school had failed to meet AYP standards for reading and math in the 2003–2004 school year, Augustine said, "The AYP piece is different for nontraditional schools because children are very fluid." She noted that the school board had voted to extend CEP's contract through 2009.

In Philadelphia supposedly independent evaluations of CEP were dependent on company-controlled data. In March Philadelphia released an evaluation of CEP's two schools, conducted by researchers at Temple University. The report surveyed 70 students and 70 parents who offered positive reports on CEP's program—a fraction of the more than 4,300 students CEP has served. In evaluating student academic growth, the report relied entirely on CEP's own Plato data, which claim astounding gains of three to four "grade levels" in reading and math for students who spend 180 days at CEP—but there's no indication of how many students actually stay that long. The school district itself partakes of the statistical spin. Paul Socolar, editor of *Philadelphia Public School Notebook*, an independent newspaper, noted that in 2004 the district issued a CEP fact sheet that excluded CEP scores on the statewide standardized test for eighth graders, which had gone down; in January of this year the district excluded results for CEP eleventh graders, which had also gone down. "It's a total manipulation of data," Socolar said. And as for meeting the AYP standards, CEP's Philly schools don't. Randle Richardson says the proof of his company's success is that districts keep renewing their contracts.

The question is how success is defined. Public schools have strong incentives to remove the lowest-performing students from their classrooms and make them CEP's problem, especially since the passage of No Child Left Behind. For Socolar, CEP is a political solution to the public system's failures: "From the beginning, the concern that jumped out about CEP is whether putting these students in the hands of private companies is a way of putting them out of sight and out of mind," he said. While the public schools are hammered by the accountability-through-testing mandates of NCLB, CEP skirts the same accountability and proves the uselessness of high-stakes testing as an education strategy. Judging CEP by its test data only seems to make sense because the company and school districts that hire it buy into that accountability measure. Test scores, in truth, can never be an end in themselves—or proof that children are learning. That's why NCLB is phony education reform. At the end of an interview, Richardson asked in almost plaintive tones, "Are we the enemy?" Well, yes and no. CEP may be doing a poor job, but it's only a symptom of the crumbling national commitment to public education, including the public schools' failure to educate huge percentages of mostly black and Latino students. Vouchers and other privatizing efforts in education have still not gained the momentum that conservatives had hoped for, but companies like CEP in the expanding private education industry help chip away at the public school infrastructure by targeting a market—the "bad students"—that has few advocates. CEP promotes privatization in a more quiet, effective way than Chris Whittle's Edison schools have. And Richardson's future ambitions reveal an astute understanding of the changing nature and needs of today's student population: He'd like to run schools for overage students—seventeen- or eighteen-year-olds who work or raise families and need flexible programming, the students who "don't fit in the box," he says. As the box holding traditional students shrinks, one challenge facing public school educators is how best to serve all students—from high achievers to the most disruptive kids like Morris Gandy's son. If the public sector abdicates its responsibility to educate all children, businessmen like Randle Richardson are ready to step in.

THE END OF ZERO TOLERANCE?

Zero tolerance discipline has a mounting record of failure as a strategy for creating and maintaining safe learning environments, and one with discriminatory outcomes for males and African-Americans in general. Indeed there is virtually no evidence that it has been successful in any of the goals it was designed to achieve. So why has it become so entrenched in our public schools? Perhaps because zero tolerance was never designed by educators with educationally sound and age-appropriate strategies in mind. Like the antidrug policies of the 1980s that spawned it, zero tolerance school policies were reactive and built on hype, not reality. "Zero tolerance started out as a sound bite. It was a political solution, not an educational solution," says Russ Skiba. "We've never gotten to the point of having accountability for it. I think it's a Berlin Wall, and one day it's just going to come down." That day may be more distant than many would like, though there are some reasons for optimism. Several national professional organizations with some measure of clout have issued condemnations of zero tolerance in schools that challenge its legal and educational underpinnings. The American Bar Association in 2001 adopted a resolution opposing the principle of zero tolerance discipline that criminalizes student behavior without individual consideration and calling for due process in handling alleged misbehavior. In 2006, the American Psychological Association's task force on zero tolerance issued a strong report calling for reforming the widespread policies and practices that were punishing students for inconsequential violations without offering constructive, effective strategies to reduce violence and improve school safety. The APA report noted the low incidence of serious violence in schools and the harmful consequences, racially disproportionate impact, and disruptive nature of zero tolerance.[15] While the report received significant news media coverage, there's hardly been a rush by schools to turn down the volume on punishments.

4 SUPERMAX SCHOOLHOUSE

You have kids in school being educated in life, and in prison you have a similar situation of people being reeducated. In theory they're not far apart. In the administrative side, you're trying to regulate and control a large group of people, so there are a lot of similarities. So if we're developing a technology, we can use it in both areas.
　　　　—Peter Cosgrove, deputy director, National Institute of Justice's Law
Enforcement and Corrections Technology Center, Southeast

I would not mind if someone said, "I heard Louis talk about shooting up the school." I would have no problem with that if they searched me. But the fact is that they promise me they don't think I'm a criminal, but they treat me as one.
　　　　—Louis Brenner, New Haven, Connecticut, high school student who
protested his school's new metal detection searches in 2006

On September 15, 2006, Louis Brenner took a stand against the new metal detectors at his school, Metropolitan Business Academy in New Haven, Connecticut. For the first few days the handheld wands were in use, Brenner, then sixteen and a high school junior, was bypassed in the random selection process, which pulled about every fifth student out of line to have bags and body screened by school security guards. "The whole time I was just talking to Nick and thinking about it: What would I do if they asked me?" says Brenner, referring to conversations with his friend, Nicholas Evans. "They finally asked me and I refused." After that day, Brenner was chosen to be screened on seven consecutive mornings and seven times he refused, claiming his Fourth Amendment right against unwarranted search. And each time the principal sent him home. "I would not mind if someone said, 'I heard Louis talk about shooting up the school.' I would have no problem with that if they searched me," Brenner says. "But the fact is that they promise me they don't think I'm a criminal, but they treat me as one."

Nick Evans's turn came four days later when a school resource officer at Hill Regional Career High School chose him to walk through the new portable metal detector. Evans, also sixteen and a junior, was more than ready to be a refusnik. After Superintendent Reginald Mayo sent out notices at the start of the school year informing students that metal detectors would be employed, Evans researched Fourth Amendment rulings involving student searches. "I have a thing about people going through my bag and stuff like that," he acknowledges. He also scrutinized the district's student handbook and discovered there was no policy permitting metal detectors and searches. "I'm all about knowing what's what. So I was kind of thinking, 'This doesn't sound right. I'm sure they can't be doing this,'" Evans says. He and Brenner had become acquainted through a mutual friend and discovered a shared passion for computers, and until then, that's mostly what they talked about. Articulate and assertive, Evans contacted the local WTNH radio and was interviewed on air about his protest. He blogged about the controversy, which was also debated on the school's MySpace page. Suddenly, he and Brenner were local media sensations—and thorns in the New Haven school board's side. "I caused the board to go into emergency session that day to talk about what to do," Evans recalls.

On a November morning a month after their two-man protest, Brenner and Evans related their story from the living room of the Evans family home on a suburban New Haven street where neighbors raked piles of leaves. Both boys had slight frames and firm handshakes, serious and self-possessed. Nick's hair was a bushy mass. His T-shirt featured a penguin bearing a "no" slash over the acronym SBC, which he explained has to do with Linux source code (allegedly) stolen from the Santa Cruz Operation. Louis wore dark jeans and a pullover shirt and sported a neatly trimmed goatee. At one point, they bantered about computer systems, revealing their geek side. Tina Evans, Nick's mother, having arranged plates of cookies and cups of tea for us, busied herself in the kitchen but popped in occasionally to add a parenthetical here, a footnote there. She was clearly proud of her son, and, with her husband, backed him up without question. Superintendent Mayo justified his decision to use metal detectors by citing several shootings of youth over the summer in Hill, a "crisis neighborhood," Tina said. She notes that metal detectors had long been in place at Hillhouse and Wilbur Cross, the largest high schools.

But there had never been a shooting in a New Haven school, and both Metropolitan and Career were small magnet schools for achievers and relatively incident-free. "When I went to a meeting to learn about this school, one teacher said, 'At this school we have not had a fight yet. This is such a friendly environment, the kids love each other here,'" recalls Brenner. "That was one thing they said to make me try to go there. They were making it sound like such a haven. I know there have been fights, but everybody doesn't get involved in it like at other schools. It's just very selective: these two kids fight and they throw them out, and that's the gist of it." Both schools reflect the whole district's demographics, with more than half African-American students. Brenner and Evans, who are white, say they'd never encountered racial tension. And like Brenner, Evans says he felt safe in his school, which saw occasional fights but never a hint of guns in his three years there. "On the first day I refused to go through," said Evans, "one of our administrators said that over his career he'd taken a BB gun, a paint ball gun, and several knives from students, but never an actual slug thrower."

Evans and Brenner thought the detectors were a political response to those summer shootings and as such their use was inconsistent and fairly useless. Scanning occurred only at the start of the day, so late-arriving students walked in freely. "In the first few days, there's a door right next to the one where we filed through and it was wide open. It goes right to the cafeteria," said Brenner. "So literally half the kids figured, 'Oh, I'm not putting up with this line,' and just walked into school." Evans said searches of book bags at Career were cursory, with school resource officers merely patting the top. "Obviously, I can't put an assault gun or rifle or sword in there," he observed. "Not many people who are going to be wielding a weapon like that are going to want any form of secrecy. That's a Columbine-type thing. If you're hell-bent on blowing a dozen people away in your school, you're not going to go through the security checkpoint."

After several weeks of protest, Evans and Brenner took different paths in ending it. Evans never returned to Career, determined not to submit to scanning and searches that he believed were degrading and invasive. He was frustrated, too, that no other students stood with him despite promises by some. With his parents' blessing, he enrolled in an adult education center and was on track to graduate a year early. Brenner chose to end his protest, concerned that he was falling behind in his schoolwork. After seven days of refusing searches and being sent home,

Brenner finally gave in. "The whole day I felt like a shell of a man. I had no personality after that," he said. "I made myself believe I would win this. I was such an optimist." But Brenner saw he would get no further in protesting the metal detectors—the school board had quickly acted to write a new policy permitting them, so he plunged back into work. "I learned so much from this experience," he said. "I used to be interested in school elections, but not as interested as I am now. Now, I'm reading as much as I possibly can because I want to get into politics. And I still will talk to kids to try to force an opinion."

Student protests against high-tech security and surveillance systems are few and far between. That's why Evans's and Brenner's defiance was news. Post–September 11, acquiescence to heightened security is widespread. And post-Columbine submission to technological fixes for problems of student behavior is taken for granted. Metal detectors and video surveillance are relatively old-school technologies, with several decades of use in public schools. Newer, emerging approaches to security and access control—who gets into a school building—are bringing cutting-edge technologies designed for military and corrections uses into our schoolhouses with little discussion of their need, effectiveness, or impact on students. One example is biometrics, which identifies individuals through unique physical or behavioral characteristics. According to the International Biometric Industry Association, biometrics are being "deployed to strengthen security and properly allocate benefits in primary and secondary schools," as well as to control students' access to the Internet on school computers. Biometric systems such as iris recognition and fingerprint scans, which have prison applications, are now in schools. Computer programs that check school visitor identities against sex offender lists are also gaining popularity, encouraged by rampant fears of predators. And radio frequency identification (RFID), developed for military applications and now commonly used by industry, is promoted for tracking students. The mantra of school safety is being used to justify technology for its own sake—and for the profits of savvy entrepreneurs.

This technology transfer into schools has been helped along with research and grants from the National Institute of Justice, the research and development arm of the U.S. Department of Justice. The trend in school violence might be continually downward, yet public fears of it remain pretty constant. More recently, fears of terrorist attacks have pumped up security concerns at schools. For the nation's $20 billion security industry, public schools are fertile ground waiting to be plowed. "There is a conflation of interests right now," says Nicole Ozer, technology and civil liberties specialist at the Northern California ACLU. "Companies want to make money and government wants to create a surveillance infrastructure. Homeland Security is sending down millions to communities that want to look like they are doing something about crime. After Columbine, people don't even question it in schools. They say one of three things to justify the surveillance: terrorism, crime, or child safety. They employ things that don't really address problems in schools. Why not more counselors?"

Counselors? Or surveillance cameras and security software? Although the two approaches are not necessarily mutually exclusive, as school violence emerged as a widespread concern, a criminal justice approach to safety and violence-prevention became the predominant model. When police were sent to quell racial and social protests in the late 1960s, the first steps to Lockdown High were taken. As the national focus on crime, and juvenile crime in particular, sharpened in the 1980s, it was all but inevitable that alternatives to that model would be marginalized. Schools typically employ counselors or school psychologists, but they have never been central to safety and security approaches. With punishment and discipline as the guiding principles for controlling students, adapting security hardware and control strategies from corrections and defense sectors followed logically.

TECH TRANSFER IN THE PRISON-SCHOOL NEXUS

In 1998, Congress reacted to a spate of high-profile shootings over the previous year by enacting the Safe Schools Initiative, a seemingly muscular program meant to show how seriously lawmakers took school violence. The shootings were indeed shocking and came in rapid-fire succession: October 1997 in Pearl, Mississippi; December 1997 in Paducah, Kentucky; March 1998 in Jonesboro, Arkansas; and May 1998 in Springfield, Oregon. Among other things, the initiative directed the National Institute of Justice to develop new and appropriate weapons detection and surveillance technologies for schools. NIJ created a

School Safety Program and made its National Law Enforcement and Corrections Technology Centers–Southeast the home for research into state-of-the-art policing and prison technologies that could apply to public schools. At the same time, NIJ funded Sandia National Laboratories, a Department of Energy facility in Albuquerque, New Mexico, to apply its expertise in security technologies to schools. Sandia is run by the defense and aeronautics behemoth Lockheed Martin under contract to the Department of Energy and primarily supports the U.S. nuclear weapons program. Facilitating Sandia's work on public schools was Senator Jeff Bingham of New Mexico, who earmarked funds to one of his home state's big employers.

Sandia's Security Technologies and Research Division had been working on school security since about 1991, according to Mary W. Green, who was among those employees involved. The division had several hundred staffers researching security for high-risk facilities, such as nuclear power plants. Green recalls that people in her unit were contacted by local school officials who asked about security technology for their buildings. "All of us were into schools. We had kids. We were these nerdy types who wore polyester. My husband's pants were about four inches too short," she says with a laugh. "We were invited to school meetings and went on our own time and used discretionary funds." Green and her bosses wanted to share what they knew, a technology transfer to schools at a time when school security had become a "hot issue," she says. Sandia undertook a pilot project at Belen High School, south of Alberquerque, funded by the Department of Energy. Later, the NIJ money funded Sandia to research and test security hardware, such as metal detectors and surveillance cameras, to determine what works and what doesn't in a school. "One of the big impetuses for us to get into this is that the security industry isn't regulated. Anybody can open up shop and call themselves security experts," Green notes. "Schools notoriously have to go with the lowest bidder, and they get the junk." She recalls visiting a Washington, D.C., school that had wired part of the building for new alarms. "They didn't bother running the wiring through the walls," she says. "They just ran it along a hallway. It broke my heart. A school can get a couple thousand and just waste it."

In 1999, NIJ published "The Appropriate and Effective Use of Security Technologies in U.S. Schools," a manual on which Green had spent a year working for schools and law enforcement. Its 129 colorfully illustrated pages detail the pros and cons of video surveillance, metal detectors, and entry control technologies. Chapter one explains the rationales for security hardware when "simply providing more adults" in a school isn't enough, including "humans don't do mundane tasks well" and "manpower costs are always increasing." Back then, security technologies had yet to become as widely accepted as they are today, a fact Green attributed to limited school budgets and experience with technology, as well as privacy and civil rights issues. So she offered counterarguments to those who opposed cameras or metal detection in schools. To the argument "This is a knee-jerk reaction," the manual recommended parrying, "This solution will take care of the immediate threat while longer term social programs are put in place." "Our school will look like a prison" should be rebutted with "Our school will look like it is well controlled." Green's manual also provides legal advice on the placement and use of video surveillance: avoid areas like gym lockers or bathrooms where there is a "reasonable expectation of privacy."

Metal detection gets a thorough examination that notes its weaknesses: "a metal detector alone cannot distinguish between a gun and a large metal belt buckle," "a metal detector is only as good as the operator overseeing its use," and the clear-eyed observation "It is very difficult to do truly random checks with any hope of locating weapons." Green's guide, though nearly a decade old, is still a widely cited resource for school security, and she believes it has had an impact. "I think some schools have gotten in some tools. I don't know if I can say a lot," she says. "Back when I first got involved, people would say, 'Cameras? Kids will think we don't trust them.' Now cameras are really common, and for that we owe a lot to McDonald's and Kinko's. Because of them it's less unheard-of in schools." Sadly for Green, the congressional fervor that pumped funding into Sandia's research cooled when school safety was no longer the "hot" issue, as Green put it. Now Sandia doesn't work on school security. "I thought it would be my life because schools need this. I'm doing mints now," Green says wistfully, referring to U.S. currency production facilities, "but it doesn't have the heart-wrenching thing."

Down in South Carolina, staff at NIJ's National Law Enforcement and Corrections Technology Center—Southeast have also been cooking up new applications of hot security and surveillance technologies for public schools. One of a half-dozen regional centers established by the NIJ, the Southeast Center was assigned the school safety portfolio as its specialty. About a fifth of its budget is dedicated to testing and promoting new technologies for school security, according to Peter Cosgrove, the deputy director. "Our mission is technology oriented toward law enforcement and corrections," says Cosgrove. Center staff attend conferences on the latest tech trends and organize annual School Safety Technology Workshops for school administrators to learn from experts. As an example, Cosgrove mentioned a conference in Pittsburgh that he attended in summer 2007 on geospacing, a technology for computer mapping of internal building spaces that was designed for prisons. "Schools and corrections facilities share something in common, in terms of crime mapping," Cosgrove says. "We're working on developing a three-dimensional building plan. That same type of technology will be useful in both prisons and schools." Locating inmates—or students—within the complex warren of cells or classrooms over multiple floors and building wings allows for tracking and identifying the populations, he explains.

Center staff go to technology shows, where they talk to vendors and compare various products. "We're not allowed to recommend anybody, but we can say, 'This is on the market and it has these advantages,'" Cosgrove says. One product the center tested is a an interactive software program called Incident Commander, which guides the user through a school-shooting event. "As you go through, it suggests processes," Cosgrove explains: "how to lock the school down, the colored papers teachers put on their doors to indicate if the room is secure or not, the role of the SRO and the administration. That's been pretty well received." At another technology conference, Cosgrove watched demonstrations of surveillance cameras that transmit to local police agencies from schools to aid them in case of an incident. "It's a fun place. It's like the *MacGyver* show, you know, how he could put something together with a piece of string," he says, referring to a TV detective series. "We kind of think, What's out there? What has the military got and how can we use this? We're trying to find new applications." Another technology with potential for school and prison applications, Cosgrove notes, is RFID— radio frequency identification, commonly used today for toll collection. But it has its drawbacks. "Here's where people start having privacy issues," he says. "I might put a chip in my dog but I'm not putting one on my kid. In theory, you could give each kid an ID card imbedded with a small radio chip of a certain frequency, and you could monitor his movements. Again, there's an analogy with prisons: you could track a prisoner within the prison. With GPS [global positioning systems], you could use it to track people. That technology already exists, but how much do you want the government to know?"

One current focus of the center's work is cell phones, an effort Cosgrove says is called Detect and Defeat: detect the cell phone and disable it without disabling communication in an entire area. Cosgrove says the technology can apply in prisons, where cell phone use is prohibited, and schools, where it is often restricted. The two institutions, he notes, have much in common. "If you want to stretch the comparison, you have kids in school being educated in life, and in prison you have a similar situation of people being reeducated. In theory they're not far apart," Cosgrove philosophizes. "On the administrative side, you're trying to regulate and control a large group of people, so there are a lot of similarities. So if we're developing a technology, we can use it in both areas." Like Green, Cosgrove thinks metal detectors aren't very effective and create the perception, not the reality, of safer schools. "Metal detection is basically a magnet. It doesn't tell you much," Cosgrove says. "Kids carrying backpacks with metal catches or even a jacket with metal buttons will set them off, and if you have to back them down to allow for that, they might not detect a Glock with only a little metal in it. Sometimes in the security business you put things up to make people feel safer as opposed to being safer."

Despite drawbacks and limitations, security technologies have been embraced by a meaningful portion of public school administrators and local officials—like New Haven's Superintendent Mayo—as a knee-jerk response to security concerns. Nearly 6 percent of public schools of all levels employ random metal detector checks on students, such as Louis Brenner faced. For middle schools, it's 10 percent; for high schools, 13 percent. Slightly more than 1 percent use walk-through detectors daily, and that increases to 2 percent for middle schools and nearly 4 percent for high schools. Security cameras are the most prevalent technology, used in 36 percent of all schools; nearly 64 percent of high, 42 percent of middle, and 29 percent of primary schools use surveillance cameras. Viewed through a different lens, 11 percent of all students attend schools that use metal detectors; 58 percent of students attend school under the watchful eye of surveillance cameras. With a total public school population of some 26 million, simple math says that for millions of children, being scanned and monitored has become as much a part of their daily education as learning to read and write.[1] Of course, not all schools have the gadgetry of Lockdown High. But in some localities, costly high-tech security, such as the newest biometric or software system for access control, are as integral to the educational agenda as new textbooks. In one indicator of how important security technology has become in schools, the trade magazine *Security* published its first ranking of the "biggest and the best security programs in the U.S." and gave public schools a prominent place on it. Called the Security 500, the list includes fourteen public school districts—six of them in Florida. Ranked 291, Houston Independent School District was tops among schools—and one step above Intel. Number one on the list was the Department of Homeland Security.[2]

Acceptance of security technology may be widespread, but resistance is hardly unknown—or futile. In a Northern California community with a conservative, small-town bent, ordinary folks started a ruckus heard around the world when the schools tagged their kids like livestock.

TRACKING STUDENTS LIKE CATTLE

Michelle Tatro remembers the day in January 2005 when she picked up her daughter, an eighth grader at Brittan Elementary School in Sutter, California, and she was wearing a new ID card. "I could see she was visibly angry," Tatro says. "She had this thing around her neck and said, 'They're making us wear this.' It was 'You'll wear this or else.'" Lauren showed her mother a lump on the back of the card and said the principal had told students that boxes installed over bathroom doors could read the cards. The purpose, he said, was to catch kids doing graffiti. Michael and Dawn Cantrall also had kids at Brittan and they were not happy about the new IDs, either. Together with Michelle and her husband, Jeff, they met with the principal. "This was the first time we heard about radio frequency identification," Michelle Tatro says. "They were talking about antennas and used the word *track*. At first they wanted to sell it as an attendance-taking device. Then they said it was for safety—if the building was on fire, they could locate students." For Sutter, a small, rural town where the entire eighth grade had just eighty-three kids, such high-tech attendance seemed anomalous, to say the least. Also at the meeting was the vice principal, a teacher, and the school district's attorney. The Tatros and Cantralls soon learned that the teacher, Doug Ahlers, had created the RFID badges for a local company, InCom. And the attorney also worked for InCom. "It's a small town," Tatro says, "and very incestuous."

RFID technology consists of a minuscule computer chip encoded with information that emits a radio signal. A reader—a stationary or handheld device—can pick up the signal if the chip is within range. While RFID makers say that range is only a few inches for typical low-frequency tags, research indicates that it is possible for a chip to be read as much as sixty-nine feet away. Originally created to identify aircraft during WWII, RFID technology has been widely used to track retail products and livestock. It's also used for quick-pass toll collection on roads and bridges, and more recently, RFID has been considered for such documents as passports and drivers licenses.[3] The encoding on Brittan students' badges was a random number, the principal told parents, but Michelle Tatro doesn't know what information her daughter's badge contained. "When we got home, we looked on the Internet to see what it's capable of," Tatro says. "People could be tracked without their knowledge wherever they go. This child is walking home from school and if he's got a badge in his backpack, it could still be read by a pedophile or by the school bully." In the two years after the Sutter incident, the privacy and surveillance issues for human use raised by parents were amplified in a succession of reports from the Government Accountability Office and the Department of Homeland Security from 2005 and 2006. They warned about breaches to the privacy and integrity of information on RFID tags, confirming the Tatros' and Cantralls' worst fears as parents. In one chilling section of a 2005 GAO report on information security, it warned: "Without effective security controls, data on the tag can be read by any compliant reader; data transmitted through the air can be intercepted and read by unauthorized devices; and data stored in the databases can be accessed by unauthorized users."

Alarmed by the intrusive potential of RFID, the parents sought help the old-fashioned way: they wrote letters to civil liberties groups. At the ACLU, their letter landed with Nicole Ozer, who had just started working as a technology and privacy specialist at the Northern California office. At the Electronic Frontier Foundation in San Francisco, their pleas reached Lee Tien, a staff attorney who had been involved in opposing a plan to use RFID in San Francisco Public Library books. Ozer and Tien went to Sutter to advocate for the families at school board meetings and public forums. "When I learned about it I was appalled," Tien says. "It was being forced on parents without their consent or approval. They were told to submit or their child couldn't attend school." Ozer's office issued a press release and Sutter was suddenly catapulted into the national—even international—media spotlight. Calls flooded in from print and broadcast outlets, including *The Today Show* and the BBC, requesting interviews with the Tatros and Cantralls. "They were the kind of people who resonate with other parents," Ozer says. "They weren't talking about some abstract civil liberties issue. They were talking about their kids being safe and not being tracked like cattle."

School administrators at first argued that the InCom system was needed for attendance, to save teachers time and insure the district would receive all the per-student federal aid to which it was entitled. But they couldn't say how much money was saved, Lee Tien recalls, so they said it was about security. Tien and Ozer learned that financial interests were really the key motivation for using InCom's system. By agreeing to be the pilot, the district got the tags and readers for free and would be InCom's model school to attract more business around California, Tien says. And if RFID attendance became mandatory at the state level, which was the company's dream, InCom would strike gold and district employees would share in the profits. "You have security as a reason to justify things, but it's all about following the money," Tien says. "It was a financially indefensible sweetheart deal, with the lawyer for the school who we dealt with acting as a lawyer for company. I just scratched my head." Ozer says that while many parents shared the Tatros' and Cantralls' concerns, others were reluctant to complain because of close connections among all the players. "It's a small town and we weren't able to identify who had invested in the company, because it's not publicly traded," Ozer says.

Over three weeks of slowly organizing parents and researching RFIDs, the Tatros and Cantralls saw their efforts pay off at a public meeting held in a church at which InCom, school officials, and parents discussed the RFID system. Ozer and Tien informed parents about the potential risks of the technology and the activist parents told what they'd discovered. "We put posters around the room: here's what we learned on the Internet, do your own homework," Michelle Tatro says of their presentation. "The majority of parents was against it—about three quarters." By then, the media swarm in Sutter had put added pressure on the school officials and InCom. At the next school board meeting, the InCom VP and high school teacher Doug Ahlers announced the company was pulling out of Sutter's school before a packed audience of parents and news media. "It was only a minor relief," says Tatro. "The company is still in business. They are as tenacious as I am." Tatro's campaign against RFIDs is still rolling several years later. She travels to Sacramento to lobby for legislation inspired by Sutter's experience that would ban RFIDs in public schools. "These children don't need to be monitored like an inmate. They have committed no crime to lose the right to security and privacy," she says. The bill was introduced by State Senator Joe Simitian and passed both houses in 2007 only to be vetoed by Governor Arnold Schwarzenegger. The Security Industry Association, a lobby group, claimed his veto as a "victory" that would cause lawmakers in other states to "listen to us on this issue in the future."[4] But it wasn't the corporate titans who sparked the Sutter story, Lee Tien notes. "What really opened up the issue for me was to see, my God, this isn't being done by the governor. It was a decision being made by one of the most local bodies, at the grassroots. It is the InComs of the world that are spreading technology," he says. "That is their modus operandi: Go to that local school board level and sell it."

In two school districts in New Jersey, a similar story of insiders parlaying parental fears for student safety into a technology venture in the schoolhouse is playing out. But so far, no Tatros or Cantralls are in sight.

THE PIG FLIES IN NEW EGYPT

New Egypt is a rural enclave in New Jersey's center where comfortable blue-collar home owners abut growing numbers of affluent urban refugees. Unemployment and crime are low, and like Sutter, New Egypt is a small, homogeneous community. Just 1,700 kids attend four schools in the Plumsted Township School District. Plumsted prides itself on "providing the highest quality programs at a reasonable cost to the taxpayer" and on being "one of the most frugal" in the state. The district works fiscal miracles with staff that "constantly write for, and receive, federal, state, and private organization grants," according to the state education department.[5] Just such an entrepreneurial spirit motivated Michael Dean, Plumsted's technology director, to send a grant proposal to the National Institute of Justice in 2002 for money to create a first-ever iris-recognition-cum-access-control system for the district's schoolhouses. In a district where, as one news article put it, "The biggest security breach in recent memory . . . happened when a parent forgot to sign in at the office before delivering cupcakes to a child's classroom,"[6] Dean's proposal could seem incongruous. After all, iris recognition is at the leading edge of biometrics, used in U.S. jails and prisons to track inmates and authenticate their identity, and piloted in some airports as a sort of E-ZPass for passengers. New Egypt schools would be the first to use it. "We thought, 'Let's see if this pig will fly,'" says Dean.

The proposal was actually a collaboration between Dean and a technology executive he knew, and was designed to tap federal funds to advance their mutual interests. "My ulterior motive was to fund fiber optics between our schools" for data communications, Dean recalls. "Ray Bolling of New Jersey Business Systems [and I] were brainstorming on how to get this fiber optics funded. Ray had seen a presentation on biometrics and iris recognition. He knew about NIJ grants." Although the iris recognition system for security was the stated reason for the grant, the NIJ grant covered the cost of the fiber-optic cable as well, Dean says. Ray Bolling was a VP of NJBS, which provided data cabling for New Egypt's schools, when he met Michael Dean. The two hit it off, Bolling recalls. "At the time, my wife and I were married a year and we were looking for a place to live," he says. "Meeting Mike and learning about the town, learning about the quality of schools, the town reminded me of West Windsor, where I grew up." As a community member Bolling had an interest in saving the schools money, and helped Dean replace a costly data and phone system with cheaper DSL. As a businessman, Bolling stepped in when Dean wanted to install fiber optics for security cameras in the elementary school. "That's work our company does," Bolling explains, and he gave a $110,000 bid. However, Bolling's father, his company's chief, had a better idea: get a grant. Bolling and Dean learned about NIJ school safety grants. But how could they stand out among all the proposals for video surveillance and student IDs? "One of my roles in the company is to look at technology in future," Bolling says. "Biometrics was one technology I wasn't familiar with, so I went to a presentation about iris recognition." Coincidentally, the presenter had worked for Bolling's father years earlier. When Bolling then saw an article about a teacher thwarting a woman trying to take her brother's child from school, he found just the hook to snare a grant. "How do we positively identify parents authorized to sign kids out of school? If we could use iris recognition, it's been proven the fastest and most accurate biometric identifier." The NIJ, which supports research into biometrics in general and iris recognition in particular, awarded Plumsted $293,360.

Dean and Bolling named their system T-PASS, for Teacher-Parent Authentication Security System, and assembled the pieces to create it. Hewlett-Packard donated a server and sold them two others. The patented iris recognition software was purchased from Iridian, and an access-control system came from a South Carolina company. Cameras installed inside and outside school entrances would check the irises of those trying to enter against a database of images obtained from teachers, administrators, and parents. The elementary school was chosen for a pilot study of T-PASS, which included iris recognition for entry and for parents checking out their kids during the school day. Parents could participate or opt out and use a buzzer system for entry, while all school employees were required to participate. The system was also installed at the middle and high schools for faculty and employee entry. Students were not part of T-PASS other than being the subjects of its supposed protective purpose. The district and its tech team spent fall 2002 and spring 2003 informing and enrolling parents and faculty into the new system, and by April 2003, T-PASS was initiated in the schools and the pilot at the New Egypt elementary commenced. The NIJ also awarded a $149,000 grant to 21st Century Solutions, a Maryland consulting group, to evaluate T-PASS. But in a district with no security problems, how could a system built to keep out the wrong people be judged a success or a failure? Ray Bolling revealed an ulterior purpose behind the T-PASS pilot. "We wanted to measure people's acceptance of technology," he says. "If people accept it in a school system for safety for kids, would they accept it for other applications? We exceeded the number of parents we thought we would enroll." And, he adds, "we got worldwide attention for the project."

Acceptance of T-PASS wasn't high at all. Nearly 60 percent of elementary school parents refused to have their irises photographed and used the buzzer entry system instead. Evaluators surveying parents, faculty, and administrators before and after the April to June 2003 pilot gleaned contradictory reactions: "iris recognition [appears] to have the twin effects of increasing perceptions of security and increasing the number of perceived problems." They called the anomaly a "'boomerang' effect" resulting from the fact that "new security technologies make people feel more secure, while simultaneously reminding them of the problems that surround them." They also noted that the system would do nothing to prevent "many forms of victimization in schools" since they are usually perpetrated by those who belong there—the very people T-PASS lets inside the schoolhouse. T-PASS's biggest fans were school secretaries who told evaluators it "significantly cut down on the amount of parents walking around the school trying to find their kids." The technology had its operating snafus, too, with outside cameras functioning poorly on sunny days and many people "tailgating"—slipping in behind a T-PASS-authorized entrant to save time.[7]

Despite these flaws and no measurable impact on school security, Michael Dean and Ray Bolling got a follow-up NIJ grant of $369,000 to install T-PASS in Freehold, New Jersey, schools in 2006. By then, they had created their own company, Eyemetric, to profit from their invention in Plumsted. "I couldn't do that as a public school district employee," Dean says. Bolling, Eyemetric president, saw in Freehold the opportunity to take T-PASS to the next level, with newer cameras, tailgating detection, and software that prints out visitor badges. But parent participation in Freehold was even lower than in Plumsted—about 20 percent. And like Plumsted, Freehold had no security problems. "In a small community like Plumsted, everybody knew everybody," Bolling admits. "The secretary knew everyone from the community." Using the federal grant as seed money for their private venture, the savvy duo revamped T-PASS to exploit a more palpable threat. "We now have deployed a new program: T-PASS for sex offenders," explains Bolling. "Our goal is to build an affordable system for schools at a cost of $2,400 per school." This T-PASS checks school visitors against law enforcement sex offender databases. Interest has been slower than Eyemetric's founders had anticipated. "A lot of that is budgets and it being the end of school year,"

Bolling explains. "We are about to do a back-to-school mailer saying, 'Here are things you should look at.'" New Egypt schools were the first to have T-PASS with Sex Offender Lookup, as it is called, even though, as Michael Dean says, sex predators aren't a problem in Plumsted Township. "But obviously throughout the nation people worry," Dean notes. "If you watch Fox News, you'd think that every kindergarten teacher is molesting six-year-olds. But the bottom line is that schools continue to be one of the safest places for kids to go."

Even Dean seems to acknowledge how silly such high-tech surveillance is, especially in low-crime communities and at a time of budget austerity. Still, when it comes to school safety, irrational fears about sex predators can trump reality—and common sense. In Lake Travis, Texas, one mother learned this lesson trying to get into her kids' school.

HUNTING PREDATORS, CATCHING PARENTS

When Yvonne Meadows went to Bee Cave Elementary School for scheduled teacher conferences on September 28, 2006, office staff asked for her driver's license. Puzzled, she asked why. "Usually, we just sign our name on a paper log," Meadows explains about a year later. "The kids have been in school there for a year. They already know me." What's more, the school already had a copy of her license on file, obtained when she registered her children. Meadows was told that the school had just installed a new computer software program from a company called Raptor. The program was V-Soft, for Visitor, Student, or Faculty Tracking, and it would check visitor identification against databases of registered sex offenders and raise an "alert" if a match was found. Either by scanning a license or using data input manually, the program transmits the birth date, license ID number, and photo of an individual to the company, which then checks them and flags any matches. That personal data is retained in the Raptor system, and a connected printer issues an ID badge for the visitor. The principal told Meadows the new policy was posted in the school and applied to all visitors—parents, vendors, and others. Meadows's gut feeling was that this was an unnecessary intrusion on her privacy. What would Raptor do with her information? "My own common sense said, 'This doesn't make sense to me,'" Meadows says. "I am a parent and I have the right to attend these meetings." She refused to submit to the check, so the principal refused to allow her general access to the school, and Meadows had to meet with her kids' teachers in a conference room.

Bee Cave is one of seven schools in the Lake Travis School District, an affluent suburb just west of Austin, Texas, and like the New Jersey schools, there was no history of security or safety lapses, says Larry Meadows, Yvonne's husband, an attorney. "When has a parent of a student ever molested a child? I know of no case whatsoever. It's a red herring," says Larry. "If a molester wanted to, they would anyway." He recalls that when their kids started at Bee Cave, there was no security at all. "People could walk in willy-nilly. Then they go to lockdown," he says. "They didn't confer with parents. They just did it." The board contracted with Raptor Technologies, a Houston-based company that has elbowed its way into dozens of school districts in Texas and other states with the pledge to make schools safer. The presumption of some school administrators seems to be that technology justifies itself, especially when the words *sex predator* are attached. "Everybody is looking for ways to keep their kids safe in light of what is happening in the world today," said one Texas principal in a news account about her school's use of Raptor's system. "It's invaluable for the safety of the kids."[8]

When on a subsequent visit to the school for a performance Yvonne Meadows again refused to hand over her license for scanning, the principal insisted on escorting her to the auditorium and scolded her for making trouble. Meadows decided to file a grievance about the new policy, requesting relief from having to submit to the screening. Her grievance worked its way through the district bureaucracy, from the principal to the assistant superintendent to the superintendent, who simply passed it to the school board to resolve. The board denied Meadows, too. So she pulled her kids out of Bee Cave and started to homeschool them while her husband filed a petition with the Texas education commissioner. The heart of his argument was that Lake Travis's inflexible policy was denying Yvonne her parental rights to be fully involved in their children's education, forcing her to choose between her privacy rights and participation at school events. He likened the district's use of the Raptor system to "an unwarranted and illegal electronic dragnet of parents." The Lake Travis board ramped up its legal defenses, hiring Giuliani & Bracewell, the Houston firm headed by Rudolph Giuliani. In August 2007, an initial ruling by an administrative law judge at the Texas Education Agency went against the Meadowses. The ruling focused on Yvonne Meadows's claim of rights to privacy for her information and asserted that the TEA had no jurisdiction to rule on that issue. The ruling then rested in the hands of the commissioner, a recent appointee of Governor Rick Perry, who could accept or overturn the decision. I scheduled an interview with the Lake Travis assistant superintendent Diane Frost about the V-Soft program but she abruptly canceled it, telling me, "Lake Travis ISD chooses not to participate in this interview." By November 2007, the Meadows family had relocated to a different town and were still waiting to hear a final decision. They were contemplating filing a lawsuit. "It's a key case. A lot of school districts are implementing this," says Larry Meadows. "What are most parents going to do? They are going to cave in because if you're against this, are you for sex offenders? That's the game they're playing. Of course we don't want sex offenders in school."

The Meadowses' fight was an uphill battle, though, especially in light of SB 9, a law enacted in June 2007 by the Texas legislature. An amendment to the Texas Education Code, SB 9 authorizes—but does not mandate—school districts to require IDs from visitors, legalizes storing the information in an electronic database, and permits checking IDs against sex offender registries. SB 9 states that districts may access state registries directly or contract with an "entity" to access the sex offender list. If the language sounds tailor-made for a private entity like Raptor, there's a reason. Raptor's CEO, Allan Measom, hired a lobbyist to promote SB 9 and had discussions with staff of the legislation's sponsor. At an education committee hearing to discuss the bill on May 1, 2007, Raptor's lobbyist attended in support of the bill. Measom has said his goal is get similar legislation passed in every state.

On the other side of Austin, in the Del Valle school district, another parent was ensnared by the V-Soft system because she *couldn't* produce a driver's license or government photo ID. She was an undocumented immigrant. Del Valle installed Raptor's product in its eleven schools in February 2007, and in April, the problem posed by V-Soft for the area's large immigrant population drew the attention of the Mexican American Legal Defense and Education Fund (MALDEF), a civil rights organization. The staff attorney David Hinojosa had heard of many other school districts using such software, and it wasn't just immigrants shut out, but grandparents and poor people who may not drive or acquire passports or other legal documents that serve as valid ID. He contacted the Del Valle administrators with MALDEF's concerns about stifling parental access. Pressured by MALDEF's threat of legal action, the administration modified its policy, Hinojosa says. Those without a license or other ID first must submit to a background check conducted at the school district office twice annually. Hinojosa said the resolution wasn't completely satisfactory. If MALDEF weren't burdened by so many other cases, especially those generated by the No Child Left Behind law, Hinojosa might have pursued litigation on Fourteenth Amendment due process and parental rights grounds. "They said the issues were safety and security," says Hinojosa from his office in San Antonio. "Normally, you go to such extreme and drastic measures when something has occurred. But there weren't child predators going in the schools. It's criminalizing every person."

In the schoolhouse, criminalizing measures and measures used on criminals are trampling on rights and privacy in the name of security— or efficiency. Fingerprinting, long synonymous with entry into the criminal justice system, is now gaining entrée to the school cafeteria.

NO LUNCH FREE FROM BIG BROTHER

Penn Cambria School District embraces 108 square miles of rural Pennsylvania in the Keystone State's western flank, where bituminous coal mines were a major source of jobs in a bygone era. The demographics of the district, thirty-five miles east of Pittsburgh and fifteen west of Altoona, are today those of working-poor whites, with an unhealthy unemployment rate of 8.6 percent. Forty-two percent of its roughly 1,800 students qualify for free or reduced-cost meals, and just 55 percent of graduates go on to college. The area's four largest employers are the state correctional institution in Cresson, the federal penitentiary in Loretto, St. Francis University, and Penn Cambria School District. The choices for Penn Cambria's graduates are starkly contrasted indeed.[9] Yet in a place where prospects are as limited as people's incomes, Penn Cambria has been an unlikely school technology pioneer. In 1999, it piloted a new system for students to buy their lunches by touching a scanner that reads their index fingerprint. Aware of the criminal justice association with the procedure, administrators discussing the new system eschewed the word *fingerprint* for the euphemisms "finger-image" and "finger-picture."[10] "Our biggest concern when we put it in was if these tiny finger scans would be read and recognized by the system," recalls District Superintendent Mary Beth Whited.

Fingerprint recognition is another biometric technology used in correctional institutions that's found commercial application in public schools. There is no security angle to fingerprint scans, though. Business is promoting biometrics as an efficient and cost-effective way to speed student lunch lines and collect payment electronically. Scanners read a student print, identifying its unique ridges and creating a mathematical correlate to the print, which is stored in a computer as the student's identifier. To pay for lunch, a student touches the scanner, which automatically connects to her meal account, and the cost of lunch is deducted. Food Service Solutions (FSS) in Altoona supplied Penn Cambria with its technology gratis, hoping other districts would buy in. The typical cost for the system's hard and software is $4,000 to $5,000, with updates needed regularly. The company website touts its biometric finger scanner for "its accuracy, speed, expandability and cost effectiveness," and promises that "Biometrics eliminates lost or forgotten swipe cards, sharing of Personal Identification Numbers (PINs), fraudulent ID card use or exchange, and card issuing or replacement costs." And as an added selling point, the company asserts that with fingerprint scanning, students will no longer "fear peer pressure for being on a Free or Reduced meal plan." With a nod to concerns about other uses of students' prints, FSS asserts that "both parents and students can rest assured that the biometric images cannot be used by law enforcement for identification purposes. Only a mathematical algorithm remains in the system after registration . . . not fingerprint images."

How a school district like Penn Cambria came to implement a sophisticated cafeteria sales system is a lesson in the power of marketing technology to fix problems that don't exist. Whited says that the district's food-service provider learned about the biometric system at a tech conference where Food Service Solutions was an exhibitor. "What they were looking for was a way to provide data and monitor lunch accounts and not stigmatize students who were free or reduced," says Whited. While the company provided the software at no initial cost, the district did have to spend several thousand dollars for new computers after a few years. She says the system works "smoothly, and we don't worry about students losing tickets or long lines." But asked about the extent and nature of the stigmatizing poor students faced for receiving free lunches, she responds, "I would not say that was an issue. It wasn't that we felt there was a problem." Asked about how fingerprint scanning has sped up clogged lunch lines, she says, "It doesn't really speed up the line or slow it down, they still have to go through the system." Whited says parents find it "useful" because they just pay into a lunch account for their children and don't have to give them lunch money. The system has expanded into all Penn Cambria's schools. Whited is proud that the district is so technologically advanced despite its rural setting. "We look at the ways we can take rural children and keep them up on things," says Whited.

Fingerprint scanning systems like Penn Cambria's are being used in hundreds of schools around the country. But not all forays into the cafeteria have been received with alacrity. Taunton Public Schools, a district about forty miles south of Boston, was set to launch a similar point-of-sale computer system with fingerprint scanning in March 2007. Pushed by a new food-service director eager to employ the new technology, the Taunton school committee voted on February 7 to approve the purchase of Nutrikids, a software system for cafeteria management sold by Lunchbytes, a company in Rochester, New York. Lunchbytes offered the district three options for student meal purchases: a card scanner, a keypad, or fingerprint scans. The district had a keypad system, which students used with their ID number. But for the new system the district chose fingerprints, and Taunton's superintendent, Arthur Stellar, told a local newspaper that student participation would be mandatory. But soon after the board vote, a slow simmer of opposition turned to a full boil when parents began to question the consequences of fingerprinting their children. Complaints reached the ACLU staff attorney Sarah Wunsch in Boston, and she did enough research to discover that the school could not guarantee children's prints would be completely secure in the database. In a letter to Stellar, Wunsch wrote, "The fact that the finger printing system does not store the actual print is irrelevant. Most fingerprint databases don't actually store the entire fingerprint either. Identity management security expert Andrew Clymer says, 'The fact that it is able to compare an input against this number and determine a match is the critical issue. It does not seem beyond the bounds of possibility that by understanding what the vital points are you should be able to manufacture a print that exhibits these points."'

Wunsch requested all documents related to the Taunton district's evaluation of and decision to buy the Lunchbytes system and information provided to parents and staff about it. Superintendent Stellar retreated from insisting that all students participate in the fingerprinting, and sent documents that reveal that only one school committee member, Christine Fagan, had questioned the security of the new system at the February board meeting. Although the committee voted unanimously to approve the new system, Fagan and several other board members began reconsidering their votes as parent protests mounted. (Superintendent Stellar did not respond to multiple requests by e-mail and telephone to comment on the district's plan to use fingerprint scanning and the resulting controversy.) "It kind of flared up," Fagan says months later. "We voted it through and it seemed harmless, but then came an outcry from the community." Fagan did her own research, attending a seminar on school law at which issues relating to fingerprinting and confidentiality of computer records were raised. She talked with her husband, a criminal defense attorney. "I asked him if police walk in one day, and say, 'We believe one of your students was involved in something,' and they have a warrant, what would happen? If we had that information, how do we say no? We had no policy on that," she says. "The broader implication was that this could go anywhere. If you watch a show like 24, you know that things we thought were farfetched aren't at all."

Fagan says Superintendent Stellar "really likes technology" and that he told committee members that the new system would speed slow lunch lines and maximize the number of poor students receiving free lunches. But she says both notions are bogus. "The problem we have is there are too many choices and kids take time choosing," Fagan says. Students key in their ID numbers for lunch—whether paying or free— so anonymity is built in, and besides, she says, "We're not the kind of community that people would pay attention to who is on free lunch." Taunton was the kind of community with high parental involvement in the schools and a willingness to question authorities—especially over individual privacy concerns. The finger-scanning debate continued over three school committee meetings and the group finally took another vote to reverse its support and jettison the system before it even started. Fagan regrets making an uninformed decision the first time around, but feels good about helping keep fingerprint scanning out of Taunton's cafeterias. "I have six sons. My youngest is a senior now and he said, 'Ma, I don't want to give my fingerprint to anyone,'" she recalls. "You know how we advise kids not to give out their name to strangers? And here we are telling them to hand out information that is uniquely theirs."

5 THE WAR ON DRUGS GOES TO SCHOOL

One of the worst decisions our children can make is to gamble their lives and futures on drugs. Our government is helping parents confront this problem with aggressive education, treatment, and law enforcement. . . . Drug testing in our schools has proven to be an effective part of this effort. So tonight I proposed an additional $23 million for schools that want to use drug testing as a tool to save children's lives. The aim here is not to punish children, but to send them this message: We love you, and we don't want to lose you.

—From President George W. Bush's 2004 State of the Union address

I'd certainly fight a drug testing program in any way I could. It's as if the youth never exist in these situations. We're talked about in this distant fashion. Even the president in his State of the Union speech said, 'We're doing this for our children because we love them.' I truly believe the government doesn't have the authority over my own mind and my own neurological pattern.

—Devon DeFazio, founder in 2006 of a Students for a Sensible Drug Policy chapter at Clearwater High School, Clearwater, Florida

Chris Steffner strode to the front of the packed audience, shunning the podium to deliver her sermon Oprah-style with a wireless mic transmitting the Word loud and clear. The pert, petite blonde is principal of Colts Neck High School in Monmouth County, New Jersey, and a true believer in the national movement to randomly drug-test students in order to save them from themselves and the perceived epidemic of youth drug and alcohol abuse. Steffner was among nine presenters at this, the second Regional Drug Testing Summit of 2007, organized by the federal Office of National Drug Control Policy (ONDCP) and held at the Hilton Hotel near Newark International Airport on February 27.

"I'm not here to tell you, 'You should drug-test your kids.' That's your decision," she declared. "It's not about how bad your drug problem is. It's about how much you're willing to do to keep your students off drugs." With a colorful PowerPoint presentation projected behind her, Steffner regaled the assembly with tales of what she was willing to do as principal at Hackettstown High School, her prior post, where she initiated a random drug-testing program in 2004 for athletes, club members, and students driving to and parking at school. There was the story of drunken students at the senior prom, whose vomiting tipped Steffner off to their condition: "I did what every red-blooded principal will do. I bend over and smell that vomit. If I do nothing, I tell those kids it's okay." Steffner also was willing to publicly humiliate students and told of calling an inebriated prom attendee's parents to cart him off before his peers. "They don't get that they can be out of control, they don't get that they can die," Steffner intoned. "That's the beauty of being a kid."

In the first year of drug testing at Hackettstown, Steffner claimed, 70 students from a pool of 1,000 were subjected to urinalysis, yielding one positive—for what drug she did not say. In the 2005–2006 school year, 740 of 1,000 eligible students were tested, producing no positives. A logical conclusion might be that the tests were a waste of time and money. But Steffner said the results were proof that testing was deterring drug use. She nodded to another presenter, "the guru, Lisa Brady," who as vice principal of Hunterdon Central in 1997 helped pioneer random drug testing in that New Jersey high school. One by one, Steffner deflected the arguments of student-drug-testing opponents, dismissing civil rights and privacy concerns, costliness, and the basic lack of scientifically based evidence that drug testing actually deters use among youth with the self-righteousness of a religious crusader.

Student drug testing has indeed become a crusade, proclaimed by former president George W. Bush in his 2004 State of the Union address and fired up by John P. Walters, director of the ONDCP, otherwise known as the drug czar, from 2001 to 2008. True, Ronald Reagan initiated the War on Drugs and the Drug-Free Schools Act of 1986, which funded drug and alcohol use prevention. And during Bill Clinton's presidency scattered local efforts were made to bring drug tests to schools. But Bush's administration, led by Walters, made student testing a strategic front in the national drug war by aggressively using legal advocacy, budgetary largesse, and publicity campaigns such as the Regional Drug Testing Summits. The Bush White House's embrace of student drug testing was the evolution of a youth-focused antidrug policy immortalized by Nancy Reagan's "Just Say No" campaign of the 1980s. Proponents say that drug testing gives students an excuse to "just say no" in the face of supposedly irresistible peer pressure to smoke pot, pop pills, or drink alcohol.

What invigorated Walters and the student-drug-testing movement was a crucial 2002 U.S. Supreme Court decision in an Oklahoma case known as *Earls*. The ruling, which gave a green light to wider student testing, has emboldened such antidrug missionaries as the Drug Free America Foundation, created by the conservative Republican activists Melvin and Betty Sembler, and its allies, like the Drug Free Schools Coalition, whose founder, the New Jersey attorney David Evans, regularly spoke at ONDCP summits. Drug testing youth is also a priority among a network of influential former government insiders and their corporate interests. For them, schools are the next logical and profitable market, now that drug testing in the military and workplace are well established. Drug testing and its related services are a billion-dollar industry and growing.

Aligned against the apostles of testing stand the American Civil Liberties Union, which has challenged student drug testing in school districts around the country, the Drug Policy Alliance (DPA), a nonprofit opposing drug-war policies, Students for a Sensible Drug Policy (SSDP), and such weighty professional associations as the National Education Association, the American Public Health Association, and the American Academy of Pediatrics (AAP). DPA and SSDP were dogged in challenging Walters and the pro-testing movement, sending organizers to the regional summits to engage participants and offer a critical view of testing. In the face of moralistic arguments and flawed research on the efficacy of student testing to deter drug use, opponents offer a reasoned, nonpunitive approach to drug-use prevention through education. "What worries me is there is an anger, a nastiness at the bottom of this that says, 'These are bad kids,'" says John R. Knight, MD, founder/director of Harvard's Center on Adolescent Substance Abuse Research and co-author of the AAP's 2007 policy statement opposing student drug testing. "I don't think that approach is useful."

LEGAL LANDSCAPE FOR STUDENTS GROWS BLEAK

The legalization of drug testing in schools is a decades-long path dotted with landmark U.S. Supreme Court decisions, the most recent of them *Earls*, in 2002. At each step of the way, the concept that students retain their constitutional protections inside the schoolhouse has been eroded.

While such an idea might seem like common sense, until 1969 schools were presumed to have legal authority over their charges under the legal doctrine *in loco parentis*—as their parents. But in 1969, the High Court established that students retained their First Amendment free-speech protections in school. It was a radical notion, born in a radical time of student protests. An Iowa student named Tinker had worn a black armband in protest of the Vietnam War, to the dismay of school officials. The Supreme Court's ruling in *Tinker v. Des Moines* contained this oft-quoted language: "It can hardly be argued that either students or teachers shed their constitutional rights to freedom of speech or expression at the schoolhouse gate."[1]

But such a liberal interpretation of students' rights was, like the protests themselves, a product of the era. With more conservative times came more conservative rulings granting more authority over student actions and privacy to school officials. In 1985, the Supreme Court's ruling in *New Jersey v. T.L.O.* established a critical precedent in the limits of students' constitutional rights, this time on Fourth Amendment protections against unreasonable search and seizure. A high school principal searched the purse of a female student (identified only as T.L.O.) whom he accused of smoking cigarettes on school grounds. Not only were there cigarettes, but also marijuana and related paraphernalia, and evidence that the girl was selling marijuana, too. She challenged her subsequent arrest on drug charges, claiming the evidence was obtained illegally in violation of her Fourth Amendment rights. The school argued, and the Supreme Court agreed, that the search was reasonable even if there was no search warrant because the principal had cause to suspect her of violating school rules.

Ten years later, search and seizure in the schoolhouse again came before the Supreme Court, this time in the context of drug testing. James Acton was a seventh-grade student in the Vernonia school district in rural Oregon who wanted to play football. His school began randomly drug-testing athletes in 1989 because faculty believed that drug and alcohol use had increased and was causing behavioral problems, especially among student athletes. Acton's parents refused to allow James to be tested, and he was kept off the football team. They filed suit against the district, claiming that testing violated James's rights under the Fourth Amendment as well as the Fourteenth, which guarantees due process and equal protection. The Actons won at the district court level, but the Supreme Court in 1995 reversed that ruling, advancing the rights of school administrators to search and seize—in this case, a student's urine—without a warrant if they have reasonable cause to suspect drug use. *Vernonia* also established that student athletes, by voluntarily choosing to participate in an extracurricular activity with rules, had lower expectations of privacy than other students and strengthened administrators' authority in controlling student behavior, laying the groundwork for increased student drug testing in the coming years.

Vernonia was strictly about student athletes, but *Earls* allows schools to cast the net wider to drug-test students in any competitive extracurricular activities. Lindsay Earls, a sophomore at Tecumseh High School in Oklahoma, was in the show choir, the concert choir (both deemed competitive), and the quiz bowl, "a nerdy activity like *Jeopardy!*," she says. The school board initiated random drug testing in the 1998 school year after football team members were caught *in flagrante delicto*, as it were, according to Lindsay's dad, David. "The mother of the quarter-back on the school football team came home and all the football players and cheerleaders were in her house smoking dope and, I'm sure, drinking alcohol. And she immediately went to the school board and demanded they do something about it," he recalls in a phone conversation from his Oklahoma home. "The school board jumped up and said, 'Okay, let's do something about this.' They had *Vernonia* in place, and the board chose, in my opinion, to overstep the bounds, saying, 'Let's test everyone.'" Aside from that incident, Lindsay says she didn't know anyone who used drugs, but drinking was common.

Lindsay didn't like the idea of testing, but she liked the idea of giving up her beloved quiz team and choirs less. David and his wife, Laurie, grudgingly signed a consent form allowing their daughter to undergo random urinalysis and paid a four-dollar fee. But David bristled at being given an ultimatum and researched case law on drug testing, learning that it applied only to student athletes. He tried to talk to the school superintendent, Tom Wilkes, who David had grown up with—everyone knew everyone in town. Wilkes wouldn't talk, and neither would local lawyers. "They didn't want to take on something that might prevent them from getting business from the school," David says. He had gone back to college to become a juvenile justice specialist and heard about the American Civil Liberties Union. "I thought they might take this on," he says.

Graham Boyd, head of the ACLU's drug-policy program, had been litigating against student drug testing for years and in the Earlses' situation saw the chance to test the limits of legal precedent. He told the Earls that if they pursued this case, it could end up in the Supreme Court because Tecumseh's testing was so much wider than *Vernonia* had sanctioned. "Graham said they were operating on a bluff, so let's call their bluff," David Earls says. Tecumseh, like most of the school districts whose random drug-testing programs he'd challenged, had no pronounced student drug problem, Boyd notes. "Why do they do it? It's for the deterrence, but also it parallels a more authoritarian model of interacting with students. It will also include drug dogs and surveillance cameras. They go hand in hand. They also don't work particularly well."

Boyd took *Earls v. Tecumseh* to federal district court in Oklahoma City in 2000 and lost. But a year later he won at the Tenth Circuit Court of Appeals in Denver, which found the Tecumseh testing program violated the Fourth Amendment. "I was embarrassed for the school attorney. The justices weren't kind to her," says David Earls of the Appeals Court. "I don't guess she ever practiced law outside of Oklahoma and she stepped into a hostile environment. One of the questions they asked her was, 'What is threatening about band kids? Are they going to step over each other if they're stoned?' When it was over, I told Graham, 'We got this hands down.' Then you go from that to the Supreme Court and it was one hundred eighty degrees. *We* got kicked around."

David Earls isn't exaggerating. In March 2002, it was Boyd and the Earlses' case that faced a hostile environment when he argued it before the court of Chief Justice William H. Rehnquist. The *New York Times* report called the justices "unusually snappish," and cited Justice Anthony Kennedy's "implied slur on the plaintiffs." *Amici* briefs supporting Tecumseh were filed by half a dozen pro-testing groups, including David Evans of the Drug Free Schools Coalition, the Drug Free America Foundation, and DATIA, the lobby of the drug and alcohol testing industry. The Bush administration weighed in with its opinion that even schoolwide testing would be legal. In June 2002, the court handed down its decision in favor of Tecumseh. Justice Stephen G. Breyer, thought to be a swing vote, instead was among the 5–4 majority composed of

Rehnquist, Kennedy, Antonin Scalia, and Clarence Thomas, who wrote the opinion. In validating random testing of students in sports and any competitive extracurricular activities, the majority focused on schools' "custodial responsibilities" and justified testing as reasonable given a "nationwide epidemic" of drug use by youth. The dissenting opinion, written by Justice Ruth Bader Ginsburg, argued that the testing of athletes sanctioned by *Vernonia* was vastly different from Tecumseh's broad testing program, which was invasive.

Lindsay Earls had just finished her first year at Dartmouth College when the decision was announced. She graduated in 2005, returning home to Oklahoma. She says she has heard rumors that the district considered ending drug testing because it's so expensive but is tied to it because of the long, public litigation. She's also heard that more students have a substance abuse problem. The rancor she faced from townspeople who thought the Earls family was wrong has mellowed, but there are still those who harbor ill will. "They think I dragged Tecumseh's name through the mud," Lindsay says. "Well, I feel they were dragging my name through the mud just as much."

THE STRAIGHT DOPE ON YOUTH DRUG USE

Like all components of the Lockdown High model of school safety and discipline, student drug testing is predicated on hype and distortion. In this case, it's the view that illegal drug use is epidemic among young people. The reality is different and more nuanced. Drug and alcohol use and abuse are harmful and have harmful consequences for thousands of people—young and adult—but among young people they are affected by myriad factors, including societal attitudes. Their substance use has been on a downward trend for years. It's a fact that even Walters, the drug czar, had to acknowledge each year that the latest study had reinforced the decrease. In a letter to summit participants, for example, Walters stated: "Recent surveys indicate that there has been a 23 percent reduction in youth drug use over the last five years—that's 840,000 fewer young people using drugs today than in 2001."

Monitoring the Future, the preeminent national survey of students, offers widely respected data on young people's drug and alcohol use by polling eighth, tenth, and twelfth graders. The MTF survey has been conducted since 1975 by the University of Michigan with funding from the federal National Institute on Drug Abuse. It has tracked the peaks and troughs of substance use, which seem to reflect varying attitudes and perceptions of the risks associated with and the acceptability of drug and alcohol use in the wider culture. In 2006, MTF showed that the use of marijuana, the most common illegal drug, decreased for the fifth straight year, most sharply among the older students. But in 2009, the survey detected a slight uptick in pot use, a change that the principal researcher, Lloyd D. Johnston, attributed in part to teens seeing less risk in using marijuana and also disapproving of it less, too. Those youthful attitudes would be consonant with the growing acceptance of marijuana use—especially for medical reasons—around the country. As Johnston said in 2009, "Changes in these beliefs and attitudes are often very influential in driving changes in use."

The MTF tracks use of other illegal drugs, including LSD, methamphetamines, cocaine, opiates, and steroids, and over the last several years has shown steady annual declines in their use among the students surveyed. For 2009, use of Ecstasy, LSD, and cocaine also declined, while other substance use stayed constant at levels well below the peaks of the mid-1990s, the survey states. Alcohol use has also been in a long-term decline over the years for all ages, according to the MTF, which measures how many kids have used alcohol at least once in the past thirty days. Use among eighth graders was 40 percent lower than in peak years, among tenth graders 25 percent lower, and among twelfth graders had one sixth the prevalence.

Legal prescription drugs were also added to the MTF survey because, as Johnston noted, they were becoming a bigger part of the whole country's "drug problem." In 2002, the survey added OxyContin to its questionnaire, and in recent years, another narcotic, Vicodin, was added, as were Ritalin and Adderall, both used to treat Attention Deficit Disorder. For 2009, the survey found student use of most of these drugs had not increased despite several years of previous increase, and several drugs, including Ritalin, showed decreased use. But OxyContin use was still higher among all age groups than in 2002, when it was added to the MTF survey. The prevalence rate—how many students had used it at least once in the last twelve months—was very low, even if too high. For eighth graders, it was 2 percent; and for tenth and twelfth graders, 5 percent.

Another national survey, by the federal Centers for Disease Control and Prevention (CDC), echoes the downward trend. Called the National Youth Risk Behavior Survey, it found a decline in current alcohol use among high schoolers from 51 percent in 1991 to 43 percent in 2005; local surveys conducted as part of this survey revealed similar declines. In New York City, for example, marijuana use declined by 6 percent and alcohol consumption by 7 percent between 2001 and 2005. Heroin use, though, increased threefold during that period, from .6 percent to 1.8 percent of students having tried it at least once.

For antidrug warriors and the student-drug-testing pushers among them, downward trends require calibrated spinning in two directions. First, they claim that decreased use is owed to the effectiveness of the drug czar's efforts, including student testing and antidrug media campaigns from ONDCP. But because no level of drug use—especially marijuana—would be considered acceptable under their zero tolerance ideology, they argue that even more testing and antidrug efforts are needed. "In some ways, the White House is exasperated by their inability to reach anything approaching abstinence. The numbers fluctuate but they don't trend all the way down to zero," says Marsha Rosenbaum, a drug-abuse prevention educator and National Institute on Drug Abuse scholar. "Some of us believe there is no possibility of abstinence in a culture saturated with legal drugs, let alone illegal ones."

Decreases in youth drug and alcohol use have myriad causes, including social and cultural attitudes. But government antidrug advertising deserves no credit. If anything, the advertising campaigns directed by ONDCP have actually *increased* the likelihood of young people smoking marijuana. That was one of the findings of a 2006 report from the Government Accountability Office to Congress on the effectiveness of the youth antidrug media campaign conducted by ONDCP. From 1999 to 2004, ONDCP spent $1.2 *billion* on persuading youth to say no to drugs, especially marijuana. The result was that there were "no significant favorable effects of campaign exposure on marijuana initiation among non-drug-using youth or cessation and declining use among prior marijuana users," according to an independent evaluation the GAO cited. It noted the consistency of declining trends in drug use nationally, but couldn't credit them to ONDCP's efforts. On the contrary, it did find "significant unfavorable effects": the more young people were exposed to the anti-pot ads, the more likely they were to think smoking pot was normal. For girls aged twelve and a half to thirteen, the ads actually prompted higher rates of initiation into pot use.[3] Not surprisingly, Walters's office disagreed with the GAO's findings that more than a billion dollars had, essentially, gone up in smoke.

One issue that is rarely addressed in discussing youth drug use and the testing movement is race and class. Testing's most fervent and visible adherents are white, middle or upper middle class, and suburban. This might seem counterintuitive to anyone who automatically thinks of drugs as a problem of so-called inner city youth, who typically are Latino and black. But it is no coincidence that Lisa Brady, Chris Steffner, and David Evans all hail from mostly white, affluent New Jersey communities. They are fairly representative of the student-drug-testing crusade in general. In Tecumseh, Oklahoma, or Hunterdon, New Jersey, white middle-class communities see in student drug testing salvation from a perceived evil infecting their youth that would make schools—not parents—responsible for policing children. Although the demographic angle seems obvious and certainly invites exploration, the testing proponents seem not to have even thought about it. At the Newark summit, for example, an attendee asked what percentage of schools doing testing were urban compared with suburban. Brady said there was no such information, but suggested that in urban areas "Parental concern could be an issue." The Education Department and ONDCP staff at the forum had no response. Surprisingly, attendance at the Regional Drug Testing Summits was dominated by white educators.

Rates of drug and alcohol abuse also are somewhat greater among white youth, according to the CDC's national data, which is one reason that communities such as Hunterdon have embraced drug testing in schools. Binge drinking and hallucinogen, methamphetamine, and cocaine use were higher for white youth than for black youth, and comparable to that of Latino youth. John Knight, of Harvard's Center on Adolescent Substance Abuse Research, says the class divide is clear among patients he treats. "I speculate that drug-use rates are higher among middle-class kids who are white and suburban," Knight says. "What we know works is parents who talk to their kids frequently about drug use, and I worry that in wealthier, suburban families, they don't want to worry about taking the time to talk to their kids. These are the same parents who want their kids sent to boot camps." A survey of drug testing in schools by the same Michigan researchers who conduct Monitoring the Future found that schools with majority black or Latino students are "slightly less likely to test" than majority white schools. Given the disproportionate incarceration rates of blacks and Latinos for drug-related crimes, it makes sense that they would perceive drug testing in school as an extension of the criminal justice system—a shortcut on the school-to-prison track for their children. That may be one reason major urban school districts, such as New York, Los Angeles, San Francisco, Chicago, and Boston do not drug-test their students.

HOW DRUG TESTING WORKS—AND DOESN'T

Student drug testing sounds as easy as A, B, C when proponents describe it. And it's true that drug testing can be a pretty simple thing. You can go to any drugstore and buy a home urinalysis kit. But the scientific and legal protocols of random student drug testing are complex and elaborate—if done correctly and in compliance with guidelines on testing and regulations on confidentiality from the federal Department of Education. "There is a fair amount of sloppiness," says the ACLU's Graham Boyd. "Schools pay attention to the issue of 'who can we test?' not the 'how we test.'" The *Earls* ruling covered only middle and high school students in competitive sports and extracurricular activities. Elementary school children, so far, are safe. Schools that test students who drive to and park at school, like Steffner's, cannot use federal funding for that part of the program. Individual states may have their own constitutional protections regarding student drug testing that would supersede what *Earls* allows. For example, in 2006, New Jersey became the first state to mandate steroid testing for high school athletes competing at state playoffs. Florida, Texas, and Illinois followed suit in 2007, adopting random steroid testing for their high school athletes to begin in the 2008–2009 school year. Missouri lawmakers contemplated a similar policy in 2008.[4]

Walters published a booklet in 2004, "What You Need to Know About Starting a Student Drug-Testing Program," a step-by-step guide. Because case law is focused on who can be tested, there are few mandated how-tos in random student drug testing. Two legal strictures, which enforce the confidentiality of test results, stem from the federal Family

Educational Rights and Privacy Act (FERPA) and the Protection of Pupil Rights Amendment. So drug-test results are supposed to be carefully guarded by school officials. Most of the ONDCP booklet offers guidance on devising a testing program that would withstand legal challenges, using federal workplace drug and alcohol testing rules as the model. A medical review officer expert in testing is required in federal testing, but recommended for schools only to insure the integrity of testing—so positives aren't false and lab protocols are followed. The guide recommends using a federally certified lab, but if schools want to simply use their nurse to check urine samples, that's fine, too. And many schools do. It discusses specimen collection, which should be directly observed to make sure students don't tamper with their sample. But that's an embarrassing situation for both the student and the nurse or counselor stuck with collection. Positive tests must be confirmed by a second, more sophisticated and expensive test at a lab, the booklet explains.

The variety and sophistication of drug tests has grown since students were first forced to urinate in cups. Federal employment and military drug and alcohol testing is by urinalysis only. But hair, blood, and saliva analysis are also used in the private employment sector, and corporate interests are pushing hair and oral swabs in schools. Urine tests are the choice for most schools, though, because they are cheaper, but not as cheap as the test pushers say. Principal Chris Steffner said at the Newark summit that drug tests are "dirt cheap" at ten dollars each, or testing "the whole school for fifteen hundred dollars." Well, that may be the simple cost per test, but it doesn't include all the additional costs of staff involved in testing, like a nurse and medical review officer, and a substance abuse counselor, as well as follow-up tests for positives. A more realistic cost provided by Robert DuPont, a pro-testing drug czar under presidents Nixon and Ford and the first director of the National Institute of Drug Abuse, is $21,000 for a high school testing five hundred students over one year.[5]

Standard urinalysis detects five categories of drugs: amphetamines (including meth and other uppers); cocaine and its crack form; cannabinoids or marijuana; opiates (codeine, morphine, and heroin); and phencyclidine, known as angel dust or PCP. Synthetic narcotics, like OxyContin and Vicodin, steroids, Ecstasy, and barbiturates will not show up in this test. With the exception of marijuana, traces of which can be detected for up to thirty days after use, most drugs leave the system within three days of use. Catching a user with urinalysis is a hit-and-miss proposition. Certain things can trigger false positives. Poppy seeds may show up as opiates, and cold medications containing pseudoephedrine may be flagged as amphetamines. Alcohol, which is linked to more deaths of young people than any drug, isn't detected by the standard urinalysis or most other tests because it leaves the system within hours. Most students do their drinking after school or on weekends, and by Monday morning, alcohol's by-products have been flushed out. Breathalyzer or saliva tests could detect alcohol but only within hours of drinking. Many testing opponents, including the American Academy of Pediatrics, believe that drug-testing students could encourage them to drink because it is easier to escape detection. Hair and blood tests are more accurate and much more expensive at roughly $75 and $100 respectively. Hair can actually provide a sort of time line of drug use extending back for months but cannot show recent use—or alcohol consumption. Hair tests have other problems: they may indicate positives from passive exposure to marijuana smoke, and react differently depending on the race and sex of the person tested.

In the past few years, a new test for alcohol has become more popular in employment testing, and it's being pushed by the drug and alcohol testing industry for schools. Called an EtG test, it detects ethyl glucuronide, a biomarker or by-product of alcohol metabolism, in urine. Pequannock Township High School in New Jersey added EtG tests to its regular drug-testing program in February 2007, hoping to improve on the alcohol swab test its schools had been using. "You have to be really drunk for that to work," says Larrie Reynolds, Pequannock's superintendent. "We investigated the new technology, and the new EtG test is one we believe works." Reynolds says about half of students in his schools drink, and some parents know but they don't care. It is the kind of affluent community where teachers have "SAT pressure, not No Child Left Behind pressure," according to Reynolds. "Parents want their kids to go to Harvard."

Pequannock's move to EtG testing caused a flurry of news media coverage, even outside the United States. But what reports and Reynolds didn't mention is that in September 2006, the federal Substance Abuse and Mental Health Services Administration (SAMHSA) issued an advisory on alcohol testing which warned that the EtG test was not accurate enough to determine whether an individual had been drinking. It warned that "Legal or disciplinary action based solely on a positive EtG ... is inappropriate and scientifically unsupportable at this time." Mouthwash or disinfectant hand wash with alcohol could show up in the EtG and be wrongly interpreted. Harvard's John Knight said the EtG is being widely used even though "there is no good science on it." "The specificity is off," he says. "Ten percent of positives are false positives. I would like to know the cutoff for specificity. I can't trust the clinical lab people. They are trying to sell us a bill of goods." He has a point. At the Newark summit, Sonia Hoppe of Southwest Laboratories raised the EtG test in her talk on the drug-testing process. She alluded to a "controversy" over EtG's accuracy, but she didn't mention SAMHSA's warning. "It is a valuable tool, a unique biomarker," Hoppe said. "Every time I go to a school I hear alcohol is the problem."

The American Academy of Pediatrics has taken a strong stand against drug testing of young people at school, or at home, because of the complex, uncertain science of testing and its many negative consequences for children. In 1996, the academy's Committee on Substance Abuse and Council on School Health issued its first policy statement firmly opposing youth drug testing in the wake of the *Vernonia* Supreme Court decision. In 2007, the committee issued an addendum, reaffirming in forceful terms its opposition to the drug testing of adolescents and dissecting the arguments of proponents. Harvard's John Knight, a co-author of the addendum, says one impetus for it was the heavy marketing of drug-testing kits by companies. "That's what makes me uneasy. There is a lot of money to be made on drug testing. I've been contacted by these people. They see us as opponents," Knight says. Another impetus was the drug czar's push on testing. "The ONDCP issued its booklet urging schools to test, claiming there is lots of scientific evidence that it was safe," Knight says. "No one has taken time to look at risks." False positives can stigmatize a child, and false negatives mean missing kids who have real problems, he says. "It's a very sophisticated science. We've done a study that showed a majority of physicians in the country are clueless about ordering and analyzing drug tests. A lot of people don't understand what they're doing and mistakes will be made."

EFFECTIVE DETERRENT OR JUNK SCIENCE?

It's more than a little ironic that the main substance of abuse for students—the one with the most dangerous, even fatal consequences if they mix drinking and driving—is the one standard urinalysis won't catch. Yet the pushers promote testing as if it is the silver bullet for any and all substance-abuse issues young people face. They cite a few studies of dubious rigor and questionable conclusions as proof that random drug testing effectively deters students from using drugs and alcohol. At the same time, testing pushers dismiss studies that find little if any deterrent benefit from testing youth as biased and lacking in scientific credibility. Theirs is a triumph of ideology over rationality and good science.

The study most frequently cited in ONDCP's literature and news media reports was done by Lisa Brady, vice principal and then principal of Hunterdon Central High School in Flemington, New Jersey, during its first three years of random drug testing, from September 1997 to September 2000. Hunterdon initiated testing for athletes as a response to a 1997 drug- and alcohol-use survey of tenth through twelfth graders, which Brady wrote "confirmed the worst fears" of the school board. A third of the students had used marijuana, more than 10 percent had used hallucinogens, and 13 percent of seniors had used cocaine. Brady surveyed students in 1999 after two years of random drug testing. Her findings state that in twenty of twenty-eight drug categories, use decreased for all students. The student-reported survey also indicated that multidrug users decreased by 100 percent in tenth grade, by 14 percent in eleventh grade, and by 52 percent in twelfth grade. Given that only a small pool of athletes was eligible for random testing, Brady's claims seem odd and are without explanation. In February 2000, testing was expanded to include students in all extracurricular activities, but in August the ACLU filed a Fourth Amendment suit against Hunterdon on behalf of three students and the testing program was halted for two years. Testing resumed at Hunterdon post-*Earls* and Brady claims that in that two-year hiatus, pot and alcohol use increased dramatically according to students' reports. Strangely, she includes no data on drug-testing results: How many positives? And for what drugs? What were the changes before and after testing? Brady's much-lauded study was never peer reviewed or published. "Lisa Brady's data is inflated beyond belief," says Rodney Skager, the professor emeritus of education and information studies at UCLA who created the California Student Survey of drug and alcohol use. "I challenged her on it."

Another favorite of the drug-testing camp is a 2005 survey of fifty-six Indiana high school principals, all but two of whom had drug testing during the previous three years. The principals' responses to questions about student drug use—alcohol wasn't included—were based on their own surveys of students and compared with results of a similar survey in 2002–2003. Joseph McKinney, chair of the Ball State University department of educational leadership, authored the survey report, which stated that 58 percent of principals reported that drug use had decreased based on their surveys; 41 percent said drug-test positives had decreased; and 56 percent said there was no change in test results. McKinney's report was never peer reviewed, but it was published in *West's Education Law Reporter.* "I remember looking at McKinney's report," says Dr. Linn Goldberg of Oregon Health and Science University, an authority on athlete drug and alcohol use. "If it's not published in a peer-reviewed journal, forget it. He's a very nice person, but these studies are all too easy to talk about."

Goldberg has done drug testing for the Olympics and was a doping control officer for the U.S. Anti-Doping Agency. He also occupies a curious place in the drug-testing debate. His 2002 one-year study of drug testing involving two Oregon schools is the only peer-reviewed, journal-published study the pro-testers cite as proving testing's deterrent effect. It was the initial stage of a three-year study called SATURN—for Student Athlete Testing Using Random Notification—funded by the National Institute of Drug Abuse and prompted by the Supreme Court's first drug-testing ruling. "I had worked in the area of drug-prevention education. We thought it behooved us as Oregonians post-*Vernonia* to look at drug testing of student athletes," Goldberg says. "We had the strictest test, did GCMS [gas chromatography/mass spectrometry] testing, not some cheapo test. We thought if you can't prove it with this, you never will." One school had mandatory testing for athletes, the other didn't, and both surveyed students for their self-reported drug use. SATURN results found "some benefit" in reducing high-end drug use, he says. "There is a deterrent. It is weak, but it's very expensive," Goldberg says.

"You get a much better bang for the buck with education." Results also revealed a strange, paradoxical finding: in the drug-testing school, athletes who were required to undergo testing came to see drug use as less risky and more acceptable—the opposite of what was intended.

Goldberg says he met with John Walters in the summer of 2006 to discuss testing. "We said, 'Why are you doing this? It doesn't work,'" he says. "They want to do testing because it's easy. Education takes time, and that's what schools do. Schools aren't the military, they're not prison." Goldberg's pleas fell on deaf ears. Today, he's done with drug testing and is focusing on drug-prevention education programs he created for male and female student athletes, called Atlas and Athena, respectively. "If you want an effective deterrent and schools are strapped for money, our education programs work," Goldberg says. "They cost about eleven dollars per kid."

The only other peer-reviewed study on student drug testing is from researchers at the University of Michigan who also conduct Monitoring the Future. Published in the *Journal of School Health* in 2003, the study garnered media attention—and the disdain of pro-testing crusaders. The authors, Ryoko Yamaguchi, Lloyd Johnston, and Patrick O'Malley, used MTF survey information from 1998 to 2001 as well as surveys of principals on drug-testing policies. They found no deterrent effect on youth drug use at schools with testing. The Michigan study had weaknesses, though, a key one being that it compared schools with differing testing policies—for cause, random for athletes, and no testing. In response to criticisms, the Michigan researchers added more schools and another year of survey information about random testing. Their findings held true.

Harvard's John Knight says when he wrote the academy's policy on student drug testing, he sought information from the drug czar's office. "I know John Walters, and Bertha Madras is a colleague of mine from Harvard. I contacted them and said, 'Send me all the research on student drug testing at your disposal,'" he says. "They sent me a huge pile of materials, and there were only two peer-reviewed studies—Goldberg and Yamaguchi. The rest was junk science, published on the web, or the very subjective opinions of school principals." Knight says because of his vocal opposition to drug testing, he has felt under attack by the testing supporters. "I am one hundred percent supported by

NIH [National Institutes for Health] grants, which gives me reason to worry," he says. "I've never taken a dime from the lab people." Knight says instead of drug testing, he is in favor of universal screening of adolescents in school health clinics, with total confidentiality and no punitive measures. "I've spent my life developing a test to identify kids early and much more cheaply," he says. "I did a simple cost analysis for a typical school that does drug testing. The lab fees are $140,000 to test half the students once a year, and another $60,000 for a nurse. Meanwhile, for $50,000, you could hire a counselor to interview students confidentially."

THE DRUG-TESTING PUSHERS

Drug testing crusaders thought that *Earls* would open the floodgates to drug testing in public schools across the nation, but that hasn't happened. Most public schools have other priorities, such as accomplishing the unfunded mandates of No Child Left Behind to raise test scores and grappling with budget shortfalls. Federal funds or not, drug testing is costly and time-consuming if done according to strict federal protocols. Some 19 percent of all schools—public and private—drug-test students for any reason; 14 percent test "for cause," when a student appears to be under the influence of drugs or alcohol; about 5 percent test athletes; 2 percent have broader testing programs, like Tecumseh's.[6] What did change post-*Earls* was the federal government's enthusiastic promotion of student drug testing, announced by George W. Bush and enacted by John Walters. "It is the office of propaganda for the drug war," said the ACLU's Boyd of ONDCP. "It is completely of a piece with them rolling out student drug testing as part of the drug war because it is profoundly symbolic—but without any impact." The Bush administration pumped millions into funding student drug testing at the local school district level through the Education Department's Office of Safe and Drug Free Schools. Starting with $2 million in demonstration grants in 2003, the office upped the ante each successive year, with $17 million in 2007 for new and continued drug-testing grants. Another $1 million was earmarked to create a Student Drug Testing Institute, to "assist schools in developing, implementing and evaluating" student drug testing. As of 2006, the department had funded close to four hundred public schools to do random drug testing.

Pushing student drug testing from his bully pulpit was John Walters, who considers drug use a public health epidemic and believes that marijuana use correlates with schizophrenia, a claim that is widely debated and refuted by some who point to the steady rate of the disease in the population—about 1 percent, despite increased use of marijuana over the years. "This particular drug czar has a penchant for testing," says Marsha Rosenbaum. Walters brought conservative credentials and a punitive approach to drug-related crimes to the post when President Bush appointed him in 2001. He was deputy to the first President Bush's drug czar, William Bennett. And when Bill Clinton took office, Walters served briefly as a drug policy director, resigning in 1993 when Clinton sought millions for drug education and prevention programs and shifted focus from the drug trafficking interdiction and commerce favored by the Reagan and Bush I administrations. In a 1996 article for the conservative Heritage Foundation, Walters criticized Clinton's approach as "nationalization" of antidrug efforts that were "primarily a responsibility of parents and local communities."

Eight years later, Walters had changed his tune about the federal role in drug prevention. In 2004, he inaugurated annual Regional Student Drug Testing Summits, staging conferences in four cities each year at which federal employees and pro-testing allies were pushing student drug testing as hard as any street corner drug dealer. The summits were well-orchestrated road shows featuring a cast of regulars from Walters's office and the Education Department, as well as civilians such as Chris Steffner, David Evans, Lisa Brady, and a local school official or two. Despite assertions that communities should debate the issue, the presenters left little doubt that there is only one opinion on testing. Presenters typically relate the parable of a good student gone bad—all due to a tragic wrong turn to drug use. At the Newark summit, Steffner told of a former student, "Suzie, who was in the top ten of her senior class," and was diagnosed as a heroin addict by the school nurse one fateful day. Evans dedicated his summit talk "to Ian Katz, who got into heroin and his mother didn't know it until she found him dead in his bed one day." Bill Trusheim, superintendent of Pequannock, New Jersey, public schools, said that they "had a couple of tragedies," which helped his district implement a testing program "rather quickly."

At the Newark summit, Bertha Madras, Walters's deputy for demand reduction, opened the event with a professorial lesson both sober and scary on the adolescent brain's reaction to drugs: "Even an acute use of drugs can in some cases lead to addiction." The Education Department analyst Sigrid Melus explained how to apply for funds to drug-test and spelled out requirements: funds can't be used for treatment, prevention programs, or "for cause" testing; confidentiality of results and parental consent are crucial. "In terms of who provides testing, it could be a drug-testing company or school staff," Melus said. "Most of our schools contract out testing." There to speak for one of those companies was Sonja Hoppe, a VP of Southwest Labs of Arizona, whose expert opinion was that "drug testing works." She breezed through a description of drug-testing methods—urine, blood, and hair analyses—and assured the audience that "there is no false positive." The New Jersey attorney David Evans, a member of the conservative Federalist Society and founder of the Drug Free Schools Coalition, covered the legal angle, with a run through case law. A self-described "recovering drug and alcohol addict," Evans took a swipe at Lindsay Earls ("She was in the choir. She described herself as a goody two-shoes. I thought of someone else had who had been in the choir—Whitney Houston—and look at her") and lobbed a potshot at the Drug Policy Alliance. ("They support legalizing pot. Some of the Drug Policy Alliance people are here today. Marijuana is a dangerous drug.") As for those concerned about civil liberties, Evans cautioned, "Don't spend time, you're never going to change their minds." Lisa Brady, whose Hunterdon drug-testing program is ONDCP's most-cited supposed success story, assured the assembly that "once the nonpunitive nature of these programs is explained, any student will tell you how grateful they are to be given the opportunity to say 'no' in that peer-pressured situation."

The Newark audience of two hundred teachers and school officials was more subdued than enthused. When Melus asked how many planned to apply for federal funds to do testing, about twenty hands went up. Less than a dozen indicated their schools were already drug-testing students. At lunch break, an exhausted Melus and two Education colleagues ate box lunches quickly in the lobby and bemoaned the third, upcoming Regional Summit—in Hawaii. Despite Madras's warm-and-fuzzy science, Evans's quips, and Steffner's tough-love sincerity, the drug czar's itinerant student-drug-testing revival meetings weren't making many converts. A month earlier, the first summit of 2007, in Charleston, South Carolina, drew about fifty people, and the reception was chilly, even for January. A local news article quoted the school superintendent dismissing drug testing as "costly" while a drug-abuse program director said testing shifts schools' focus wrongly from prevention to policing. And the DPA analyst Jennifer Kern was quoted on drug testing as ineffective and harmful to the learning environment. Kern, an upbeat and indefatigable twenty-four-year-old, had been hopscotching around the country, attending six of the summits from 2006 to 2007. She set up tables for DPA materials that counter pro-testing arguments. In Newark, summit organizers shunted Kern's table to a distant corner, but she deftly worked the crowd during breaks to discuss the issues and found many testing critics and skeptics.

Bill Sciambi was among them. A New Jersey parent with kids in the Delaware Valley Regional schools, Sciambi is one of those civil rights defenders that stymie Evans and his cohort. Sciambi helped organize parents to debate drug testing in his district after the idea surfaced in 2004. "Random drug testing for a lot of people seems to be a silver bullet, a bandage on the problem. I don't think it works," he says. "We all agree there have to be comprehensive programs starting with parents, substance-abuse counselors in schools, and activities to keep them involved. It takes a wide range of things." Sciambi recalls that David Evans came to school board meetings to push drug testing, even though he lives outside the district. But Evans brought along Robert Aromando, who did live in the district and had been the CEO of American Bio Medica, a drug-test manufacturer, and head of Roche Diagnostics drug-abuse unit—where Evans had also worked. Aromando was then a trustee of Evans's Drug Free Schools Coalition. "There were parents who clearly saw the conflicts," Sciambi says.

Drug testing was shoved to the back burner until the 2006–2007 school year, when it resurfaced. Sciambi e-mailed and distributed flyers to turn out parents to debate the proposal at the first board meeting. Of twenty-five parents, only two spoke in favor of testing. The school board listened attentively and considered information from DPA and from Evans. Then it voted 6–2 against testing, despite what Sciambi thought must have been "psychological pressure" to approve testing, given that three neighboring districts did it. One of the board members told

Sciambi later that Evans "really turned him off with his heavy-handed tactics." In Sciambi's affluent, exurban corner of New Jersey, "we're more libertarian. Less government is better, stay out of my business." Drug testing, he says, sets up an institutionalized system of suspicion. "You're telling kids, 'It's 1984. You're not responsible for what you do, you'll be on camera all the time.'"

BEYOND THE PUSHERS' HYPE

For every story told by drug-testing proponents about its success in deterring drug use and cost benefits for schools, there are many more about the flaws of testing from schools that have tried it. The Drug Policy Alliance tallies schools that have considered random drug testing, adopted it, or abandoned it. Dozens of schools from Texas to Wisconsin to Virginia tried and then dumped testing programs over cost, ineffectiveness, flagging support from school officials, or a combination of concerns. Drug-testing pushers peddle testing as needed for a safe learning environment, welcomed by students as an "excuse" to resist peer pressure to use drugs and alcohol and as a strictly confidential process. But the reality of drug testing and its consequences are often far different.

Take Hackettstown High, where Chris Steffner initiated testing in 2004. Christopher Lauth was a sophomore then, a member of the anti-drug group TREND—Turning Recreational Events in New Directions—and on the staff of *Tiger*, the school newspaper. School administrators said "they'd love student input, but they sugarcoated things," Lauth recalls. "They said, 'Don't worry, it will be wonderful. You'll be called from class, it will be confidential.'" Lauth went to the Drug Policy Alliance website and got information that worried him. Of course other students would find out if you tested positive if you didn't show up to team practice or to a club activity. He also saw statistics indicating that false positives were not uncommon. But most worrisome for Lauth was what drug testing could do to the climate of trust in school. "Hackettstown had a very strong relationship between faculty and staff. I felt very safe and could talk to administrators," he says. "I thought it was a great school. Go down the road to Warren Hill [a neighboring school], and you had people getting beat up." He'd never been offered drugs and no one he knew was using, either.

Lauth started a petition and got a hundred signatures, but Steffner launched the program so quickly that most students had little time to form an opinion. She held three forums to discuss drug testing, all around Christmas—one of them during a snowstorm, he recalls. By the end of 2004, testing began. Many students were blindsided when they got notification of the new program. Some got angry, he says, and by his senior year Lauth saw changes in the once-cohesive school community. "I noticed more problems with discipline. Things being stolen in the locker room, acting out," he says. "I noticed lunches got more out of hand and out of control." Steffner ordered new laminated ID cards and required students to display them, another first, Lauth says. After graduating and going off to college in Florida, Lauth kept watch over his high school by checking its website. He saw reports of sex in the locker room and police being called a number of times for robberies. His analysis? "The school feels it has no problem searching students' things, so students now feel they can take things, too," he suggests. Meanwhile, Lauth notes, while Steffner chased federal money for drug testing, the school's roof had been leaking for years, so the ceiling was falling and "they have to put buckets around to catch the rain."

Dublin, Ohio, "a pretty well-to-do district," according to the deputy schools superintendent, Mike Trego, had drug and alcohol testing from 2000 to 2002, before *Earls*. Like the Tecumseh district, alcohol, not drugs, was a problem among students. The district's athletics contract stipulated that if school athletes were found in proximity to any alcohol—say, at a party where a few kids were drinking beer—they would be considered guilty and penalized. "There was a lot of push back from the community. They thought it was unfair," Trego says. "They said, 'You need something more concrete.' So, the recommendation was, let's do drug testing." After studying the issue, the school board adopted a random drug-testing program for athletes, who paid an annual twenty-five-dollar fee toward the cost. A company came weekly to conduct tests for drugs and alcohol, and in two years, Dublin found twenty-one positives. "Most were marijuana, one for steroids, and one for amphetamines," Trego says. And alcohol, the chief substance being abused, got a pass because students did their partying on weekends and alcohol leaves the system quickly.

When the school board changed, a new superintendent was hired in

2002 and brought a different perspective, Trego says. She thought drug testing was a parental responsibility, and the new board backed her up, ending a program that had taken $65,000 from the school budget. The district's Code of Conduct Committee, which Trego chaired, considered renewing testing, but there has been no community pressure or board interest. "When we look at the University of Michigan longitudinal study, there doesn't seem to be a real impact on those who use testing," Trego says. "It becomes a cost factor, and a resource—almost an excessive resource. We now have [federal] Safe and Drug Free Schools money for parent education and intervention. It's more a question of do you make prevention the focus or wait until kids have a problem?"

The Guymon School District, in Oklahoma's panhandle, thought drug testing would work as a deterrent, just as John Walters claimed. The school board adopted random testing in 1999, the year after Tecumseh schools did, for athletes and students in competitive activities. An outside company was hired to do monthly testing. Guymon has a population of 11,000 with a small school district of 2,400 students. The town sits on Highway 54, "a big drug crossroads," according to Scott Dahl, who was a school board vice president and then president. But after three years, board and community members became alarmed at the unforeseen consequences of testing students. It wasn't deterring drug use, but it was encouraging some students to engage in even more harmful behavior to beat the test. "I had parents calling and saying, 'I caught my daughter drinking Clorox because she was going to be drug-tested,'" Dahl recalls. Dahl and others also noticed that testing was discouraging students from joining sports and other after-school activities. "I'm thinking, a lot of extracurricular kids are so busy, they're not out on the streets doing this stuff," he says. "We're probably missing the kids who are."

Guymon was spending $18,000 to $20,000 a year on testing, and many former proponents began questioning just what kind of "bang for the buck" they were getting, according to Dahl. The tests picked up a few positives, mostly pot, and those students were offered help, not punishment. "Maybe it worked for a few, but most kids were trying to beat the test." For all the money and effort, board members simply lost faith in drug testing. In 2002, Dahl proposed ending the program and the board supported him unanimously. "I like George Bush. It's not that I'm against drug testing," says Dahl years later. "But we think there are better ways to spend the money." Guymon hired a school liaison officer with a drug-sniffing dog. "That way you're covering the whole school," Dahl says. Health classes now have a greater focus on drug education. School administrators, meanwhile, have far more pressing problems to address, chiefly the testing mandates of No Child Left Behind, says Dahl: "We call it No Child Left Untested."

In the last two years, since Barack Obama entered the White House, the student drug testing movement has lost its main public champion, John Walters. The new head of the Office of National Drug Control Policy is Gil Kerlikowske, former police chief in Seattle, Washington, whose orientation runs more toward prevention than criminalization. The budget for student drug testing has not disappeared but it has been slashed dramatically. For fiscal year 2010, the Department of Education's Office of Safe and Drug Free schools had a budget of $7.3 million for random drug testing—$10 million less than for 2007. And that represented continuation grants to schools already funded under the Bush administration to do testing—not new awards.

Still, even if the student-drug-testing crusaders no longer have a bully pulpit in the White House, their chief power and momentum has always been at the local level, in school districts and communities, where the most potent policies of student discipline and school security are being forged.

6 THE PROFITEERS OF LOCKDOWN HIGH

The market for security is about $17 billion in the United States [in 2007]
and it is growing by a factor of 20 percent a year, among the fastest growing
industries. My impression is that schools are way behind the curve. They
don't understand the risks involved in having a thousand kids on campus.
Yes, they are scrambling to catch up but they aren't there yet.
    —Security International Association researcher Linda Yelton

The exhibit hall of San Francisco's sprawling Moscone Convention Center was bustling with conference-goers on the first day of the National School Boards Association annual gathering in April 2007. The NSBA drew 6,800 school board members and superintendents from around the country to its signature event of workshops, seminars, luncheons and notable keynote speakers, such as Bill Clinton, to ponder public education. Nowhere was the excitement as palpable as in the hall, that great marketplace of vendors hawking their wares directly to the people who control school district budgets. According to the NSBA, the total buying power behind those collective purse strings in 2007 totaled $280 billion. Throughout 55,000 square feet of exhibits, 355 vendors courted potential customers, displaying tables laden with bowls of bite-sized candy bars, eye-catching key chains and sleek ball-point pens emblazoned with company logos. Participants jostled along crowded aisles, bearing tote bags bulging with trinkets and glossy brochures describing the latest in playground equipment, the newest software for payroll management and computer-chip-carrying IDs to monitor student attendance. Here, the well-aimed sales pitch might hit just the right target who, back home, would lobby the local school board to invest in that newfangled technology, this appealing gadget.

A tour of the exhibit hall could easily fill hours with a mind-numbing variety of products both real and surreal—with sales raps to match. Over at Fisher Labs, the oldest manufacturer of hobby metal detectors in the country, a full-fledged, walk-through, portable metal detector beckoned attendees. This was definitely not for finding lost coins and jewelry. Fisher jumped into the security-related metal detector business only five years ago, according to its pitch woman Eva Shea. Now 28 percent of its customers are schools, mostly colleges, "but we're moving into high schools and middle schools," Shea adds. The portable display model sells for $5,000. Business is best on the East Coast and is aided by police departments that partner with school districts to buy Fisher's detectors with federal grant money. Shea says her company's participation at the NSBA convention evoked a few raised eyebrows at first. "I got some weird looks. People were surprised we would be here," she says. "One woman said, 'oh, this is terrible.' But then I explained why we're here."

Inner Link, a company based in Lancaster, Pennsylvania, promises "smart solutions for a health future" through a panoply of "web-based health and safety technology solutions," according to literature at the company's booth. Dr. Robert Gillio, a critical care doctor, founded the company in 2002 because "he wanted to bring health and education to students," says Rod Schoening, a project manager. One product, TeamPrepared, is designed to aid schools and emergency responders during crises by helping them prepare for same. Command management, preparedness, resource management and communications and information management are among its key tools, but exactly how it works is not immediately evident by reading the brochures or talking with Schoening. One popular selling point, though, is the product's ability to provide school building floor plans, which Schoening says helps in "building a community alliance" during a crisis. InnerLink charges $2,000 per school building in licensing fees. "We've had 258 people request information about it," says Schoening, "and we've had pretty good buy-ins from Jane's and NASRO." He refers to the defense intelligence and analysis organization, whose databases can be accessed through TP and to the national school police organization. "NASRO is interested in using a piece of our program for training," he says proudly.

Scholar Chip is a Long Island, New York, company founded in 2000 by a former Brookhaven National Laboratory physicist. The chip refers to the radio frequency ID tags that the company promotes for a variety of uses in student surveillance. "We track the bus and provide real-time data for students," says Terrence McGivney, a salesman. "We take attendance on the bus and at the building. We send an alert if a student was suspended and is on the bus, if they cut class yesterday or if it's their birthday." Acknowledging that this technology application stirs up some civil liberties issues, McGivney notes that "RFID tracking of students as if they are commodities is being challenged. A California town is challenging it." He is referring to Sutter and the fuss kicked up by Michelle Tatro. Scholar Chip has not made the leap to tagging young people—yet. But for an average of seven dollars per student per year, the company is providing its less controversial technosolutions to keeping track of scholars.

Stopware sent Roberta Sosbee and Eric Chang to pitch to the NSBA crowd. Their product checks IDs of visitors to schools or other buildings and issues badges. Stopware has been servicing clients, among them Fortune 500 companies, for ten years and wants in on the public school market. The hot ticket now is checking for registered sex offenders at schools, and that's where Stopware is looking to boost business. "We created a whole new product this year for schools," says Chang, referring to the sex offender look-up and a feature that links students to those parents or guardians approved to pick them up at school. Chang says the company revised the product to comply with new state laws like Florida's Jessica Lunsford law on registered sex offender screening. Just 5-10 percent of the company's business is with schools, but Chang is confident that will grow in the next decade. "We're educating people about the need for this," he says.

In the last decade, the U.S. security industry has increasingly targeted public schools as a vast, rich market for its hardware and software, products and services. Schools still represent a small fraction of the industry's gargantuan market, estimated to approach $20 billion annually and increasing by 20 percent a year, according to the Security Industry Association (SIA), a trade group. But that fraction has been growing from a sliver to a meatier slice of the pie. The SIA considers school security one of its key "Industry Issues," and tracks proposed state and federal legislation related to it, offering assessments of how it will benefit or hurt business prospects of SIA members. *SDM* magazine, a security industry publication, surveyed businesses about their growth markets. The survey found that the education market, which includes grades K-12 and colleges, was the third-fastest-growing market in 2007, with a 15 percent annual sales increase, behind commercial real estate and retail customers, at 30 percent and 21 percent respectively. The magazine noted that a recent shooting at Virginia Tech University helped rivet attention on school security in general.[1]

News reporting on the rare act of school violence—particularly shootings—not only rivets attention but spurs spending by schools that might make officials feel better but won't actually make students safer. For example, a week after the April 20, 1999 Columbine tragedy, Texas-based Garrett Metal Detectors was reportedly "awash in new orders as principals and teachers across the country try to shake feelings of vulnerability in the wake of the Columbine High School massacre."[2] In the previous four years, schools had become Garrett's largest single market, comprising 25 percent of all sales. And that was before September 11. Today, the industry promotes its technology to schools with the language of homeland security as well. Not only must schools protect students and faculty from the terrorists within—the bad, violent students. They must protect them from the terrorists without—whether jihadists or sex predators.

This seamless melding of marketing narratives, that sell terrorism as an everyday threat—in schools, in communities, nationally—is a core feature of our post-September 11 surveillance society. Embracing this wider definition of school safety, the federally created National School Safety Center offers a guide to "safeguarding schools against terrorism." In it, the center warns that schools face terrors from every quarter:

> Terrorism takes on many faces, forms and missions, from the international terror groups led by such individuals as Osama Bin Laden, to domestic terrorists such as Timothy McVey [sic] (convicted of blowing up the federal Murrah Building in Oklahoma City) or Buford Furrow (responsible for the Los Angeles Jewish day care center attack), to the notorious school shooters from Columbine High School.[3]

That rhetoric practically guarantees that schools can never do enough to safeguard their students, however many emergency plans they concoct or cameras they install. How can schools prepare for bin Laden and still be schools? They can't. But school administrators can use security technology to protect themselves from charges that they were unprepared for that rare incident of violence. A terrorist attack on a U.S. school has never occurred, but such a fact matters little. Standing ready to exploit public fears of the next Columbine and supply a dizzying array of security fixes are the profiteers of Lockdown High. They work the system at every level of the security economy—as consultants, entrepreneurs and corporate chieftains. They are fluent in government funding and legislative processes, many having exited public service to more lucrative opportunities in the private sector. These cogs in the free-market security economy have billions of reasons to keep public fears of student drug use, school violence, and now terror threats, in a state of high alert. Here are sketches of just a few of the many individuals and companies that perpetuate the mythologies of violent schools and substance-abusing students—while also making a living off the Lockdown High approach to school safety.

THE CONSULTANTS

THE GO-TO GUY

"I'm not here to sell anything," declared Ken Trump, surveying the three dozen people gathered in a Moscone Center meeting room on April 13. "This is not a sales speech today." Kenneth S. Trump, age forty-three, stout and portly, was presenting at the National School Boards Association 2007 conference. The topic was "School Security and Emergency Preparedness Planning: Safe Schools in a Post-9/11 World." In truth, Trump was selling something. Trump, a self-described "politically incorrect" master of the media sound bite, was selling himself as an expert on school violence and security. He is among a cadre of former school cops turned school safety consultants, and certainly one of the most widely quoted by the news media. He started his business, National School Safety and Security Services, in 1997 in Cleveland, Ohio, after running an antigang unit for that city's school district. When a federal grant paying his $60,000 salary ran out, and a clash with the school superintendent boiled over, Trump was out of a job.[4] So he hung out a shingle and parlayed his gang-buster experience into a consultancy on school safety at a time when the field was virgin territory. As fate would have it, a string of impending school shootings would send reporters scrambling for quotable experts. Trump was there and soon became the "go-to man," as one profile described him, his standing affirmed and amplified each time he was identified as an expert on school safety.[5]

Trump has a talent for sounding the alarm in colorful language about the lack of school preparedness, especially after school shootings. At the

April 2007 session, he told school board members he understood that safety was one of many problems they contend with. "It's easy for this to get lost in the busy agenda of running a school district," he said, "but the question isn't whether it's a wake-up call. The question is whether you're going to hit the snooze button six months after an incident. How do you keep this on the front burner when it's not a crisis?" The alarm clock analogy is a Trump favorite. Weeks after the Columbine incident, Trump told an Associated Press reporter, "We keep getting asked, 'Is Littleton a wake-up call?' My question is, are we going to hit the snooze button and go to sleep?"[6] Five years later, Trump reprised this theme in a Columbine anniversary article: "It's really not a question of whether Columbine was a wake-up call, but whether we've hit the snooze button and gone back to sleep."[7] After a mentally disturbed man shot and killed students in an Amish schoolhouse in October 2006, Trump intoned to a reporter, "We are still, seven years post-Columbine, suffering from Mayberry syndrome. If it can happen in a one-room Amish schoolhouse in rural Pennsylvania, it can happen anywhere."

As a for-profit consultancy, Trump's business rises and falls with the level of school crime—or at least the perception of it. When the school districts snooze, Trump's business will lose. Perhaps that is why Trump told his audience that the nationwide decade-long drop in school crime and violence, documented extensively and irrefutably by many sources, is a fallacy. "How many people have heard that crime is down fifty percent in schools? That's based on a hodgepodge of statistics and crime reporting," he declared. "The federal data is flawed and outdated." He was referring to the federal Department of Education's National Center for Education Statistics' "Indicators of School Crime and Safety." The reports debuted in 1999 and include data from three major sources that survey tens of thousands of individuals. But Trump, who runs his business with his wife, Carol, likens such research to "going to the mall and asking people about crime. It's absurd." Trump does his own research, the methodology of which could be qualified as hodgepodge: "I monitor it nationally, from school resource officers and from media reports." Trump blamed fickle politicians who let school violence fade from their radar when it is no longer a hot-button issue with the public. "The school emergency planning grants have been cut from $39 million in fiscal year 2003 to $24 million in fiscal year 2006. It makes no sense to cut funding to protect our schools," he said. As a service to potential customers, Trump's website provides information about applying for federal emergency planning grants, which can be used to pay for his services.[8]

SCHOOL COP BEHAVING BADLY

Forty-five-year-old Curtis Lavarello looks like a former cop and sounds like a conspiracy theorist. He is both. He partnered with Ken Trump at the April 2007 NSBA conference to talk about school safety, and especially about terrorism. "I'm even more of a conspiracy theorist than Ken. I truly believe the next area of attack will be on our children," he told the audience of school board members, adding enigmatically, "I never have to step foot on your school to attack your children. I can contaminate your sugar supply." Lavarello, of Sarasota, Florida, started his for-profit consultancy, the School Safety Advocacy Council, in 2005. Since both men claim to be the leading expert on school safety, they could be competitors. They aren't. Trump that year sat on Lavarello's advisory board, which is heavily weighted with policemen and sheriffs, particularly from Florida. His firm does swipe at other competitors on its website: "While others may boast on the fact that they are a not-for-profit organization, the fact remains there are no other individuls [sic] in the nation have the reputation and experience as those who serve for the School Safety Advocacy Council."

Lavarello's breezy and rambling presentation on April 13 began with a jokey story about his self-described clueless debut in school policing in Fort Lauderdale, right out of the police academy. "The first week, I walked around thinking there was only one bad kid," he recalled. "I kept hearing 'special ed, special ed.' And I thought, why don't we just get rid of Ed?"

He spent eighteen years as a school resource officer and advocates a "proactive, not reactive" SRO program, which he calls the "Officer Friendly" approach. Lavarello believes that Officer Friendly should be armed, and advised his audience that, "If you're in one of those districts where SROs can't have guns, you should go back and do something about that." Like Trump, Lavarello disparaged the credibility of multiagency federal surveys on school crime, and believes school crime is going up. He trusts his own survey of SROs: "Last year we did a national survey of school-based officers, and asked them, 'Do you think crime is being underreported in your school,' and ninety-seven percent said 'Yes.'" He said school administrators fear their school being labeled persistently dangerous under the federal No Child Left Behind law. So, to avoid that stigma, they "sweep some crimes under the carpet."

Lavarello has firsthand experience with the stigma of crime. His audience was probably unaware that he was arrested for drunk driving just two years earlier. The burly law enforcement veteran was a part-time deputy in the Sarasota Sheriff's Office when he was stopped at a DUI checkpoint at 2 a.m. on March 18, 2005. According to a news account, "Officers noticed Lavarello's breath smelled of alcohol and that his speech was slurred. . . . During every portion of his sobriety test, Lavarello swayed and couldn't keep his balance, reports show." The school safety expert refused to take a breath test. The Sheriff's Office fired him the same day. Yet Lavarello told the reporter that it was "politics," not drunk driving behind his arrest: "I was very involved in Sheriff Balkwill's campaign," Lavarello said. "The deputy who filed the charges was very, very involved in his competition's campaign." Lavarello later pled guilty to reckless driving and the DUI charge was dropped, reportedly because of the lack of breath-test evidence needed for conviction. Lavarello received one year's probation, fifty hours of community service, and mandatory attendance at DUI school.[9] Not long after his arrest and firing, Lavarello was hired as executive director of the Sarasota Coalition on Substance Abuse, a nonprofit that "promotes substance abuse free environments." Among the organization's projects is educating youth about the perils of drunk driving.

But Lavarello did not find himself clear of controversy. At the time of his arrest, he was also the paid executive director of the National Association of School Resource Officers—NASRO—the largest school police membership organization. Shortly after Lavarello's arrest and firing from the Sheriff's Office, NASRO dismissed him, too, with a negotiated settlement that kept the actual reasons for his firing a secret and paid him $125,000, plus $400 monthly for health insurance until he landed another job. A noncompete clause stated Lavarello's agreement not to "form, create, or operate, or assist in the formation, creation or operation of any association . . . which competes with [NASRO] . . ." for a one-year period. Yet at the time Lavarello signed the termination agreement, he had already created the School Safety Advocacy Council which, soon after his termination from NASRO, began offering the kinds of SRO training courses and school safety programs that were NASRO's bread and butter. So, in early 2006, NASRO filed a civil suit against Lavarello, charging he violated terms of their agreement by creating SSAC and using "confidential and proprietary information" from his NASRO job, such as membership lists, training contracts, and program materials. And, the suit charged, he continued to collect monthly health insurance payments even after taking the Coalition job, which provided health benefits. Lavarello's legal response denied that he had violated their agreement. The suit was still pending in the Twelfth Circuit Court in Sarasota County as of May 2010.

At the NSBA school safety presentation, Lavarello ended with a nonsales pitch for Raptor, the Houston-based sex-predator-screening software company. "This is not a commercial for Raptor. I just think it's good software," he asserted. "Do any of you work with the Raptor system? You in Texas know the Raptor system. In Florida we have the Raptor system." What Lavarello did not say is that Raptor Technologies is a "partner" of the School Safety Advocacy Council, and Raptor's founder and CEO Allan Measom, sits on its advisory board.

THE ENTREPRENEURS

FROM ENRON TO RAPTOR

Allan Measom has seen catastrophe create opportunities. He's also seen it wipe them out. He is an American businessman, with a keen eye for market trends and public neuroses. Using entrepreneurial savoir faire, Measom founded Raptor Technologies, the Houston-based company that mines gold from the most unlikely and sordid of materials: state registries of convicted sex offenders. Targeting public schools, Measom's company sells an internet-based software program V-Soft. Measom's product is not the only access-control software system that screens for sex offenders, but he has aggressively pursued alliances with law enforcement and school security consultants, such as NASRO and the School Safety Advocacy Council, tapped federal grants and, most impressively, lobbied politicians for state legislation that opens school-house doors wide to a kind of surveillance that some consider intrusive and unnecessary. And Raptor has benefitted from the kind of generous, mostly uncritical news media coverage that money can't buy.

Raptor's genesis was in the events of September 11, 2001. Measom was then a consultant to Enron, the defunct Houston corporation now synonymous with financial wrongdoing. After New York's twin towers were destroyed by terrorism, Measom was asked to develop a software program that would track who entered and left Enron's headquarters. Three months later, the accounting misdeeds of Enron's chieftains sent the company tumbling into bankruptcy, and left Measom in his own financial morass. "Sitting at Enron one day realizing they would not pay us all they would owe us," Measom recalled in a phone interview from his office, "I was curious about school districts and if they are wondering who is coming and going. I visited with one district police officer and he said the biggest issue was keeping up with registered sex offenders moving in and out of a district. After Megan's Law, most police districts send a picture, but the school secretary sticks it in a drawer. She won't remember." Measom and his partner, Justin Waldrip, the software's developer, went to Austin and bought the Texas database of registered sex offenders from the state department of public information. Measom began attending local school PTA meetings. "I'd start talking about what we'd do and the PTA head would say, 'Stop, let me write a check,'" Measom said. "I knew there was a nerve I had touched." That nerve was public fear of sex predators, and it stretched beyond Texas to the rest of the nation. The nerve became more raw, too, after the horrific 2005 murder of nine-year-old Jessica Lunsford in Florida by a convicted sex offender. The state passed the Jessica Lunsford Act, which requires background checks for school employees, among other things. And it generated much publicity—and school contracts—for Raptor.[10] Measom told me V-Soft was in four thousand schools in thiry-seven states. The initial cost is about $1,500 plus an annual fee of $432 per school. Raptor and Measom did well, earning an estimated $2.5 million by 2005. What a change from the early lean times when he lived off credit cards. "I was $250,000 in debt when I started the company," Measom said. "The first year, when my wife and I went to the movies, we had no money."

That was then. Now, Measom has ten employees and anticipated selling V-Soft to a thousand schools in 2008. "I have no real competitors. There are a couple of guys but they don't have the hands-on thing," he said. "We've become the go-to for sex offenders." One reason is glowing and frequent news coverage of Raptor. "We've been blessed by the press," Measom said. Another is his cultivation of relationships with law enforcement groups, especially NASRO, whose state and national conferences he often attends. It pays off. In 2006, the federal National Institute of Justice awarded Raptor a $52,675 grant through its School Safety Technologies program because of Measom's marketing-networking strategy. "We were up at New Jersey NASRO," he explained. "I was doing my dog-and-pony show, and one of the guys in the room was from the DOJ [Department of Justice] and he knows people from the School Safety Advocacy Council." Raptor was one of just two grantees that year. The grant funded a proposed "School Safety and Sex Offender Screening Project," at fifty schools across the country chosen by NIJ to get Raptor's V-Soft. "We didn't make any money on this. We sold everything at cost," Measom said. "But every time we went out to a school, the media was there. It was worth its weight in gold to get the media attention." Raptor's website offers "facts" about V-Soft and sex offenders that seem scary: of all registered sex offenders (RSOs) logged in Texas schools with V-Soft, 73 percent committed crimes against children, whose average age was eleven; and most RSOs were parents or guardians of a student at the school—people who visited the school regularly. But there is no information on when this data was collected or how many RSOs were logged out of all visitors. In 2007, Measom claimed that V-Soft had identified 1,100 RSOs, of whom 10 percent were from out of state and failed to reregister. As an adjunct to the criminal justice system, his product may be useful, but Measom cannot claim to have prevented any crimes in school. Indeed, the majority of sexual abuse and assaults of children occur in or near their homes—Jessica Lundsford was murdered by a neighbor. Given the hysteria around sex offenders, though, the logic of employing V-Soft is not so important.

Measom's "hands-on thing" includes lobbying state legislators for laws that would ease Raptor's entry into schools. "I just got legislation passed in Texas," he said, referring to Senate Bill 9, passed in 2007. "It had four lines in it about schools having the right to ask for ID when someone comes on campus, and they have the right to check databases. Now I'm working for each state to put it in their legislation for purposes of security. I don't care if you're from Mexico or Zimbabwe. You have to show ID if you want to go into a school." Measom knows his technology raises privacy concerns. Some people are reluctant to have their private information scanned into Raptor's database, where it is stored indefinitely. He said that only birth dates are stored by Raptor and that his systems are encrypted and firewalled. "Big brother people are scared. But if you aren't doing bad, what do you care?" he asked. "I go around with the ACLU. I'm dying for them to make a big stink. Then I can go on O'Reilly or Oprah. I'd love to go on Oprah, and she'll tell people to go out and buy the system." Raptor is a harder sell in the northeastern states, where "you have the civil libertarians," Measom acknowledged.

But Athens, Georgia, is where Raptor got its first bad press and was summarily kicked out of a school—and not by the ACLU. "As I saw it, the principal went a little rogue," said Jason Winders, then the executive editor of the *Athens Banner-Herald*, in a telephone interview from the newspaper. In early May 2007, Principal Ken Sherman of Clarke Middle School installed Raptor's V-Soft, scanning all visitors and parents. Sherman was under pressure after a March incident in which a thirty-one-year-old man got into the school and assaulted a twelve-year-old student in the girls' bathroom. "The man snuck in. He wouldn't have been scanned in first place," said Winders. And the man had no record as a sex offender, so V-Soft would have let him pass, Winders noted.

Sherman learned about Raptor through the school district's security chief, who in turn had learned about NIJ grants funding Raptor in schools from a University of Georgia security employee. This man, according to reporting by the *Banner-Herald*, is on the advisory council of NIJ's National Law Enforcement and Corrections Technology Center, and he filed a grant request for Sherman. Weeks later, Raptor—not the NIJ—contacted Sherman to tell him that he'd gotten the grant and V-Soft would be installed shortly. But Sherman had never consulted or notified the Clarke County Board of Education—let alone parents—about Raptor. And when one parent balked at having her ID scanned, Sherman pulled rank, according to Winders. "His attitude was, 'Don't question my authority,'" Winders said. (Contacted for comment, Sherman responded in an email: "This is a pending legal matter and a highly sensitive case. Therefore I am not at liberty to share any information.") The angry parent called the newspaper, and Winders put reporters on the story. "We started asking questions and that's when the school board learned about it," Winders said, "and the board was offended and downright angry. The public was infuriated that it had been done in secret." Very quickly, the board ordered Sherman to stop scanning visitors. Winders wrote about the events on his daily blog, chastising Sherman for his unilateral action. "Our principal wasn't versed on this," Winders said. "He couldn't tell me if data was stored by Raptor." Greg Goedeke, who does marketing for Measom, responded to the *Banner-Herald* reporting and the public backlash with a letter to the editor that was by turns sarcastic, angry and threatening. Goedeke belittled Winders' call for "public debate," writing, "why even have a school Principal, a Superintendent or other school staff if they can not make decisions about the safety of 700+ children and staff. I look forward to the debate on switching from steak fingers to chicken fingers in the cafeteria." "The company was just assholes—no other way to put it," Winders said. "If they had played their hand right, they might be in the schools now. But there was a combination of circumstances: a parent who asked a question, a principal who got his back up and a company that was an asshole."

LEADER OF THE DRUG DOG PACK

Man's best friend can be a student's Fourth Amendment nightmare when the dog is a drug-sniffing detective. Interquest Detection Canines has built a national business deploying drug dogs in schools, a practice challenged in the courts for trampling students' constitutional protections against unreasonable search and seizure. Indeed, the Houston company's advertising brags that its service was a "key element" in a civil rights case brought by students whose school was among the first to use drug dogs more than thirty years ago. The case was *Horton v. Goose Creek Independent School District*, filed by three students at a Baytown, Texas, high school. In 1978, the district contracted with Security Associates International (SIA), a Houston firm, to do random drug sweeps with dogs. The plaintiffs Robby Horton, Heather Horton and Sandra Sanchez sued the district for violating their Fourth Amendment rights, describing the dog-sniffing of their possessions and persons as embarrassing and disruptive. In testimony, Heather recounted that "we were in the middle of a major French exam and the dog came in and walked up and down the aisles and stopped at every desk and sniffed on each side all around the people, the feet, the parts where you keep your books under the desk." A dog mistakenly alerted to Sandra and Robby, so school officials searched her bag and his pants pockets, legs and socks. No drugs or alcohol were found on them or anywhere in the school.

A district court judge ruled against the students, but on June 1, 1982, the Fifth Circuit Court of Appeals in New Orleans reversed that judgment on a key issue: dog-sniffing of cars and lockers was acceptable, but not of students themselves, without individualized suspicion that they possessed contraband. The ruling stated in part: "The use of the dogs to sniff the students presents an even clearer instance of a search within the fourth amendment. The students' persons certainly are not the subject of lowered expectations of privacy. On the contrary, society recognizes the interest in the integrity of one's person, and the fourth amendment applies with its fullest vigor against any indecent or indelicate intrusion on the human body . . . when there is no individualized cause to justify the sniffing, the Constitution prohibits the intrusion." The security firm, SAI, calibrated its dog-sniffing to parameters *Horton* helped draw. "We don't necessarily make sniff searches of students, so it came out OK for us," said Rick Newman, owner of SAI, in a news article about the ruling.[11]

Interquest was whelped by Debbie Farmer, a dog handler in the canine detection unit of SAI, and her partner Mike Fernandez. The company website states that Farmer helped establish "policies and procedures" that withstand legal challenges in the courts. Schools comprised most of their clients from the beginning, and today Interquest is a twenty-five-franchise concern, contracting with twelve hundred schools in twenty-seven states. Franchise fees cost between $40,000 and $60,000, with total investment costs of up to $100,000. Call it the McDonald's of drug dogs. And like McDonald's, Interquest is good at marketing, sending dog-and-handler teams to conferences where school police, educators and school board members congregate. At the National School Boards Association 2007 conference, Interquest's booth was a popular stop in the exhibition hall. There, a drug-sniffing mutt lounged lazily while his handlers were the barkers, extolling the benefits of random drug sweeps in schools. "We start by bringing dogs that have a friendly appearance, like Labs and Goldens, not scary ones," explained Marygrace Huber, whose Interquest business card identifies her as "Supreme Empress of Administration." "It's up to a district to sign up for so many visits a year, but the best way is to do it twice a month, random and unannounced. The school doesn't even know when we are coming." Cost is $280 to $600 for a day of sniffing. Interquest's canines are trained to alert to various drugs, and marijuana is most common, representing about 30 percent of alerts. Alcohol comes next, at 28 percent. How many positive drug or alcohol discoveries do Interquest's doggy detectives yield, say, in a typical sweep of a typical school? If the dog searches are meant to deter student drug use on campus, do dog alerts decrease after Interquest sweeps begin? Such statistics could certainly be a helpful promotional tool. This line of questioning flummoxes Debi DeShon, a franchise owner in California's Central Valley. Finally, she explains that school districts don't need "selling" on Interquest services because the services sell themselves.

Interquest grew about 12 percent a year, says Huber, and had opportunities for explosive growth, but "we don't want it to be out of control." Most franchises are in the south and west, and Huber would like other areas of the country that haven't been exposed to detection to see how "fun it can be." There are barriers, though, which she initially hesitates to articulate. With the caveat that it was her opinion, not the company's, she suggested that "in the northeast people are more aware of their rights, so much so that they go to the other extreme." Huber's view was echoed by Glenn VadeBonCoer, manager of Interquest of Chicagoland, in Illinois, who presented at the NASRO conference in Orlando in July 2007. At a workshop titled "Canines for Reducing Drugs, Violence and Bullying," VadeBonCoer said, "Down south tends to be a lot more tolerant of this. In Texas, [drug dogs] are everywhere in the schools. You try to bring this in the north and you'll be in trouble if the ACLU gets ahold of it and starts bullying the school to get the program out." Despite such rights awareness, random drug-dog sweeps have become fairly commonplace, with more than 21 percent of public schools using them regularly. Geography isn't the only factor. Urbanization is key: just 11 percent of schools in cities use drug-dogs, while 31 percent in rural areas and more than 32 percent in towns use them. And income levels matter, too. Schools with more than 50 percent of students eligible for free lunch— an indicator of poverty—or fewer than 20 percent poverty-level students—are least likely to bring on the dogs. It's the schools sandwiched in the middle-income level that most commonly use drug dogs.[12]

As a private company, Interquest has an edge over drug-dog sweeps done by local police agencies, which are held to much stricter legal definitions of reasonable suspicion of drug or alcohol possession and unreasonable search. The courts grant school officials wide latitude in enforcing school rules, and random dog-sniffing by outside contractors is now widely accepted. That's good for business. "We really like doing it," said Huber at the close of our interview. "We have a really good thing going around."

THE INDUSTRY

THE TESTAHOLICS LOBBY

The drug-testing industry was a mere acorn just two decades ago, far from the mighty, towering oak it is today. From corporate giants like Quest Diagnostics and LabCorp, to mom-and-pop Internet purveyors of drug test kits, this powerhouse industry generates some $6 billion annually.[13] Key to that robust growth is the industry's cultivation of ever new markets. The U.S. military was the literal testing ground for mandatory drug-testing in the 1970s, followed by workplace testing, which was a hallmark of the war on drugs unleashed during the Reagan presidency. Reagan's 1986 executive order mandating drug-testing policies in federal agencies was followed by passage of the Drug-Free Workplace Act of 1988, aimied at private companies receiving federal funds. Acquiescing to the anti-drug drumbeat emanating from the industry and its Washington allies, private sector employers climbed aboard the drug-testing bandwagon. In 1987, 21 percent of employers did any drug-testing; by 1996, 81 percent did. But as a costly and fairly pointless exercise, testing's popularity among employers has been plummeting, and in 2004, 62 percent of employers were doing it.[14]

As employer testing crested and began to fall, a glistening new horizon beckoned the testing industry and its government enablers. By the mid-1990s, concern about youth and school crime was sharpening, and the antidrug warriors turned their gaze to the schoolhouse. The 1995 U.S. Supreme Court ruling in *Vernonia* which permitted random testing of school athletes created legal leverage for testing proponents and economic incentive for the nascent industry. That same year, the drug-testing industry came of age, forming a lobby known today as the Drug and Alcohol Testing Industry Association—DATIA. Four years later, the Columbine High School attacks provided a political rationale for testing that meshed with heightened fears of school violence. On April 29, nine days after the infamous event in Littleton, Colorado, Pennsylvania Rep. John E. Peterson held a press conference to announce a bill he'd authored to fund random drug-testing for students in grades 7 to 12. Peterson, a conservative Republican from the state's rural northwest corner, called his bill the "Empowering Parents to Fight Drugs Act of 1999." A year earlier, Peterson had introduced a more stringent version of the legislation, which would have "required" schools to drug-test students—not simply to provide funds to encourage schools to test. Exploiting the Columbine tragedy and dismissing evidence that neither of the assailants had drugs or alcohol in their bodies, Peterson declared that reducing student drug use would prevent future school shootings. "The only way to have drug-free school is to follow the successful program of the military and the workplace," he told reporters.[15] The *Drug Detection Report*, a newsletter on workplace drug-testing, reported on the reaction to Columbine among student-drug-testing proponents: "In the wake of the shooting tragedy in a Colorado high school, national leaders are looking for ways to stop the carnage in American schools, including curbing drug abuse in schools through drug-testing programs."[16]

Still, it wasn't until George W. Bush became president that the stars aligned for drug-testing proponents eager to push onward into the schoolhouse. Bush included funding for student drug-testing in the No Child Left Behind Act, and appointed a drug czar who was gung-ho on testing. John Walters used his Office of National Drug Control Policy to proselytize and fund school testing programs in concert with the Department of Education. And when the court of Chief Justice William H. Rehnquist agreed in 2001 to revisit student drug-testing in the *Board of Education v. Earls* appeal, anti-drug ideologues and their industry compadres finally had their day in court. Bush's Justice Department filed an amicus brief in support of the Tecumseh school district testing program of students participating in a broad array of extracurricular activities. The New Jersey lawyer and drug-testing activist David Evans wrote an amicus brief on behalf of drug-testing proponents that garnered support from an interlocking directorate of drug warrior groups, including the Drug Free America Foundation and its spinoff Institute on

Global Drug Policy, DATIA, and Rep. John Peterson. DATIA trumpeted its participation in the *Earls* brief in a January 2002 newsletter to members that distorted both the legal issue at stake (the limits of search and seizure in the schoolhouse) and the position of the ACLU, which brought the original suit against student testing: "This case is important because it will decide how much of a drug problem a school has to have in order to drug test students. The school in this case had minimal drug use and so the court did not allow testing, however, this is not the situation with many schools in the US. The ACLU has taken the position that a school has to be 'out of control' with drugs before testing can take place." (The ACLU's oft-stated position is that random drug-testing in schools is a punitive approach that does not reduce drug use and harms the learning environment.)

When the Supreme Court ruled in June 2002 against Lindsay Earls and for the school district, the testaholics were gleeful. DATIA was described as "delighted by the ruling," with its spokesperson Laura E. Shelton sounding philanthropic. "We've heard from a lot of school people who wanted to put testing programs in place but were waiting to see how the court ruled in this case," she said. "We are so excited to be able to present this much-needed information to testing and education professions. Drug and alcohol testing has shown to be a very effective means of deterring drug use, and the nation's children need to live healthy and drug and alcohol free lives."[17] Shelton, a registered lobbyist for DATIA, was probably excited about the ruling's impact on the industry's bottom line, too.

In 2002, DATIA identified "student drug-testing" as one of four specific issues it was trying to get Congress to support, and the *Earls* decision sent the trade group into high gear. In July, DATIA organized a conference for two hundred members who "came to Washington to learn how they might profit from the Supreme Court's new permissive stance on school-based drug-testing," according to one news account. The keynote was the Keystone State's very own John Peterson. "Folks, it's saleable, but we have to stand up and sell it," he said. Peterson issued a press release the same day announcing yet another version of his student-drug-testing bill, which would provide $100 million in federal funds.[18] In October, four months after the *Earls* decision, Shelton, exhorted drug-testing companies to win a piece of the student business by improving their marketing to school districts. In an interview with the Drug Detection Reporter, Shelton noted that only 5 percent of the nation's fifteen thousand school districts did student drug-testing, and suggested that companies needed to educate local communities and school boards about the "benefits" of testing, as well as "what to look for in a drug-testing company."[19] With roughly 55 million public school students, the potential school drug-testing market would rightly make the drug-testing industry salivate.

Student drug testing ascended high on DATIA's agenda for the next five years, along with such top priorities as promoting hair, saliva, and sweat testing as alternatives to urinalysis, and backing legislation to crack down on products that thwart drug tests. When President Bush included student drug-testing in his 2004 State of the Union address— and earmarked millions for grants in his next budget—DATIA members stepped up to do their part. DATIA's board chairman Joe Reilly, who runs the company Florida Drug Screening in Palm Bay, and board member Elaine Taule, president of NMS Management Services, a testing services company in Delray Beach, created Student Drug Testing of America to "assist" public and private schools to do testing. The "coalition," whose name and website suggest a nonprofit group, included several other DATIA members. The scheme paid off. In October 2005, the federal Office of Safe and Drug Free Schools awarded the front group a three-year $137,000 grant for drug-testing at three Florida schools. Reilly sent out a press release announcing the news and stating that he and Taule would administer the grant award. "The major goal is to reduce drug use among the target population of students by 5 perent annually," Reilly wrote. Not bad for their business, either.

In 2007, student drug testing was number seven out of seventeen DATIA action items: "Support legislation and initiatives aimed at furthering school drug-testing. Work to increase public perception and acceptance of school drug-testing and to increase the amount of funding and technical assistance available to school systems that want to establish drug free school programs . . ." With 1,300 members—from the testing behemoth LabCorp to the just-plain behemoth ExxonMobil to the niche hair-testing corporation Psychemedics to the small-time operator Florida Drug Screening—DATIA was now a strong voice in the chorus clamoring for student drug-testing. Not surprisingly, they were in perfect harmony with long-time drug-testing zealots whose ideological commitment to student testing was also harmonious with their ability to profit from it.

AGING DRUG WARRIORS

Before there was a drug-testing industry, there was a cadre of warriors in the earliest stages of the War on Drugs. Their fealty to conservative Republicanism was wedded to loathing for the counterculture of the 1960s and 70s and its perceived identification with drugs—especially marijuana. They were government men, political appointees in research, law enforcement and policymaking agencies who devised the infrastructure of drug-testing policy and practice that now encompasses children. Today, they are a mostly grizzled and graying bunch but their reach within government and the private sector is still long. They are part of an intertwined and extensive network of drug-testing consultants, lawyers, researchers, activists and lobbyists. By helping to lay the legal, legislative and political infrastructure, these warriors have assisted the rise of a drug-testing industry in which they have clear financial interests, and provided the ideological cover for student drug testing.

Call Robert L. DuPont the godfather of the drug-testing movement. A Harvard-trained psychiatrist and addiction specialist, DuPont was the founding director of the National Institute on Drug Abuse (NIDA) in 1973 and the second national drug czar, appointed by President Richard Nixon and serving under Ford and Carter until 1978. DuPont's long career and professional accomplishments also include his close association with controversial Republican Party operatives Mel and Betty Sembler and their antidrug efforts. The Semblers' drug rehabilitation program for teens, called Straight, Inc., was founded in 1976 and DuPont was its consultant. But reports of physical and psychological abuse of teens by Straight employees triggered multiple civil suits against the company, which had received glowing media coverage and support from the Reagan White House. According to reports, DuPont testified on behalf of Straight as an expert witness and has remained a staunch ally of the Semblers. Straight was dissolved in 1993, but the Semblers reemerged with the Drug Free America Foundation in 1996, with DuPont on their advisory board. Student drug-testing is one of its key issues.[20] DuPont wears many hats still. He partners with Peter Bensinger, former head of the Drug Enforcement Administration under President Ford, in their private consulting firm, Bensinger, Dupont & Associates, which advises clients on employment drug-testing programs. DuPont has also been the scientific advisor to Pyschemedics, the for-profit company that does drug-testing on hair and whose majority shareholder is H. Wayne Huizenga, the Florida billionaire entrepreneur and Republican Party associate of the Semblers. DuPont runs a nonprofit, too, called the Institute for Behavior and Health in Bethesda. In 2003, this DuPont creation received $346,775 from the federal Office of Safe and Drug Free Schools to "implement, enhance, and evaluate the effectiveness of student drug-testing programs through a design involving eight high schools." DuPont was one of just two grant recipients that were not schools chosen in that first year of grants. A staunch advocate of drug testing of students, DuPont was an expert for the Vernonia, Oregon school district when its drug-testing program was challenged by James Acton. And he signed onto the amicus brief filed in support of testing for the *Earls* case—as former NIDA head and as Bensinger & DuPont Associates, for good measure. A perennial favorite at DATIA conferences, DuPont was a luncheon speaker at the trade group's 2006 regulatory summit where he spoke of the need to revise government rules to allow drug-testing of specimens other than just urine, such as hair. At DATIA's 2008 annual gathering in Dallas, DuPont led a two-part workshop on "The Future of Student Drug Testing" for companies interested in diving into that rich market.

If Robert DuPont is the godfather of drug-testing, J. Michael Walsh might be considered the consigliere. The highlight of his substantial career in the federal government surely was a stint at the NIDA as director of its applied research unit. From 1980 to 1989, Walsh, who has a doctorate in psychology, directed research on drunk driving and drug policy, and oversaw the development of the drug-testing guidelines that ultimately were adopted by all federal agencies under his coordination. This fierce drug warrior was rewarded with an appointment by President George H. W. Bush as executive director of the President's Drug Advisory Council from 1989 to 1993 (including a brief tenure as deputy at ONDCP, the drug czar's office). Walsh left public service to use his drug-testing expertise in service to himself, creating the Walsh Group, of Bethesda, Maryland, whose motto is "Advancing Public Policy Through

Research." Walsh is also invested in advancing the broadest, most intrusive uses of drug-testing. In 2002, Walsh was funded by the Robert Wood Johnson Foundation to research so-called per se laws against "drugged" driving, which is defined as a person having any amount of drug or alcohol in his/her blood. Under Walsh's direction and reflecting his own ideology, the consensus report recommended that states consider adopting laws prohibiting driving "when any amount of a drug is present as measured in blood, urine, saliva, or other bodily substance," and that refusal to consent to a test would be the same as testing positive. Walsh's promotion of this extreme approach to enforcing safe-driving laws was effective, and almost a dozen states have adopted such "zero tolerance per se" laws.[21] Walsh's for-profit consultancy has several large corporate clients, such as *The Washington Post*, Hoffman-La Roche pharmaceuticals and the National Football League. But not surprisingly, the former government insider has major governmental agencies still paying his salary. Among his public clients are the National Department of Transportation, the Small Business Administration, ONDCP, the National Institute on Drug Abuse, and the Department of Education. DOE gave Walsh $401,241 in 2003, to run and evaluate student drug testing in three high schools in Hunterdon, New Jersey—where ONDCP's favorite principal, Lisa Brady, began testing years earlier. His grant was the only one to a private, for-profit entity, and with Robert DuPont's grant, the only two DOE grants that did not go directly to school districts.

David G. Evans, though not a veteran of the earlier drug wars, has certainly distinguished himself as the Zelig of the student drug-testing movement and a member of more drug-related organizations, real or virtual, than any other drug-testing advocate. Evans is a suburban New Jersey lawyer, member of the conservative Federalist Society, and former researcher in the New Jersey Health Department's alcohol and drug abuse unit. His tall, thin bespectacled persona and snarky presentations were a regular feature of John Walters's Student Drug Testing Summits from 2004 to 2008. His embrace of student drug-testing came about some twenty years ago, he says, when his children were students in New Jersey schools. Evans chaired the Student Drug Testing Task Force at Hunterdon Central High School, which created its student random testing program, and was involved in bringing testing to two other schools in the area. He founded the Drug Free Schools Coalition, a New Jersey entity led by Evans, and is a special advisor to the Drug Free America Foundation of the Semblers. He's also head of the DFAF's Legal Foundation Against Illicit Drugs, and calls himself "a leading member" of the National Student Drug-Testing Committee, which appears to be a website offering outdated news articles and research from DFAF, Lisa Brady, and Evans himself and links to other antidrug groups. His presence in cyberspace is widespread.

Evans' real-life credentials are impressive, too, but he doesn't talk about these endeavors in his public talks about student testing. After leaving the health department, he turned to law and "built his legal practice by representing manufacturers of testing devices and other pro-testing interests," according to the *Drug Detection Report*. Evans worked for Roche Diagnostics' drug-abuse unit as a legal consultant and did state and federal lobbying on its behalf. Also working at Roche was Robert Aromando, Evan's neighbor in Flemington, New Jersey, and an executive at several other pharmaceutical companies. Evans also works for Aromando, who started his own lobbying firm, K Street Associates of Flemington, which specializes in "consulting and support services for healthcare policy issues," according to Aromando's lobbying registration report. In 2008, K Street's clients included J. Michael Walsh and a group called the Private Sector Oral Fluid Testing Advisory Board, which would like the feds to approve saliva for drug-testing, thereby exponentially increasing the business prospects for drug-testing companies. Aromando, in turn, sits on the board of Evans's Drug Free Schools Coalition, and has lobbied New Jersey school board members with Evans to adopt testing—without disclosing his financial interest.

Evans's zeal for student drug-testing is real. He wrote the amicus brief filed in support of the Tecumseh High School's random testing program, the signers of which are a who's who of the drug war movement. As a speaker at DATIA's 2003 annual meeting in Nashville, he was optimistic about the prospects for achieving universal testing in schools: "All the stuff that I heard fifteen, twenty years ago about employment testing, I'm hearing about student drug-testing: privacy issues, technology issues, process issues, legal issues—it's all coming up, and we're getting it resolved in almost the same order . . . I have no doubt about it, and I think five, ten years from now—maybe sooner—everybody's going to be doing it just like we are doing it now in the workplace, because the effectiveness is going to be demonstrated."[22]

The buoyancy and determination of antidrug warriors like Evans and the school security industry benefit from a friendly administration in Washington, D.C., such as that of former President George W. Bush. But they were around before him and they will continue on through an Obama administration and whoever follows. There are healthy profits to be made.

7 POLICING THE SCHOOLS, ARRESTING DEVELOPMENT

You've got people in your schools right now plotting a Columbine. Every town, every university now has a Cho, and in every state, we have al Qaeda cells thinking of it. Every school is a possible target of attack . . . You've got to be a one-man fighting force. . . . You've got to have enough guns, and ammunition and body armor to stay alive . . . You should be walking around in schools every day in complete tactical equipment, with semi-automatic weapons and five rounds of ammo . . . You can no longer afford to think of yourselves as peace officers . . . You must think of yourself as soldiers in a war, because we're going to ask you to act like soldiers.

—John Giduck, keynote speaker at the 2007 National Association of School Resource Officers conference, in Disney World, Orlando, Florida

The police immediately came toward the African-Americans and started hitting us with billy clubs and handcuffing innocent people who were not even involved in anything, simply trying to go to their classes. They slammed students up against lockers, put guns to students' heads, and handcuffed innocent people. There were many people who got hit with batons. I person-ally got hit with a baton.

—JR, a student, describing a ninety-officer police action at Thurgood Marshall High School in San Francisco on Oct. 11, 2002, that resulted from two students fighting.[1]

At 6:40 a.m. on November 5, 2003, a SWAT team from the Goose Creek, South Carolina, police department stormed into Stratford High School from all directions in a commando-style drug raid you might expect to see at a crack house. Principal George McCrackin, who had requested and orchestrated the raid with police, marched around the school's hall-ways with Stratford teachers and staff participating in the action. About two dozen cops, their semi-automatic handguns drawn, shouted "Get down!" and "Put your hands on your head!" ordering children down on the floor—tossing some of them there—or shoving them against walls with guns pointed in their faces or at the back of the their heads. A group of students in the cafeteria was rounded up, cuffed with plastic restraints and herded into the hallway with the others. The students were then ordered to their knees, facing the wall, hands behind their heads, and forced to remain there until 7:40 a.m. A large drug-detection dog was led down the row of students to sniff their backpacks and bags. Poorly trained and unresponsive to commands, the dog pulled and lunged and tore at some students' bags. It signaled drugs twelve times, but nothing was found. Drug sniffing dogs are notoriously unreliable.

For the 107 Stratford students held captive in the hallways of their school that morning, the invasion by the armed men was a nightmare. "I froze up. I didn't know what to do," one fifteen-year-old boy told a reporter. "Everybody thought it was a terrorist attack." A girl leaving a bathroom saw cops in the hallway with guns drawn and later said, "I assumed that they were trying to protect us, that it was like Columbine, that somebody got in the school that was crazy or dangerous. But then a police officer pointed a gun at me." Although only 20 percent of Stratford's students were black, about two-thirds of those cuffed and searched were African-American because the buses serving the predominantly black neighborhoods were usually the first to arrive at school. McCrackin hatched the scheme after a student supposedly tipped him off to drug dealing by another student. Attorney Marlon Kimpson, of the law firm Motley Rice, which would represent student-plaintiffs, said McCrackin had "twenty-plus surveillance monitors in his office." The Goose Creek drug raid was fully documented by the video cameras, and when a tape of the event was leaked to the media, it caused a national sensation as images of children cowering before gestapo-like cops burst on the evening news. McCrackin resigned as principal in the wake of widespread condemnation of the police and school officials, and the ACLU, Motley Rice and a Charleston attorney Gregg Meyers brought a class-action lawsuit charging violations of students' Fourth Amendment rights against unreasonable search and seizure and Fourteenth Amendment guarantees of due process. The outcome was a $1.2 million settlement with the school district and police department, and a consent agreement on proper policing procedures in schools. "It was embarrassing to the school district and the police," says Meyers. "If they had found a single kid with drugs, it might have been different. But to go through that whole hullabaloo for nothing?"

The Goose Creek police raid on Stratford High could be an iconic event, if not quite as infamous as Columbine, because of the graphic and shocking images that catapulted it into the news and the egregious threats to children's safety and well-being. But it isn't. How many people today recall the incident? True, no lives were lost, there was no carnage and the physical injuries Stratford students suffered were minor. But the execution of an over-the-top SWAT action in a public school with no significant history of student violence, crime or drug use should have shocked the nation into rethinking approaches to school safety. The incident was dramatic evidence that policing in the schoolhouse has veered dangerously off course in many communities. Columbine is an iconic event because it reinforced popular notions about schools and youth as dangerous, while the Goose Creek raid was dismissed as just an aberration because a critical mass of Americans believes many schools are violence-ridden. They have no problem with a heavy police presence. The raid on Stratford High was an extreme example of aggressive school policing, yet smaller-scale incidents occur daily in districts around the nation as part of the Lockdown High model of school safety and security. Policing in schools is one of the key components of the school-to-prison pipeline, as officers supplant educators in dispensing discipline, redefine youthful misbehavior into misdemeanor crimes, and turn students into suspects. Instead of helping educators create safer learning environments, aggressive policing can actually make some students feel less safe and less trusting of law enforcement, as occurred in Goose Creek. "You have an overlay of the law enforcement paradigm in classrooms. You create a police force with a presence on campus and shift away from a child-centered and education-centered model," says Deborah Fowler, legal director of advocacy center Texas Appleseed. "It becomes the kind of focus you would expect to see in a juvenile detention model."

Policing in public schools has a history that stretches back fifty years, with the first officer assigned to a school in Flint, Michigan in 1953, according to one account. The rumblings of concern over juvenile delinquency, gangs and truancy in urban areas were reverberating in post-war America, and schools were one locus for tamping down the youthful misdeeds. In the mid- to late-1960s, police presence in schools increased in reaction to the vibrant social and political activism of students, some of which had clear racial dimensions, as discussed in chapter one. It wasn't until the 1990s and the fears of "superpredator" youth that gripped the nation that policing in public schools was seen as more urgent and began receiving more substantial support through policy and funding at every level. Columbine cemented the deal. In April 1999, immediately after the tragedy, the federal Department of Justice started the COPS in Schools program, building on its Community Oriented Policing Services (COPS) initiative. Since its inaugural year, COPS in Schools has doled out about $800 million to 3,000 school districts around the country, which in turn have hired 6,500 school resource officers (SROs). The grants paid out $125,000 for each SRO hired for a three-year period. Although launched during the Clinton administration, the budget for COPS in Schools doubled under Bush. Another $10 million out of the Safe Schools/Healthy Students program, a joint program with the departments of Education and Health and Human Services, paid for another 100 SROs.[2]

At the state and local levels, police and sheriff's departments often place officers in schools, as San Francisco does. School districts also create their own police departments, as in Palm Beach County, one of the country's oldest autonomous school police departments. In some localities, the officers are armed; in others, they are not. There are no centrally tabulated statistics on the total number and types of officers policing public schools. The federal agencies that fund them don't request that information from schools, even though they mandate data collection on incidents of student violence or crimes. One statistic, gathered by the Department of Education's National Center on Education Statistics, gives some sense of the scope of policing. A NCES survey in 1999 found that 54 percent of students surveyed stated that their schools had assigned either police officers or security guards. In a 2005 survey, 68 percent of students said they had them.[3] Federal funding wasn't the only force expanding cops' role in public schools. Legislators, also reacting to Columbine, enacted laws in many states that require school administrators to report student crimes or violations to the police. Although Congress has channeled millions into SRO programs, there have been few attempts to assess how effective they are in creating safe climates in public schools and how they affect students' education. A federal study was commissioned by the National Institute of Justice in 2005 and surveyed students about the SRO programs at their schools in four districts. The study focused on just two questions: what factors in an SRO program affect students' comfort level for reporting crimes, and what factors in it affect students' perception of safety. Its key findings were that students were more comfortable reporting crimes when they had a positive opinion of the SRO, and that their perception of safety was linked to the level of crime in their neighborhood—something that no number of SROs could change for the better. Interestingly, though not surprisingly, the study noted that white students were more comfortable reporting crimes to an SRO than non-white students, which likely reflects a generally less positive image of the police among black and Latino communities. The study recommended further study "to determine the best method for SROs to create a positive image."[4]

Other studies of SRO programs have been conducted at the state level and their findings have been just as inconclusive and limited. Six state-level SRO studies undertaken from 1996 to 2001 showed them to be popular among parents and school staff but less so among students. More important, though, none of them proved that SROs reduced school violence and disruption. At best, several suggested reductions.[5] Another more recent study of SRO programs in two dozen Pennsylvania school districts was commissioned by the Pennsylvania Commission on Crime and Delinquency to assess their value and to identify what makes them successful. This 2005 report, which surveyed teachers, students, parents, principals and SROs, listed as one of its key findings that school administration support for SRO programs was strong. As to the more relevant question of whether SROs actually make schools safer—the ostensible reason they are there—the report stated: "this study did not examine the impact of the presence of SROs on school/youth violence and associated negative behaviors ... Further study is warranted to establish the degree of a causal relationship between the reduction in negative outcomes and the presence of SROs in the school setting."[6]

For those who support the concept of school policing, such studies reinforce their value without tackling the core issues raised by making policing and the criminal justice system part of the educational system. Policing in the schoolhouse changes the role of teachers and principals in maintaining safe schools, and in some school districts, police have usurped authority from school principals over dispensing discipline, a situation that fundamentally alters the school climate, and not for the better.[7] When police enter the schoolhouse, they come as law enforcement agents trained to see the world in terms of "suspects" and "perpetrators," "victims" and "cooperators." Some SROs may have special training to work with children and adolescents in a school setting and see their role more as benevolent counselor than hard-charging cop. Others see schools as an extension of the streets they police and view students, especially black and Latino, as fodder for the criminal justice system. That mentality was exposed graphically when a Houston police officer handed out twenty copies of a "ghetto handbook" he'd written to help other school cops "learn to speak ebonics as if you just came out of the hood . . ." The eight-page booklet was set up like a dictionary, offering definitions for slang: "dis: (diss) v. that or disrespect someone [*sic*]," "foty: (fo-tee) n. a 40-ounce bottle of beer," "hoodrat: scummy girl" and "po: (p-o) a. broke." The cop was suspended.[8]

Not surprisingly, the presence of police in public schools has led to rising rates of arrests of students for minor violations of disciplinary codes or simple youthful high jinks. Making arrests, after all, is what police do. The idea of the "teachable moment" which enlightened educators employ to turn student missteps and errors into learning opportunities, gets squeezed out in a schoolhouse where handcuff-wielding cops get to teach the lesson. "Things a police officer might not arrest someone in a bar fight for, you're seeing them make arrests in schools for. There are a lot of children arrested for disorderly conduct, which has a very subjective definition. Whoever is standing there gets to define it. It could be a student who refuses to sit down in class, or the spit ball," says Judith Browne-Dianis, of the Advancement Project. "When you are a child of color and your community has a distrust of police, introducing the same police officer into a school environment has an adverse impact," she says. "Our stance is not necessarily to take police out all together but to train them to deal with adolescents. Like having a community policing model in schools where they are accountable to students."

A community policing model for schools might work, but who would do the training? Who shapes the vision and philosophy of school cops and sets the tone for how they maintain safety in our schools? At the annual confabulation of NASRO, the largest SRO membership organization in the country, answers to those questions abound. Current approaches to school policing are on display in workshops to train SROs in the latest trends, the hottest issues in school safety, and the most high-tech gadgetry. If the 2007 NASRO convention was any indicator, a high-octane, Goose Creek model of school policing is favored over community policing among this constituency.

SHEEPDOGS PROTECTING THE SHEEP?

They came from Rome, Georgia. They came from Roanoke, Virginia, Billings, Montana, Hollywood, Florida, and Howell, West Virginia. They came from up and down the east coast and parts south and west. They were sheriffs and police officers and school safety agents of various stripes, about fifteen hundred in all. They came to the National Association of School Resource Officers seventeenth annual conference, held in July 2007 at Disney's Coronado Springs Resort in Orlando, Florida. Milling about the registration area on opening day, the school cops were a sea of khaki uniforms, some wearing holstered handguns. Mostly they were male and white and more then a few had shaved heads and bulging bellies or biceps. Some had both. If drug tests had been required for registration, odds are a few steroid-positives could have resulted among the more muscular attendees. It was the largest NASRO conference to date, boasted organizers, proving their claim that school policing is the fastest-growing sector of law enforcement. A nonprofit membership group formed in 1990 and based in St. Paul, Minnesota, NASRO claims nine thousand members with state-level chapters around the country. Its primary activity is offering SRO training and certification. Institutionalizing school policing, extending it deeper into the schoolhouse through "partnerships" with principals and educators, is NASRO's goal. "The law enforcement officer must consider his or her administrator their 'partner' as they consider and treat the school as their 'beat' or 'patrol district,' " wrote NASRO's executive director, Dick Castor, in the group's quarterly journal, *School Safety*. In NASRO's world view, school violence has not abated, another Columbine is around the corner and policing should be as integral to public schooling as standardized testing.

NASRO's president, Carl Osburn, began the opening ceremonies in a packed auditorium with a color guard marching on stage as a bagpipe whined. Sheriff Ricky Barrie of Orange County kicked off a parade of speakers (most representing companies selling security-related products) with a pep talk. "A lot of people think if you're not a SWAT guy, you're not with it," he told the crowd. "Your work is as critical to the mission of finding violent crimes as any tactical unit in any agency. We see that. You help us all to share in what's critical, critical, critical to the foundation of our democracy as we fight violent crime, terrorism. You play a vital role." Barrie's boosterism hit its mark among these tough guys who apparently have to grapple with feelings of inferiority in comparison with regular police officers. The subtext of many workshops and addresses during the conference seemed designed to fortify their self-esteem and the image of school cops in general as SWAT-guy worthy. There was no better cheerleader for this morale building than the day's keynote speaker, John Giduck, author of a book about the school siege in Beslan, Russia, by Chechen terrorists, titled *Terror at Beslan.* His biography in the NASRO program stated that he has "trained law enforcement departments of all levels" and "holds the highest level certification in Homeland Security." Giduck himself declared that he has never been a cop, but that he had lived the last nineteen years in Russia and had been to both Chechen wars. How that experience is relevant to U.S. school cops is, well, irrelevant. Giduck enthralled the assembly with a testosterone-heavy talk that managed to touch on Chechnya, Columbine, sheepdogs, Virginia Tech, Sun Tzu, and Al-Qaeda. He foretold a coming apocalypse in schools from a variety of terrorist forces, and portrayed school violence as endemic, with homicides practically epidemic. "There are people who are not willing to accept the reality that Al-Qaeda can come take our children," he said. "Our schools are under threat today, right now. We're seeing seven-hundred-something assaults a day. We see an average of forty-six children murdered every day in our schools . . . Every school in America has little Klebolds and Harrises in them. Every school has kids who have gone to the trouble of working up a Columbine plan." (Note to Giduck: There were fourteen student homicides in schools for the entire 2005–2006 school year.)[9]

Giduck had salt-and-pepper hair, a trimmed beard and mustache, and a gut hanging over the top of blue jeans whose bulging crotch was dead center on two humongous video screens at either side of the stage. He paced back and forth, gesticulating with his hands, his delivery dramatic and modulated between soft and loud for emphasis. If he were selling salvation he'd be good, too. But Giduck was selling a Dirty Harry-meets-Terminator approach to policing schools, equating international terrorism with school shootings by disturbed youths. And his audience ate it up. "The question is, are you adequately prepared? Are you psychologically ready to deal with Kleblod and Harris times three? I work with SROs all the time and I see you don't wear body armor in schools. Do you have body armor that can stop AK-47's automatic rounds? Whether it's Al-Qaeda or our own disaffected kids, are your ready to deal with them? Do you have enough rounds? Is it enough to deal with armed, trained terrorists?" he asked. "In my opinion, you should be walking around in schools every day in complete tactical equipment, with semi-automatic weapons and five rounds of amo." Approving chuckles and a surge of applause erupted around the room. One minute he quoted Sun Tzu ("Cut off the head of one person and a thousand people will obey you") the next he likened school police to "sheepdogs, protecting the sheep." He warned that "Osama bin Laden promised to kill four million Americans, including two million children," a threat Americans were ignorant of because "the Western media . . . is very gentle with terrorists."

Giduck's three-hour presentation was a chilling call to militarize school security, and numerous workshops over the next three days repeated the message. At "The SRO and Preparation for Mass Violence," Don Alwes, of the nonprofit National Association of Tactical Officers, lectured an overflow room of school cops on preparing for terrorist attacks. First, Alwes declared, "Schools are safe. The probability of an attack at any particular school is very remote. A lot of you work in a place that is safer for kids than at home." But moments later, he disparaged a report out of a Kentucky center on school violence that stated the likelihood of a nuclear bomb going off in a school was twice that of a school shooting. School deaths and violence were up, he insisted, and began discussing the need to prepare for a terrorist attack à la Columbine or Virginia Tech with regular lockdown drills and site surveys by tactical, that is, SWAT, teams. He urged the audience to do threat assessments at their schools when they returned to work and to devise emergency plans that include the "active shooter" scenario. The active-shooter drill was inspired by Columbine and is now a staple of school police training through NASRO and at local police agencies. Alwes concluded by taking a line from Giduck: "You're the sheepdogs protecting the sheep from the wolves."

A workshop titled "Team Effort to Reduce Violence and Suspensions" promised a different approach, perhaps one featuring conflict resolution and peer mediation. But it wasn't. Scott Martzloff, operations manager at Edison High School in Rochester, New York, was there to promote his high-tech, aggressive policing approach to security and, not incidentally, a book he'd written about his experience. Edison is a vocational school where student violence was on the upswing in a city that Martzloff said was the "per capita murder capital." Edison also was a dangerously over-crowded school at 2,400 students, about 400 over capacity, according to news articles Martzloff distributed, which arguably increases the risks to student safety. But creating smaller schools and less crowded classrooms wasn't on the agenda. With a grant, Martzloff set about redesigning Edison to address safety, installing fifty-two cameras ("I can't imagine life without cameras") and an access control system with ID card readers, and maintaining a closed campus with locked doors during school hours. Zero tolerance is "the cornerstone policy." "We're pro-arrest and pro-suspension," he said. "If you fight, you go to jail in handcuffs. There is no desk appearance ticket." His philosophy resonated throughout the NASRO conference.

Of more than fifty workshops presented during the five-day NASRO conference, only one focused specifically on conflict resolution and peaceful strategies for addressing school violence and safety. Titled "Building Healthy Relationships: Prevention Instead of De-escalation," the workshop described a curriculum created by Lighthouse Ministries, a Mennonite group, and taught in afterschool programs where it reportedly reduced student aggression and conflicts by 80 percent. But this philosophy was swamped in a sea of tough talk on the aggressive policing of schools. Columbine was the thematic thread running throughout the event, invoked over and over again by speakers and workshop leaders. It's no wonder. Columbine was school policing's Waterloo, an historic failure, so they obsess over Klebold and Harris and vow "never again" even while acknowledging that such tragedies can't be prevented with cameras and metal detectors and arrests. The sheepdogs can easily become the wolves in the Lockdown High model, and forget to protect the sheep.

PALM BEACH STORY

Sabrina Houston was a senior at Palm Beach Garden High School in November 2006 when, one day, she made a fateful fashion choice that nearly derailed her graduation. She showed up to school wearing a new top that revealed her bare midriff with a jacket on top, in deference to the school's strict dress code. "The rules say if you have something like that and you have a jacket, it's fine," Houston says in an interview nine months later. "I wasn't showing anything. The jacket covered my shoulders and everything. It was hot, and girls often wear shirts like that." But a gym teacher confronted her in the girls' locker room during her first-period phys-ed class, ordering her to the lobby to get a different top supplied by the school for just such dress code violations. "Then I see another girl dressed just like me, so I called my mother and said, 'They're trying to give me a dress code [violation]," Houston says. "I said it's not fair." Houston put on her gym shirt and refused to leave, so the teacher called a male administrator who barged into the girls' locker room and grabbed the girl when she resisted going with him. When Houston broke free from him, the man put her in a chokehold and called two officers. They arrested her for battery on a school employee, the school suspended her for ten days and then she was expelled. The administrator who had choked her, leaving marks on her throat, faced no discipline. But for wearing a summer top, Sabrina Houston was banned from all Palm Beach District schools, just months from her high school graduation.

The teen acknowledges that her attitude toward the school authorities was defiant but denies assaulting the administrator. "I'm not going to lie. When somebody gets on me, I'm going to question them," she says. She paid the price. A good student with no previous entanglements with the juvenile justice system, she was tried in a youth court, sentenced to community service and ordered to attend anger management classes. Exiled from her home district, Houston was able to complete twelfth grade at an alternative school in Okeechobee where she had a 4.0 grade average and earned ten awards, including one for best behavior. She became a role model for younger children at that school and although she missed graduating with her friends in Palm Beach Garden High, the alternative school arranged a graduation ceremony just for her. Without the support of her family and the Legal Aid lawyer Barbara Briggs, there might not have been a graduation, and Houston could have been just another drop-out statistic. Instead, she got a job to earn money with the goal of attending community college. Houston's detour into the criminal justice system was brief, and she has determined to put it behind her. "All over a dress code violation. It sounds stupid when you say it out loud," she says. "Anytime something happens, or you don't follow directions, they will call the police and have you arrested."

Palm Beach County School Police Department is considered a model for school policing, piloting state-of-the art electronic security and surveillance systems, conducting yearly training in the latest policing techniques and issues, and with a force that ranks fourth largest among Florida's law enforcement agencies. The department has also been investigated as a model of the aggressive policing that funnels too many students into the school-to-prison pipeline with high arrest rates for minor violations. As in other school districts, black students, especially those with emotional and learning disabilities, are arrested and disciplined at rates much higher than white and Latino students. The racial dimension of Palm Beach County's schools and policing is inextricably tied to their history. The district is located in West Palm Beach, a town built in the late 1890s by Standard Oil's co-founder Henry Flagler. The tycoon designed it as a company town for employees of the luxury resort he built in Palm Beach. De facto segregation evolved in the worker city with its high percentage of African-American residents. Fast-forward to the early 1970s when court-ordered racial desegregation was imposed on Florida's public schools. The race riots that flared up in school districts were answered with policing, and in 1972, the Palm Beach County School Police department was created. Officers were initially brought in as liaisons between the schools and regular police agencies and acted as a mobile unit, moving among troubled areas. From an initial force of four officers, the department had some 185 members and a $10 million budget in 2007.[10] "I think the legacy of Flagler lives on," says Barbara Briggs, the attorney.

Briggs has been an education advocacy specialist at the Legal Aid Society for a dozen years, and as a court-appointed attorney, about 80 percent of her clients land in court because of problems at school. In her previous career, she taught special education. She represented Sabrina

Houston through her ordeal but many of her clients have severe disabilities and fare worse in encounters with the school police. "I think Sabrina is so impressive. She has moved on; she's not bitter, not holding a grudge. Her maturity level is far above most adults I know," Briggs says. "But I have clients with mental retardation or illness and on medication, and what they experience in a psychotic episode is not a crime. Yet they will be charged with battery on a school employee." Forty of her disabled clients had that same experience. Legal Aid filed a class action lawsuit in the late 1990s against the Palm Beach school board and the school police department alleging discrimination because police were filing charges against students with disabilities at five times the rate of other students. They were typically for property crimes, Briggs says. "One kid had lined up some soda cans on a chain link fence in back of the school where portables were set up and he was throwing rocks at them," she says. "He was a twelve-year-old with ADHD [Attention Deficit Hyperactivity Disorder] who couldn't read. And he was charged with a second degree felony for throwing a deadly missile into an occupied dwelling." Briggs believes school policing became even more heavy-handed in Palm Beach County in the wake of Columbine. "It has been a constant. That started the zero tolerance language for weapons and it really has morphed to zero tolerance for students, zero tolerance for mistakes, for behavior typical of adolescents," she says. "That is when the school police started their real crackdown. The active shooter training, the catastrophic mind-set that has developed came about after that. That was a bad year. They forget they are in schools with kids, most of whom are just trying to get through the day, worrying about who will sit with them at lunch."

Two years after Columbine, the arrest rates in Palm Beach County schools had skyrocketed. The district, now eleventh largest in the state with nearly 170,000 students, had come under scrutiny and criticism in preceding years for its differential treatment of African-American students in academics and in discipline. The Palm Beach schools story was on the radar of the Advancement Project, a policy and legal advocacy institute in Washington, D.C., as it began one of the first investigations into what it called the "schoolhouse to jailhouse" track. Judith Browne-Dianis, then senior attorney, authored a groundbreaking report that revealed how policing of schools was "derailing" students from their educations into the criminal justice system. Conducting on-site research and interviews with school administrators, school police, lawyers and advocates in the juvenile justice system, she wrote of a "runaway problem" in Palm Beach County schools. The report, "Derailed! The Schoolhouse to Jailhouse Track," lays out a national context of zero tolerance and policing in schools with data from Baltimore and Houston. "I got into this because I was working with a Mississippi district where the school policy was that any student involved in a fight—even kids in arguments—had to be sent to youth court, where they could get fined 150 to 500 dollars or probation of six months to a year," Browne-Dianis says. "Everybody is blaming the kid when we need to look at the institution and change it so we don't arrest kids. I never suspected when I looked at this data that we would be finding children arrested for disorderly conduct, or battery on school board employee. Public defenders say that is a common charge." The report found that post-Columbine arrests by Palm Beach school police grew 11 percent from 1999, reaching 1,287 in 2001. The majority fell under the categories of "miscellaneous" simple assault, which would include disorderly conduct and disruption. The racial disparities were glaring. Although black students were about a third of the student population for that period, they were 60 percent of students arrested.[11] Released in May 2003, the Advancement Project report drew attention from the press, the school board and Chief Jim Kelly of the school police, who dismissed its findings as inaccurate. Nonetheless, Barbara Briggs thinks needed pressure was brought to bear on the rampant arrests. Data from the last few years show a drop in student arrests: 896 in 2005, 745 in 2006, 783 in 2007. Still, Briggs believes the role and orientation of the Palm Beach school police is fundamentally misguided. "I think Kelly is pretty arrogant. We approach things from such a different perspective, we're not on the same page," she says. "No one said there shouldn't be consequences for things students do wrong. It just shouldn't be juvenile justice."

Chief Kelly has a perspective on his department's role in Palm Beach schools that is, to say the least, at odds with that of Sabrina Houston and Barbara Briggs."I know how to provide a service that's not threatening," says Kelly. "I go for the win-win. I'm always looking at how I can help the other person." Kelly heads one of the oldest autonomous school police agencies in the country, and he's been there since its inception, with a brief time-out to earn a law degree. He's been chief since 1989, so its reputation and record sit squarely on his shoulders. I took a break from the NASRO convention on a day given over to a members' golf tournament to drive down and visit the Palm Beach school police, welcomed in advance by Kelly who was happy to show off his department over the course of a day. Its headquarters, in the district's administrative offices in West Palm Beach, is a high-tech operation. We walked through a surveillance center, with monitors displaying real-time video fed by cameras around the district and staffed by an employee. All school buses have cameras and schools have intrusion alarms to protect equipment. The surveillance system uses motion detectors to allow police to track people from room to room to room, and the department was about to initiate a project with Boca Raton schools and city police to install a wireless system. "All our campuses are fenced in. Our high school we built like a fortress," Kelly notes. "Design is important. We're not preventing the terrorists from coming in. We're making it more difficult." Kelly's cops have pioneered protocols now taught by NASRO, the prime example being the so-called active-shooter, which has been replicated around the state and country. "After Columbine, I'd been working to get SWAT guys together," he says. "We brought thirteen SWAT teams from different departments and trained over three days. We did two days in the classroom and then a scenario day, kids with wounds, et cetera." The lesson learned from Columbine: "The strategy is you go in, you can't wait. You have to stop the shooter."

That steamy July day, a two-week summer training session was underway at the department's Del Ray training center, the wrestling facility for a former high school across the street, and Kelly stopped to visit. Palm Beach SROs receive at least 140 hours of training annually in both policing tactics and more esoteric subjects, such as cultural diversity, intergroup conflict, sexual harassment, gangs, and verbal judo. Kelly is big on verbal judo, a technique to de-escalate conflicts. Inside the main gym, eight officers, including several women, were practicing real judo, wrestling in pairs. Another group waited in the hallway to take turns in a different exercise called "dark shooting," which is essentially the active-shooter but at night. I was invited to participate, so donning some protective gear, I joined as two SROs worked their way through a room, using flashlights to illuminate a series of life-size cardboard cutouts of people, some "good," like a woman with groceries, and some "bad," like a youthful looking perp. They are armed with air pellet handguns, and the trainer, a former major in the Palm Beach County sheriff's office, shouts out as they muddle through the darkened room. At the end of the course, we emerge into the light and the major offers critiques. Kelly says he has high standards for his recruits. "I don't hire rookies. Fifty-five percent of my officers are on their first twenty years of policing," he says. "A lot of skill sets from policing can be transferred to school policing—the people skills. Academics is very nurturing and I want the nurturing ones. You have to care for kids. You can't just want the day shift."

Such talk of nurturing seems incongruous with advocates' complaints about the aggressive policing by Palm Beach SROs. Kelly is clearly adept at public relations and a convincing advocate for his department. Tall, trim, with the kind of golfer's tan found on denizens of Palm Beach, he was polished and sharp in a crisp blue suit, looking and sounding more like an attorney than a police chief. He was particularly proud of initiatives that are more social work than police work, such as a program to decrease violence and bullying that is run in conjunction with the district's Safe Schools office. He booted DARE—Drug Abuse Resistance Education—one of the oldest and most popular anti-drug programs in schools, which he described as a "big money-making thing" that "doesn't have benefits." He and the Safe Schools director Alison Adler brought in a "single school culture" for students and teachers to create a uniform policy on tardiness and discipline. "Elementary school is where you start that because it is more touchy-feely," he says. "If everybody is on the same page as far as discipline, we can be out there doing other things." His department also began a Teen Drug Court for students who fail drug tests multiple times, and in 2007, the Intake Program, which channels cases that officers believe should not be prosecuted. "An example is a kid who was wearing an iPod in class and the teacher yanked the earphones. It prompted a confrontation in which the kid pushed her arm," he explains. "She demanded he be prosecuted for assault, but it ended up in the Intake Program." Kelly says the program had led to forty-three fewer student prosecutions since it began.

Legal advocates for students like Barbara Briggs are not persuaded by Kelly's PR on the Palm Beach school police. "Instead of school police doing the Intake Program, why not have non-police do something with restorative justice?" Briggs says. She thinks the SROs are too ready to arrest students while school administrators ignore a more pervasive problem right under their noses. "The lower level bullying and harassment is something the schools don't address," she says. "They say 'Kids will be kids.' From kids I talk to that's what I hear." Whatever improvements the Palm Beach school police are achieving in school violence and discipline, Briggs has not seen much change at her end. "My client load is pretty constant at one hundred to one-twenty a year," she says. "Right now I'm looking at some kind of strategy long-term that might have an impact. Anything that would stem the flow of kids with disabilities into the juvenile justice system."

SAN FRANCISCO: GOOD COP, BAD COP?

Goose Creek had its Stratford High police incident. San Francisco had its Thurgood Marshall High incident. Some have labeled what happened on October 11, 2002, as a police riot. By any measure, the events on that day seem to qualify as the largest police action at a single U.S. public school, as at least ninety San Francisco police officers and sheriff's deputies, some in riot gear, and multiple helicopters descended on the school campus located in the southeast neighborhood known as Bayview-Hunters Point. The story is a complex but important one of a changed school culture topped by a new principal and an inexperienced SRO who triggered police fears of a gang threat that was exaggerated. The incident occurred in a wider context of rising concerns about increased policing in San Francisco's public schools at the expense of other needed resources. The reaction from students, parents, youth advocates and school board members was a concerted push-back against over zealous policing which produced some reforms in the role of SROs and regular San Francisco police in the schools. "Our concern before Thurgood Marshall happened was about the allocation of resources to policing and the increased willingness to push disciplinary issues into the hands of the police," says NTanya Lee, executive director of Coleman Advocates for Children and Youth, a San Francisco nonprofit. "A resource-strapped dean who has two kids fighting will just say to an SRO, 'Here, you handle it.' "

The SRO program in the San Francisco Unified School District was begun in 2000 with a grant to the city's police department from the federal COPS in Schools program at the Justice Department. The initial funding placed twenty-six officers, all carrying handguns, in public schools around the city. By 2007, thirty SROs were assigned to the unit, and the funding continued until 2009. The city's police department also had a program called Car Twenty-Nine, which deploys twelve officers to patrol around schools and offer primary response to reported incidents. Together, the two programs received $3 million from San Francisco's coffers at a time when the schools, which serve some 55,000 students, were strapped, and the system was shrinking through school closures. Thurgood Marshall Academic High School was created as a college preparatory program to serve the African-American neighborhood in which it sits. It would be comparable to Lowell High School, a public school considered the top choice of academically motivated students, and although black students make up about a third, it has a diverse student body, with neighborhoods students and applicants from elsewhere in the city each comprising roughly half of its population of about 800 students. When the fall 2002 semester began a new principal came aboard and with her all new counselors and a different attitude about security. "She had a meeting with the PTSA [Parent Teacher and Student Association] and told us she'd met with the police and that they'd told her there was a brewing gang problem at Thurgood and several other schools," says Kim-Shree Maufas, who had just started her first term as president of the PTSA. "That was news to every single PTSA member. My daughter was a sophomore at Thurgood Marshall. She hadn't heard anything like that." The principal said she wanted to hire five more security staff to take precautions and made a racial comment about the problem being with black students. "We looked at each other dumbfounded," she recalls. The principal replaced the existing SRO, who Maufas described as "a peace officer in the highest sense of the word" who had an excellent relationship with students, and two other SROs were brought in. The next combustible ingredient added was 200 students who were displaced when their school was closed, raising Thurgood Marshall's population to 1,000. The new students weren't well oriented into their new school and its college prep philosophy. The dynamic began to sour, and Maufas's daughter was reporting that fights were breaking out two and three times daily. "Teachers were emailing me every day. Things seemed out of control. I had a meeting with the principal and she told me, 'We're handling it. Relax, Ms. Maufas," she says. "So I went to the school on October 10 and stayed the entire day. I was floored. Everything I'd heard was true. Passing time was chaotic. Fights breaking out. Posters torn down. Teachers barely able to teach, doing classroom management." At the end of the day, Maufas tried to meet with the principal about the "crisis" she saw in her school but was brushed off again. A day later, the crisis exploded.

In the morning on October 11, Kim-Shree Maufas was at work in her job with the city's Department for Women and Girls when e-mails started pouring in from frantic teachers at Thurgood Marshall stating that they had locked their students in the classrooms because the police were outside and something bad was happening. The came a call from her daughter who was screaming about being hit by the police. Maufas rushed to the scene to find the streets around the school blocked by police and helicopters hovering overhead. "The scene was a mile wide. There was chaos in the enclosed area," she says. Making her way into the school, she found her daughter crying and describing how an officer had hit her in the chest with a baton. Other students Maufas knew as "excellent students, well-behaved," were in the school office with similar tales of being assaulted by the police. Over the course of the next few hours, police milled around outside and then inside the school hallways, physically and verbally abusing students and teachers who came to their defense, according to dozens of firsthand accounts. One African-American teacher who attempted to videotape the events was battered by police and arrested. He was taken with as many as thirty students to the Bayview police station where they were kept in a holding cell for three hours. Four students were sent to juvenile hall and the others were released. Only after months of community activism were charges against all of them dismissed.[12]

What had caused this terrible police action at a school with no prior history of violence and a reputation for high academic standards? The immediate trigger was a financial dispute between Asian-American students and a black student that began off-campus but then continued at school and became a physical altercation. The SROs broke up the fight and took the students to the main office, but soon afterward a second fight flared between a cousin of the African-American student and friends of the Asian American. Maufas says accounts indicate that one of the new SROs called on her radio for backup with the code used for an "officer down" situation. The sheriff's department had deputies in the area, and about thirty of them joined in, thinking that their fear of gang troubles had blown up, Maufas explains. African-American students bore the brunt of the police brutality even though Asian-American students were equally involved in the initial conflicts. That night at a community meeting in a nearby chapel, police officials, school administrators, parents and clergy met in a tense environment to find resolution. But there would be no clear settlement for many months, as Maufas, NTanya Lee and lawyers from the ACLU pressed the city police department to address the wrongdoing by police and to clear the records of those students wrongly charged and detained. "Parents of the jailed students were threatened by the police, so they wouldn't come forward to file suit against the department," says Maufas. "By 2003, after several protests and going to the police commissioner every week, led by the PTSA, we devised a safety committee. It was multiracial, a model for the city."

The Thurgood Marshall police riot roiled the city and made national news, just as Goose Creek did, but its implications were more widely felt because it occurred in a major urban school district and one where citizen activism for change is well-established. "The SRO program got a wake-up call. The whole department was shamed," says NTanya Lee. "We heard from police around the country who thought it was outrageous." The incident was a catalyst for a successful ballot initiative, Proposition H in 2003, that changed SFPD leadership by giving the board of supervisors power to appoint three of the department's seven police commissioners; the mayor previously appointed all of them. "We hoped to change the top, to improve oversight of the police," says Maufas, who was elected to the Board of Education in 2007. "But what was evident from Thurgood Marshall was that we were going to have a new MOU [memorandum of understanding] about the police's role on the school campus. During the incident, no one knew who was in charge." There had been an MOU about policing, says NTanya Lee, but school principals were by and large reluctant to challenge SROs and regular police authority. By spring 2003, the San Francisco Board of Education, prodded by several new members, had adopted a resolution calling for renegotiating the MOU and reallocating money for SROs into hiring more school counselors. The first part of the resolution found traction while the second—trading cops for counselors—just wouldn't fly, even in a supposedly liberal city like San Francisco. Over the course of two years and many coalition meetings, a new MOU was hammered out that resulted in some qualitative improvements, Lee says, even if all the changes that parent and student advocates wanted were not part of the final agreement. "The first few drafts of the MOU were tough but to get it passed—it wasn't going to happen," says Maufas. "Those old board members were beholden to the power structure."

The new MOU, signed in September 2005, nearly three years after the Thurgood Marshall events, stipulates that students may not be arrested on campus; that during any police questioning an adult ally chosen by the student must be present; and it guarantees students' due process rights. But according to data provided by the SFPD, SROs continue to make arrests of students at schools for incidents that occur there: in 2006, there were 194 arrests; in 2007 there were 232; and in 2008, there were 205.[13] A report Lee authored for Coleman Advocates that provides a detailed account of events on October 11 and analysis of underlying problems in what transpired also lays out a number of recommendations for improving the SRO program. Among them are creating rules limiting police use of force against children in school settings; more and better training for police working in schools; and the assignment of an investigator within the SFPD's Office of Citizen Complaints to handle complaints against police on school campuses. Most were ignored, but Lee says that since then SRO training has improved. "We found that the best SROs are the ones that students feel act more like support staff and don't take a harsh approach to dealing with kids."

At Abraham Lincoln High School in San Francisco's Sunset neighborhood, Officer Tom Lovrin would agree with NTanya Lee's profile of the best SROs and he'd say he aspires to be one of them. He has been there full-time since 2001, when he applied to work as an SRO despite the general sentiment among San Francisco police that real police don't work in schools. "When it comes to the police department, most officers don't see going into a school as doing what we're supposed to do—uphold the law," he says during an interview with him and Principal Ron Pang in Pang's office. "Here, you're not constantly looking for trouble.

We're here to help the kids. We're counselors, parent figures and police. We're a resource for them." Lovrin is an affable and non-threatening figure, aside from the Glock semi-automatic holstered on his belt. Without the uniform, he could easily pass for Mr. Lovrin, history teacher or guidance counselor. His wife is a middle-school principal and he seems in tune with Pang's philosophy—he had worked with him when Pang was a principal of Hoover Middle School in the 1990s. "Mr. Pang is the best. He's out there every morning at the gate welcoming them," Lovrin says. "We tell them from the beginning of the school year, 'This is a safe school.' Many kids come here because it is a safe school."

Lincoln wasn't always that way. In 1992, there was a shooting outside the school and Lincoln was considered a "stay away" school, Pang notes. He has been principal since 1998 and he calls safety "my priority." Unlike public schools in many urban settings, Lincoln and the rest of San Francisco's schools do not have metal detectors, a policy that seems to be validated in Pang's school. "When they get metal detectors, that's when I retire," he says, "because of the perception it gives to parents and students." Changing demographics along with Pang's administrative leadership no doubt have transformed Lincoln's reputation so that it receives among the highest number of applicants, seven for one available seat. At 2,400 students, it is "like a small city," Lovrin says. Lincoln is a majority Asian school, with 53 percent Chinese, 7 percent African-American, 11 percent Latino, 9 percent white, and a mixture of other racial and ethnic groups. And because admission is selective, Lincoln may not receive some of the most difficult academically challenged students. "Even our hard-core kids are not as hardcore as other schools have to deal with," Pang admits. Still, his school had the highest number of reported incidents in the previous year, most of them inappropriate touching behavior and some alcohol and drug violations, nothing harder than that, the principal says. Fights occur maybe twice a month. "I'm not going to hide it. I tell parents I would rather they learn an important lesson," Pang says. As a consequence, suspensions are up. But Lovrin says arrests are a rarity, about five or six a year for robberies or assaults with a deadly weapon. But no guns —"we haven't had guns in years."

Lovrin's gun is the exception, of course, and he says he has never drawn it in school. His arrival at Lincoln coincided with the creation of the Wellness Center, which has a nurse, counselors, and a peer mediation program. But for some parents and students, the arrival of an SRO was not a welcome development. Policing in the public schools is, Pang acknowledges, controversial in San Francisco. "The Board of Education tends to be very political. Some members are very anti-police on campus, some board members are very supportive of police," he says. "When Officer Lovrin first got here, there was a big thing about having an officer, but that has decreased. And after Thurgood Marshall, we had a lot of meetings with the police commissioner." One flash point was whether SROs would be uniformed or in plain clothes and armed inside schools. Some argued that officers should leave their guns in their patrol cars. "We said, 'No, we're police officers and along with all that comes the uniform and the gun," Lovrin says. Pang believes that most students view Lovrin in a positive light, not "as someone who is here to get them." "Students who supported the SROs come from schools that had them and those who opposed them didn't have SROs in previous schools," Pang says. "Trust is the basis."

8 BUSTING OUT OF LOCKDOWN HIGH: ALTERNATIVE PATHS TO SAFE SCHOOLS

The reason why we are creating the student union is because of the experience of many students in NYC. When we walk into school the first thing we see is a metal detector, cops and x-ray machines that the city believes will help the kids and the school. WE DISAGREE!! We believe what the city does in our schools actually makes kids want to be more violent. It doesn't give us any privacy at all, and it just scares us. Having so many cops in one building intimidates and agitates students and increases tension rather than decreasing it. The basic point of the union is to show and explain to the city of New York that it is better to decrease the metal detectors and cops and look for other ways to decrease conflict in our schools and increase true safety in learning.

—From the mission statement of the Urban Youth Collaborative,
a New York City student organization formed in 2004

Herb Mack recalls the first day he and Ann Cook, co-founders of the Urban Academy, came into the old building that now houses their alternative public high school. "I took the hand-held metal detectors and locked them in a closet," says Mack. There were walk-through scanners, too, installed at entrances to the old Julia Richman High School, on Manhattan's Upper East Side. A dozen School Security Agents, as the school police are known in the Big Apple, used to search students every morning with both kinds of scanners. It took six months to get permission from the city's Board of Education and then Mack had the scanners torn down from the doorways. Until then, they were never used. "We didn't for a day walk through the things. You couldn't possibly have a welcoming school if you lined kids up to be searched. Our feeling is the only way to have safe schools is to have the kids be willing to talk to you and to the security folks about the problems they anticipate," Mack says. "We have probably a hundred windows at ground level. We have thirteen entrances to the building. If they want to get a gun in, they can push it through a window. The scanners are such a political decision." Then there was the "cage," an eight-by-twelve foot, floor-to-ceiling wire box that occupied part of the old guidance counselor office. "We thought that it must have been a storage space and thought it was strange that there were no shelves for papers or boxes. We didn't know what it was," Mack recalls. "A year or two after we'd been here, a woman came in who used to be the assistant principal for guidance. She said, 'This was my office.' We asked her about the metal box and she said, 'Oh, that was the place we locked the kids up in until the police came.'" Mack and Cook tore the cage down, too, and made the office into a large, open space for teachers' desks and a common room for students.

The Urban Academy opened in 1995 as the anchor among six alternative public schools—four high schools, a pre-kindergarten through eighth grade school and a program for autistic children—that operate as autonomous entities within the eighty-year-old building, now known as the Julia Richman Education Complex. Altogether 1,800 students attend classes in the complex, a haven for students who may not fit in the traditional setting offered in the city's regular public schools. The Urban Academy, like its founders, is a pioneer in the small school movement that has been embraced by progressive educators and, in a limited way, by New York City's education officials as an antidote to the impersonal, overcrowded and ineffective high schools that came to dominate the largest public school system in the nation. The Urban Academy's 120 students are a diverse swath of the city itself, and many landed there after unsatisfying stints at other schools that failed to engage them or stifled them with regulations. While the school is nationally recognized for its success as a small school, one component of the philosophy behind Mack and Cook's success that often escapes detection is their approach to security and discipline. Tearing down the scanners was both a literal and metaphorical statement of the Urban Academy's rejection of an authoritarian, corrections-like strategy for making their students and classrooms safe. "There is a difference between security and discipline," says Mack. "Discipline is talking to kids. We have a culture but it certainly isn't one in which the normal discipline takes place."

Security in the old Julia Richman building was under the direction of school security agents, who were put under the control of the New York Police Department in 1998 by Mayor Rudolph Giuliani. A dozen SSAs would supervise the morning ritual of student scanning and searching, after which six officers were dispatched to other duties, leaving a full-time staff of six. One long-time female SSA who had good rapport with students and embodied the approach to security that Mack and Cook favored was made supervisor, after lobbying by the co-directors. She sets the tone for the other officers by dealing respectfully with students. "We work closely together. She understands that security is provided by her talking to the kids. It's a very important part of the building," Mack explains. "We don't take any transfer agents. We take them right out of the training program so they haven't been socialized into abusive practices. Our supervisor makes them understand that there are no confrontations with kids. We've had situations where they'll say, 'You have to watch out for so-and-so because there might be a problem.' Kids are our best safety valve. And that's because they know they can talk to us." Each of the schools within the Julia Richman complex has its own culture and its own principal, who can make decisions on everything, including dress codes. So when the city police decreed that students were forbidden to wear "do-rags" on their heads because they said it was gang attire, Urban's administrators first checked with their constituents. "We went to kids and said, 'Do you think we should outlaw do-rags?'" Mack says. "They said it's not a gang thing, and we agreed with them. We became the only school in the building that didn't outlaw do-rags. The other schools went along with the ban. That meant our security agents had to be willing to let us ignore what the police were saying. They were able to differentiate our kids from the others. We've established that the principal, not the SSAs or the police, run the school." As for incidents of violence or disciplinary problems, which Mack is required to report to the city Department of Education, well, he says there aren't any. "I've never had any kind of incident to report. If the security agents get weapons, I haven't seen them," Mack says.

For Ryan Kierstedt, the Urban Academy's rejection of scanners was a key reason he became a student there. The Bushwick, Brooklyn, resident had been attending high school in East New York but was fed-up with how students were treated and the poor quality education. He just quit going to school for a whole year. "Since I was thirteen years old, I've been going through scanners at school and I never thought much about it until I realized that not everyone goes through them," Kierstedt says. "They don't trust us, so we don't trust them." He talked about his experiences at a press conference called by the New York Civil Liberties Union in February 2007 to discuss its report, "Criminalizing the Classroom." Kierstedt was one of a half-dozen students who spoke about the impact of scanners, aggressive policing and harsh discipline in the city's public schools. "I decided I wasn't going to school any more because no one was teaching me anything. I decided to go to the bookstore and just read," he says. Then a family friend told him about the Urban Academy, a school totally different from the one he'd left. "We have no metal detectors, and they actually teach me. Nobody at school is afraid of being stabbed and there's no animosity from the security agents," he says. As a senior at the Urban Academy, Kierstedt was a member of the poetry club and planned to go onto college, which 94 percent of the schools' graduates do.

In a city whose schools and students are stereotyped as violent and failing, the success of the Urban Academy and students like Ryan Kierstedt gives the lie to the rationales behind the Lockdown High model in creating safe and secure schools. In fact, a mounting body of research contradicts the fundamental principles behind punitive, zero tolerance strategies as the most effective approach to school safety and discipline, while also revealing their harmful effects on children. Authoritarian strategies have been predicated on a faulty foundation—the idea that school violence is epidemic and growing worse and demanding drastic measures at the cost of student rights and educational quality. Now, while it is true that violence and disciplinary problems have been and will always be present in schools to a greater or lesser degree, communities and administrators can choose to address them with strategies that are more appropriate to the basic mission of schools: to educate. By surrendering to the Lockdown High model, school board members, principals and teachers have abdicated their responsibility and lost the opportunity to make safety and discipline part of the curriculum. It is true that the zero tolerance is an appealing and often easier choice when schools face intense pressure to perform under federal testing mandates and budget cuts force out programs considered nonessential. And the political pressure behind punitive discipline policies and security fixes, such as metal detectors, can be enormous. But the failure of zero tolerance, reflected in the epidemic of students suspended and pushed out of schools, is becoming harder to ignore.

One of the first and now most widely cited studies on school violence and strategies for creating safer schools was published back in 1999 by Matthew Mayer and Peter Leone. The authors, professors of education, analyzed data on school crime from the National Crime Victimization Survey, which queried public school students from twelve to nineteen years old. Their findings suggested that schools with "a higher level of disorder" had more security measures, including metal detectors, locked doors, and security guards or other staff patrolling hallways, and that those very security measures may actually contribute to the school's disorder. They called it a "cycle of disorder" in which restrictive controls in school create a "reciprocal, destructive relationship" with students, who "tend to engage in more acts of self-protection and live in a heightened state of fear." Acknowledging that some might argue that the presence of high-security measures is a necessary response to the disorder and violence, Mayer and Leone suggest a different interplay: "Creating an unwelcoming, almost jail-like, heavily scrutinized environment may foster the violence and disorder school administrators hope to avoid." Schools with the least disruption, they found, were those where students understood the "system of law"—the rules of conduct. The solution, Mayer and Leone state, is "for schools to focus their efforts; effective communication rather than control is the best way to establish the legitimacy of the school's system of law in the minds of students."[1]

A 2002 study of school violence and prevention by a private contractor and funded by the U.S. Department of Education offers a more nuanced and complex profile of conditions in schools than the view publicly espoused by education officials. It also offers more evidence to bolster Mayer and Leone's theory that high security measures may be a cause of—not a solution to—school disorder. The DOE study surveyed public high school principals about crime in their schools and found that 60 percent of violence was concentrated in 4 percent of all schools. While urban schools with large numbers of low-income and non-white students tended to have the highest levels of crime, 36 percent of schools with high crime rates were in rural areas, contradicting "the image of school violence being solely restricted to central cities," the study stated. And as in the Mayer and Leone study, it found that schools with higher crime rates were more likely to use security measures such as random metal detectors, police and security personnel. By contrast, schools with lower or no violent crime put a higher priority on counseling and violence-prevention education, including peer-mediation and conflict-resolution programs. Unfortunately, the study's scope was limited and did not go beyond merely describing what exists to begin to answer the all important question: "whether programs were implemented in an effective way and/or significantly reduced the amount of violence in the school."[2]

After nearly two decades of zero tolerance and authoritarian discipline, the paradox persists. Why do schools with the most security measures and most punitive discipline *still* tend to have more reported incidents of violence or crime? If the punitive, policing approach were effective, then incidents and student suspensions should be going down. The fact that juvenile crime rates outside the schoolhouse continue to fall makes the situation inside even more incongruous. In 2006, the preponderance of evidence that students and academic achievement were being damaged by the continuation of punitive discipline motivated the American Psychological Association to weigh in on the issue. At its annual convention, the professional organization released a report by its Zero Tolerance Task Force that gleaned evidence from two decades of research into school climate and discipline. Called simply "Are Zero Tolerance Policies Effective in the Schools?," the APA taskforce, which included Indiana University's Russell Skiba, answered the question with a resounding "No." The report identifies and then rebuts the fundamental premises behind zero tolerance policies, including the idea that serious school violence is "out-of-control"; that suspending students for misdeeds creates a better learning climate for other students; that punitive discipline is a deterrent to future misbehavior; and that parents and communities overwhelmingly support zero tolerance. The report also highlights the lopsided impact for black students, a result it attributes to poor teacher training and lack of cultural competence with diverse student populations. And most important, the psychologists address child and adolescent development and how zero tolerance is an inappropriate, even harmful strategy for correcting behavioral problems, especially those with emotional or neurological roots. The report prescribes a series of reforms to school disciplinary policies, recommending a drastic scaling back of the most harsh punishments and adopting flexibility in disciplining individual students. In place of zero tolerance, the task force called for strategies to reconnect alienated youth within a school community that fosters connectedness among teachers, students, parents, and administrators. Improved training for teachers in classroom management and cultural competence is also vital.

Strong evidence that zero tolerance and prison-like security not only don't make schools and students safer, but can actually be detrimental, isn't sufficient to cause a revolution in policy and practice. There are equally strong forces that keep the Lockdown High philosophy in place as an expedient solution to the challenges of public school discipline. Earlier chapters revealed the profit motives and widespread misinformation that keep school violence on the front burner of public awareness and anxiety. But another factor alluded to in this book has also been at play, especially since the passage of the federal No Child Left Behind Act in 2001. That is the high stakes testing mania that has public schools in a choke hold in the name of higher achievement and accountability. Testing and accountability are the core principles in NCLB, which received a less extensive test-run in Texas when George Bush was governor and presided over education reform. With its demand for Adequate Yearly Progress goals at schools, endless testing, and the threat of escalating sanctions and punishments, including labeling schools as "persistently dangerous," NCLB as pedagogical reform is to the public school system what zero tolerance is to students: a one-size-fits-all, tough-love approach that makes accountability an end in itself. In a 2004 article, Mayer and Leone revisit school safety and violence by examining the "fit" between a school's agenda and the needs of students and their families. If there is a significant disconnect, it can result in problem behaviors, the authors argue. The pressure exerted on teachers and school administrators by high-stakes testing and the accountability movement, especially since the passage of NCLB, can add to the bad fit between students and the school environment, leading to suspension and, ultimately, academic failure:

> Taken together, these developments, along with increased pressure to demonstrate improved individual school and district outcomes, create a scenario in which students who are marginally successful in school may be at increased risk for exclusion and may be disciplined for negative behaviors disproportionately, relative to the entire school population . . .

schools desperately seeking to improve their test results may embark on an unwritten campaign to drive academically and behaviorally at-risk students out of the school. This could set the stage for increased acts of aggression and violence around school as these students are marginalized academically and socially.[3]

A great irony in the Lockdown approach to school safety is that it has escaped the kind of testing and accountability for results that is applied to the educational components of public schools. One probable reason is that it has always been more of a political solution than a practical one, so it "works" as far as assuaging irrational fears about youth violence. Metal detectors, student drug testing, suspensions, and policing—there is no evidence-based research that these costly and invasive strategies do our schools or our kids any good. But there is good research on a range of strategies and programs that not only can create the kind of safe learning environments on display at New York's Urban Academy but that help young people learn to make sound judgments. There is reason to be hopeful that the zero tolerance mania has reached its apex and that movement toward those alternatives is gaining critical mass in communities around the country. Students and their allies are organizing to oppose heavy policing in schools and to oppose the suspension-and-arrest epidemic that feeds the school-to-prison pipeline. Drug education programs that engage youth instead of preaching at them, peer-mediation and conflict-resolution training, restorative justice and positive behavior supports are among the alternatives gaining momentum and adherents in the public school system. Local organizing among students and parents is feeding into national networks of educators and legal advocates who have made their goal the abolition of the school-to-prison pipeline. In New Orleans, Oakland, New York, Chicago, Los Angeles, and Denver, alternatives to Lockdown High are under construction.

RESOLVING CONFLICTS, TEACHING PEACE

The scene in the second-grade classroom is pretty common: two students are in a tug-of-war over a book, each insisting to the other, "It's mine!" What happens next is not so common. An educator from the Morningside Center for Teaching Social Responsibility steps toward them, takes the book and says, "Okay, we're having a problem here. Would you like a teacher to help you? Or would you like to go to the peace corner?" Both the boy and girl say they want to go to the peace corner. There, two other students, the peace helpers, take turns listening to each student's story of what happened and how they felt during the incident. "So you had a book and a girl snatched it from you? How do you feel?" asked one peace helper. "I feel mad," answered the boy. Next, the second peace helper turns to the girl, asking her first if she wants help, and then listening as she recounts what happened and how she feels. The peace helpers, just seven or eight years old, mediate the conflict according to their training: Ask if the parties want their help; ask them what happened, and paraphrase it back to them; ask how they feel and paraphrase that back; and finally ask how the student could solve the problem, repeating that back, too. All of this is being observed by the entire class and a fifth grader who is actually conducting a "mini-lesson" for her younger schoolmates.

A tussle over a book becomes a teachable moment, an opportunity to incorporate conflict resolution into the curriculum at P.S. 24, a kindergarten-through-fifth-grade public school in Sunset Park, Brooklyn. Once labeled as "failing" for not meeting adequate yearly progress under the No Child Left Behind, P.S. 24, whose students are primarily low-income Latinos, now meets its NCLB goals and has been graded "A" by the city education department for academic excellence. One component of its success has been the integration of what's called social and emotional learning, which includes mediation and negotiation, communicating clearly and active listening, understanding and expressing feelings and valuing diversity to counter prejudice. Conflict resolution and peer-mediation training are one important part of that approach and are key to creating a safe learning environment with students who will know how to defuse clashes and avoid violence as they graduate to middle and high schools. Morningside Center's educators have worked for years in P.S. 24 training students and staff in the Resolving Conflicts Creatively Program. Created back in 1985 by Tom Roderick, executive director of the center[4] and Linda Lantieri, then a curriculum specialist at the city's Board of Education (now called the Department of Education), RCCP has been taught in more than sixty of the city's public schools and annually trains a thousand students and teachers, and has trained thousands of young peer mediators. It is a model program that has been practiced in more than four hundred schools around the country and twelve school districts, from Anchorage, Alaska to Modesto, California, to Newark, New Jersey. The scene described above is captured in a video made at P.S. 24 in 2007 by the George Lucas Foundation to highlight the philosophy of social and emotional learning. To see children in action, practicing their mediation skills and treating one another respectfully and thoughtfully makes zero-tolerance discipline seem downright medieval.

The Resolving Conflicts Creatively Program is among the most widely practiced programs of its kind in schools and certainly the one with the longest track record. It is also one of the few to have undergone a thorough evaluation of its effectiveness in reducing aggressive behavior and violence in school. In 1999, after a spate of highly publicized school shootings placed school violence on the front burner of public awareness, the National Center for Children in Poverty at Columbia University published its findings from a two-year study of five thousand elementary school students in fifteen New York City public schools. The researchers found that an average twenty-five lessons from the RCCP curriculum each year mitigated children's aggressive thoughts and behavior in school. Not only that, students' standardized test scores improved and teachers rated their social behaviors and emotional control higher. The report concluded by noting that while an estimated two thirds of schools have violence-prevention programs, "it is important for school decisionmakers to select and implement programs whose effectiveness is supported by rigorous independent evaluations such as the RCCP." Among its many pluses, the RCCP is low-tech and lost cost and enhances, instead of competing with, academic achievement.[5]

But even RCCP's proven successes were not sufficient when the political agendas of New York City's schools chancellor and mayor eliminated the program's office and budget in fall 2002. The RCCP's $1.8 million budget was dispersed to local school districts and the infrastructure of conflict-resolution training that its staff had built was severely undermined. Shortly after, then-Mayor Michael Bloomberg and the schools chancellor, Joel Klein, held a press conference to announce Operation Safe Schools, a get-tough public relations effort to deploy 129 more security guards and add surveillance cameras in eleven high schools.

Not surprisingly, statistics on school crimes released a month before the city's new school security initiative was announced showed a 14 percent drop for the year in the six major crime categories., while rates at the ten highest-crime schools dropped by an average of 46 percent for the year. Among those schools were five slated to get surveillance cameras. The Morningside Center continues the RCCP and other programs to promote social and emotional learning among students from its base at Teachers College at Columbia University. Supported by grants and school-based funding by supportive principals, the conflict-resolution program's track record grows longer and it continues to plant the seeds for ever more peace helpers in classrooms around the city.

REALITY-BASED DRUG EDUCATION

"I met some friends on campus at lunchtime and we drank gin. I took one big sip and I was feeling tipsy," the teenaged girl says. "Then when I was in my fifth-period class, my friend pulled on my hair and I fell over! The teacher came over and I told her I was drunk. I begged her not to call security. So the teacher said if I went to talk with Chuck, she won't report me." The girl is a student at Oakland High School, in Oakland, California, and Chuck is Chuck Ries, the executive director and founder of UpFront, a program that turns the "just say no" approach to drug education upside down by dealing with the reality of drug and alcohol use in young people's lives. The girl was sitting with Ries in UpFront's office, which occupies the high school's former automotive shop build-ing. A bubbly, articulate African-American girl, she promised to attend counseling sessions for the rest of the school year and as a consequence, faced no punitive sanctions. "I don't want to go that way," she says of her experimentation with binge drinking. "I can't predict the future, but I hope I don't. They give me ideas of why not to drink. I told my friends they should try it, too, but they say everything Chuck says is a lie, they'll fill your head with lies." Ries looks on and nods his head. "That's the fallout from their early drug education," he says.

UpFront is Ries's brainchild, a small program that is generating big results and excellent ratings from state evaluators in providing what's called a reality-based approach to drug education. At a time when random drug testing is being touted as the silver bullet to deter youth drug and alcohol use, UpFront offers students honest inquiry, not threats, in understanding substance use and abuse. Absent are the moralizing, preaching, and scared-straight tactics that characterize conventional drug-education programs. "We have to undo all the indoctrination they've had, like DARE," says Ries. "It creates a top-heavy, authoritarian approach. It also creates curiosity about drugs. I would never come in with pictures of all those illegal drugs. Who would do that?" Ries is a tall, gregarious man in his early fifties with an easy manner and obvious affinity for the young people he works with. He dresses casually in jeans and a shirt with sleeves rolled up, an earring in one earlobe and a beard that, like his hair, is touched with some gray. His background includes a degree in addiction studies and "nineteen years of using experience," he says of his own years of substance abuse. Honesty is indispensable to the program, so when students ask about Ries's drug use, "I tell them the truth. I never bring it up unless they ask because I think it's inappropriate. It takes a mindful person to tell a story without bringing out the drama."

The girl who was drunk in class is among the roughly 5 percent of students who are referred to UpFront's programs as disciplinary problems—the "you got caught" kids. The rest participate voluntarily, usually with a class whose teacher makes the sessions part of the curriculum. During the school year, the UpFront crew—Ries and his three counselors—is at Oakland High four days a week providing forty hours of programs, including groups with classes, workshops, and a lunchtime drop in group for students. "This year, we have twelve or so at lunchtime. We feed people and pay other students to facilitate," Ries says. "We have a discussion but it is a social thing, they make friends and we offer a safe place to come for lunch." In the course of the year, 400 to 500 of the school's 2,000 students will come through one of UpFront's programs. "Some people really hate it," Ries admits. "And almost all say it was valuable, even those who say they hate it." The UpFront approach begins with the students—what they know, what they think, and what they feel about drugs and alcohol. Their feedback, obtained through regular surveys, helps Ries and his colleagues design the program. The reality of these students' lives is that drugs are omnipresent, and many if not most will have tried them in their adolescence, marijuana, alcohol, and Ecstasy being the main ones. Ries and the other adult facilitators guide discussion, but it is the young people and their experiences that shape what happens. "What we do is try to reframe the conversation, being one in which drug use is a personal choice. When we are in group, we like to feel our experiences are important, our voices are important, but also we want to know that the group is managed and it's safe," he says.

There are ground rules. Cell phones must be turned off and no student will be permitted to criticize or put down anyone else. And all the discussions are strictly confidential: what is said in the group must stay in the group so that everyone feels safe to be as open as they want to be. The only exception is if a student poses a danger to himself or herself or others, in which case the facilitator is obliged to report the problem to school or law enforcement authorities. The meeting room is large enough to fit about thirty chairs around its perimeter but small enough to encourage a sense of group intimacy. Signs taped to the walls say "Agree," "Disagree," "Strongly Agree," and "Strongly Disagree." At the first group session on one April 2007 morning, a statistics class of thirteen, most of them seniors, files into the room and takes their seats. It is four days after a tragic shooting at Virginia Tech by a mentally disturbed young man and the students are all abuzz about it. Like Oakland High, the group is mostly African-American and Asian students with a smaller fraction of Latinos. Ries skillfully draws out the teens, getting them to talk about senior stress, and their sense of powerlessness in life and the pressure they face from their parents. He uses the Virginia Tech incident to inquire about bullying and students feeling alone and isolated. One seventeen-year-old African-American male talks articulately and movingly about the stress he feels at home, especially from his mother, whom he calls a hypocrite for doing things that she criticizes him for. This day, drugs and alcohol are not mentioned explicitly, but the weekly sessions build a dialogue among students that allows open communication about all facets of the teens' lives, even when they choose risky behavior. Harm reduction is the operating principle. "Curiosity drives adolescents. They're dying to talk about their drug experience, some of which is driven by the need to self-medicate or kill pain. Exploration is also a big part of it," Ries says. "If the expectation of drug education is to indoctrinate people not to do it, we'll always fail. Adolescence is a time of risk taking. If they're going to take risks, we want them to take as few as possible—and to learn from them. Here, we present a foundation of knowledge so that when they do go into a situation where they are confronted by risks, they can make good decisions."

The cost for UpFront is a relative pittance—$50,000 to $80,000 a year in Oakland High School. Ries said his program has been rated as exemplary by two outside evaluators sent by the state education department. UCLA professor of education emeritus Rod Skager, who has researched and written on drug and alcohol education programs, cited UpFront as an example of an alternative to zero tolerance approaches in his handbook *Beyond Zero Tolerance: A Reality-Based Approach to Drug Education*.[6] The program was set to expand into other district high schools when California was hit by a budget shortfall that put education into austerity mode. But for now, UpFront is a small but effective alternative to the well-funded and politically popular programs that leave young people misinformed and unprepared to make intelligent, healthy decisions in their lives.

HARD TIME IN BIG EASY SCHOOLS

It's difficult to believe that New Orleans public schools could have gotten any worse, but after Hurricane Katrina washed away the city on August 29, 2005, that is what happened. Pre-Katrina, 102 of 128 New Orleans public schools were academically failing and the whole district had one of the lowest high school graduation rates in the country.[7] A quasi-public charter school system, with selective admissions and vast funding resources, was getting all the attention and higher achieving students as a second, parallel system continued to deteriorate. In 2003, the state created the Recovery School District in response to the abysmal state of public education, empowering the new entity to take over the worst performing schools. After Katrina, seventeen schools initially opened under RSD control, a fraction of what existed before flooding made many schools unusable and scattered about half the student population beyond the city's boundaries. The RSD's poor performance lost all semblance of educational normalcy after the Katrina flood waters receded. What was left of the RSD schools was, by the accounts of students who slowly returned to them, a purgatory of chaotic, filthy conditions, outdated books and, perhaps worst of all, a flood of untrained and armed security guards who treated students like prisoners in a detention center. In many ways, that is exactly what they were.

Confronted by a crisis in its schools, which were severely understaffed by certified teachers, the RSD superintendent Robin Jarvis reacted with a Lockdown approach. She signed a $20 million contract with the Guidry Group, a Texas-based corporate security firm, which subcontracted with Day & Zimmermann, a firm that provides security at U.S. military and research facilities. Before Katrina, New Orleans spent $2.9 million on security for all its schools. The astronomical increase for security sent 259 armed security guards trained for military operations into schools serving just 9,500 students—and some 70 vacancies for teachers went unfilled. The ratio of guards to students averaged 1 to 37 in the RSD's schools. In John McDonogh High School, 35 private security guards and several off-duty New Orleans police officers were posted, surpassing the number of teachers in classrooms. Reports of security guards strong-arming and abusing even elementary school kids were spreading out from parents to community organizations. "It was a crisis. Kids were being handcuffed, they were forced to undergo strict security procedures to get into their schools. The guards were mostly eighteen- and nineteen-year-olds who had no training," says Ellen Tuzzolo, a youth advocate at the Juvenile Justice Project of Louisiana. The heavy policing was producing results, but not educational ones: student suspensions, expulsions and arrests were continuing at their high, pre-Katrina levels, with up to a third of all juvenile court referrals originating in the schools. The JJPLA began working with students and with other community groups, including the Downtown Neighborhood Improvement Association and Friends and Family of Louisiana Incarcerated Children, to force the RSD to slash the security contract to Guidry and channel the money into more teachers and counselors for students. A study by Louisiana State University which found that 54 percent of children returning to New Orleans after Katrina were experiencing emotional trauma and in need of services added to the urgency of ejecting the policing strategy, which could only worsen students' well-being.[8]

On October 9, 2006, a newly formed student organization, the Fyre Youth Squad, staged a press conference in front of McDonogh High to condemn the conditions inside their school and other RSD schools and to demand an end to the "prisonlike" environment fostered by metal detectors and armed security. The Squad continued to meet under the sponsorship of the DNIA and the coalition of youth advocates forced meetings with RSD administrators and school board members. Slowly but surely their applied pressure began to pay off. When Paul Vallas, former Philadelphia school district head, was hired as RSD superintendent in 2007, the advocates pushed him to rethink the approach to security and start putting resources into the children. "We organized with parents and students and had a press conference asking that Vallas end the contract with Guidry and start an in-house system of security," says Damekia Morgan, an organizer with FFLIC. "We met with Eddie Compass, the RSD security person, who was chief of police before Katrina. His budget is now eight million dollars [for the 2007-2008 school year]. They are also using a new system of training for the new cadets coming in, and we asked to participate in those trainings. We're trying to reduce the number of security personnel while also improving discipline." Morgan, who was a New Orleans teacher before Katrina struck, describes her organization's work as two-pronged: to reform Louisiana's prison system and the schools where students risk increased contact with law enforcement or being pushed out onto the streets and into trouble. "We're looking at ways to keep kids in school and not getting suspended or expelled," she says.

The broad coalition of student and community activists scored a significant victory in early 2008 when the RSD administration adopted a vastly improved student disciplinary code. Ellen Tuzzulo and the JJPLA issued a brief about the high rate of student suspensions and expulsions, which led to a meeting with district administrators. "A fellow advocate told me about a statute in Louisiana that requires a district to rewrite its disciplinary code annually. So I brought a copy with me and waved it at people in the meeting," she says. "We met with many people over many months. It's not as perfect as I'd like to see, but it's just leaps and bounds ahead of what was in place before." The revised code applies to RSD schools, where the highest numbers of suspensions and expulsions occur, and took effect in the 2008-2009 school year. It does not include a protection of students' due process rights or a detailed section on the role of security and police and strategies for reducing arrests, Tuzzulo notes. But what it does do is significant:

• Reduces instructional time lost to unnecessary removals by reducing the number of school-based infractions that are "suspendable" and "expellable" and by increasing the use of school-based interventions and alternatives to suspension and expulsion.

- Infuses the Student Code of Conduct with useful and family-friendly information for parents and students about their rights in discipline proceedings.

- Aligns the policies in the code of conduct with the principles of school-wide positive behavioral supports, an approach to school discipline that emphasizes students' strengths and achievements instead of their failures and mistakes.

RESTORING DIGNITY IN THE SCHOOLHOUSE

New Orleans is among several large urban school districts in which community and student activism against runaway suspensions and skyrocketing police arrests is leading to a change in disciplinary policies. In June 2007, the Chicago Board of Education did what would have been unthinkable just ten years ago when it adopted a new student code of conduct. Four years of organizing by student advocates, including Parents Organized to Win, Educate, and Renew, led to an important first step in 2006 when the board removed zero tolerance language from the code. The revisions adopted a year later incorporate into the code the principles of age-appropriate discipline and restorative justice, an alternative to punitive discipline that allows wrongdoers to acknowledge and remediate misbehavior before a jury of their peers. "Back when I was in high school, you could be expelled if you had drugs. But today, kids are suspended for talking back to teachers, even for being tardy or skipping classes," says Christine Agaiby, a restorative justice specialist at Alternatives, a Chicago youth agency who was involved in writing the new code. "Chicago Public Schools was being held accountable by police who were sick of making arrests in schools. The arrest rates were incredible." Alternatives had been doing restorative justice work, which had been written in the juvenile justice code in 1999, organizing peer juries as an alternative to juvenile detention. "In 2000, the Chicago Public Schools central office took notice of what was happening, and other people were telling CPS of the benefits of restorative justice."

Alternatives got a contract to do restorative justice work in twenty schools, which included creating an advisory board of attorneys, judges, and community organizers. In 2007, the program was in forty-three Chicago schools, and the impact on student discipline has been dramatic,

Agaiby says. "I can tell you that for last school year [2006-2007], because students went to peer jury, we avoided 1,026 suspensions. That is counting thirty-one schools. We'll probably avoid more than that because recidivism isn't high." And the program has an 89 percent completion rate for students who are "sentenced" by their peer juries to community service or other works. But there is much more that has to be done. Alternatives is hoping to bring conflict-resolution programs into the elementary schools as a natural precursor to peer jury programs in the higher grades. Not all of the forty-three schools with peer juries are working at the optimal level, and there's a need for more training of teachers and other school staff. And even though the student code now states that restorative justice should be used when appropriate, the culture change is not embraced by all school administrators and the zero-tolerance mentality persists. "This morning I was speaking with a community organizer who said a five-year-old was taken out of school in handcuffs. People are unaware it still goes on," Agaiby says. "There are principals who think youth aren't equipped to make decisions. Adults giving up a little power is a difficult thing." Still, she is hopeful that Chicago is modeling positive change: "I hope other cities are noticing it and paying attention."

Denver, Colorado, was just steps behind Chicago. The Mile-High City's public school system was a case study in the school-to-prison-pipeline phenomenon—literally. The Advancement Project in Washington, D.C., had partnered with the Denver community organization Padres and Jovenes Unidos to document the epidemic of suspensions and police ticketing of students, disproportionately Latinos. Their findings were published in 2004 in the report "Education on Lockdown: The Schoolhouse to Jailhouse Track," shining a spotlight on the negative effects of zero-tolerance policies on student academic success. That year, Padres and Jovenes began working with the school district's committee on discipline to reform policies that were clearly unsuccessful. In August 2008, organizers celebrated the adoption of a new Denver Public Schools disciplinary policy that contains significant improvements:

- Schools are now encouraged to work with students and parents on preventing disciplinary problems with early interventions.

- In-school suspensions and other school-based programs, including restorative justice, are alternatives to out-of-school punishments that disrupt education.
- Fewer out-of-school suspensions and expulsions will mean fewer police referrals, which should be reserved for only the most serious misconduct.

Los Angeles Unified School District has also taken a giant step forward toward an enlightened disciplinary policy for students when the Board of Education voted in 2007 to implement Positive Behavior Support (PBS) as a district-wide policy for every school in the district. In a public school system where suspensions, arrests, and academic failure are undermining the mission to educate, the LAUSD action is radical indeed. And as in other cities, the change was propelled from the grass-roots by parent, student, and community organizers. "It is a paradigm shift," says Maisie Chin, a co-founder of CADRE, a parent membership organization founded in 2001 to address problems in the LA public schools. Discipline and security were always a key issue, Chin says, and activism to change the zero-tolerance approach has been a way to engage parents in the schools to advocate for their children. "We're going to monitor the new policy heavily in District Seven, which has some of worst schools in the city. This is a litmus test for us. We're going to train parents. It will be harder to escape criticism. For positive behavior supports to be effective, it has to be whole climate change. We want suspensions reduced. It is going to be a hard fight."

The new policy lays out very specific school-based plans for using PBS, which include teaching school rules and social emotional skills; reinforcing appropriate student behavior; using effective classroom management; providing early intervention for misconduct; and appropriate use of consequences.

"It's a major step forward in Los Angeles," says Liz Sullivan, coordinator of the Dignity in Schools campaign of the National Economic and Social Rights Initiative (NESRI), a New York-based organization. The Campaign worked with CADRE in documenting abusive school discipline in LA schools and published a report on discipline problems in LA and New York City schools in March 2007.[9] In the 2007–2008 academic year, the LA school district began training administrators in the PBS approach in order to reduce suspensions, Sullivan says. In fall 2008, the LAUSD began implementing the new policy district-wide. "CADRE will be monitoring progress to see if it has an impact on suspensions," she says. "Just the fact that there was a movement, pressure from the community that had support from the teachers' union, as well as progressive people in the city's education department, put pressure on the Board of Education." Dignity in Schools campaign partners represent civil rights and educational reform groups around the country, reaching nearly 40 member groups by 2010.

Dignity in Schools has targeted the push-out problem in public schools, fed by high suspension rates and zero tolerance, casting it as a key component of the school-to-prison pipeline. Throughout 2010, the campaign built momentum to petition Congress and President Barack Obama to make fundamental changes to No Child Left Behind (NCLB), which is due to be reauthorized. Although Obama as an Illinois senator had authored legislation to promote positive behavioral supports as an alternative disciplinary policy for schools, as president his education agenda so far has been disappointing. With former Chicago super-intendent of schools Arne Duncan as Obama's secretary of education, there has been continued emphasis on testing and competition—among states and schools—for federal funding. Duncan's Race to the Top, a $4 billion funding program, has pitted states against each other to compete for funding at a time of economic recession.

NCLB was President George W. Bush's revision to the Elementary and Secondary Education Act of 1965, created to address inequalities in education for low-income children, mostly black and Latino. But since NCLB was approved in 2002, Dignity in Schools argues, the law has done more harm than good and opened wider inequalities with a relent-less focus on high-stakes testing and punitive approaches to student, teacher, and school-wide achievement. In a joint position paper authored by six member groups—the Advancement Project, Fair Test, the Juvenile Law Center, the Education Law Center, the Forum for Education and Democracy, and the NAACP Legal Defense and Education Fund—Dignity in Schools makes the compelling case that Congress must investigate how NCLB has failed to narrow educational achievement gaps: "No Child Left Behind's 'get-tough' approach to accountability has led to more students being left further behind, thus feeding the dropout crisis and the School-to-Prison Pipeline." The policy paper argues that "a revised ESEA could, through affirmative measures, bolster graduation rates and academic achievement by addressing the policies and practices that have resulted in overuse of punitive discipline, school exclusion, and justice-system intervention."

The prescription for revamping NCLB includes a de-emphasis on testing—especially the high-stakes testing that acts as a cudgel for students and administrators alike—and development of other assessment tools that use multiple factors in rating student and school achievement. It also calls for alternative disciplinary systems that replace zero tolerance with policies that emphasize prevention. And the paper calls on the government to put resources into improving the school climate, with extra help going to schools with high rates of disciplinary problems, so those schools can keep their students in classrooms, not jail cells.

Sullivan believes that a critical mass for change is taking root because the failures of zero tolerance are reaching a tipping point. "People are seeing the impact it's having on kids, and not just isolated cases. Zero tolerance is effecting the educational environment badly," Sullivan explains. "Teachers are getting fed up with it as well. We found that teachers were police-supportive because they don't have support staff to help. So having safety agents in the hallway in a chaotic environment is better than nothing. But we now hear teachers say, we know it isn't addressing students' needs, but that's what we have. One teacher says he feels safer with metal detectors, but then he sees the harassment of kids coming through the detectors. They are torn."

The campaign is trying to support local efforts to reform but also to change the national dialogue. "We want to encourage school districts to take on new approaches to discipline," Sullivan says. "Use discipline as a constructive part of learning, make it part of kids' social-emotional development—that is how we should be talking about safety and discipline."

NOTES

CHAPTER ONE. A BRIEF HISTORY OF SCHOOL VIOLENCE

1. Jonathan Messerli, *Horace Mann* (New York: Knopf, 1972), p. 373.
2. David Nasaw, *Schooled to Order: A Social History of Public Schooling in the United States* (New York: Oxford University Press, 1979), p. 75; Michael B. Katz, *The Irony of Early School Reform: Educational Innovation in Mid-Nineteenth Century Massachusetts* (Cambridge: Harvard University Press, 1968), p. 164.
3. Cited in Ira Katznelson and Margaret Weir, *Schooling for All* (New York: Basic Books, 1985), pp. 68–69; from a Chicago Board of Education member, quoted in Edith Abbot, *Truancy and Non-Attendance in Chicago's Schools* (Chicago: University of Chicago Press, 1917), p. 85.
4. Lawrence A. Cremin, *American Education: The National Experience, 1783–1876* (New York: Harper & Row, 1980), p. 395.
5. Cited in Stuart G. Noble, *A History of American Education* (NY: Holt, Rinehart & Winston, 1954), pp. 513–14.
6. Warren Burton, *The District School as It Was* (Boston: Carter, Hendee and Co., 1833), pp. 25–26, 46.
7. "My School-Boy Days in New York City Forty Years Ago," in *New York Teacher and American Educational Monthly*, March 1869.
8. Loulie Ayer Beall, "A Webster County School," *Nebraska History* 33, July–Sept. 1942, p. 200.
9. I. L. Kephart, "Barring Out the Teacher," in Asa Earl Martin and Hiram Herr Shenk, eds., *Pennsylvania History Told by Contemporaries* (New York: MacMillan Company, 1925), pp. 393–96.

10. Richard V. McCann, *Delinquency: Sickness or Sin?* (New York: Harper & Brothers, 1957), p. ix.

11. Martin H. Neumeyer, *Juvenile Delinquency in Modern Society* (Princeton: D. Van Nostrand Company, 1949, 1955), p. 3.

12. McCann, *Delinqency*, p. 55.

13. Sheldon and Eleanor Glueck, *Unraveling Juvenile Delinquency* (New York: Commonwealth Fund, 1950).

14. D. J. R. Bruckner, "Daley Loosed a Terror That Won't Go Away," *Los Angeles Times*, reprinted in *Washington Post*, April 21, 1968.

15. Charles G. Bennett, "Lindsay Moves to Thwart Rising School Violence," *New York Times,* March 11, 1969, p. 37.

16. Leonard Buder, "Study Opens Here on School Unrest," *New York Times*, Nov. 8, 1969.

17. Marin Weil, "Teachers Demand Steps to End School Violence," *Washington Post*, Jan. 27, 1969, p. A1.

18. Lawrence Feinberg, "Slain Student 1st Killed in D.C. Schools," *Washington Post*, Jan. 6, 1970, p. A5; Douglas Watson, "22 Students Held in DuVal Clash" and "D.C. Schools to Get Director of Safety," *Washington Post,* Jan. 13, 1970.

19. Wayne King, "Schools Hire Own Guards as Violence Rises Sharply," *New York Times*, Jan. 12, 1970.

20. UPI, "Study Cites Surge In School Violence," *Washington Post*, Jan. 13, 1970.

21. Rowland Evans and Robert Novak, "High Schools Becoming Battlefield of the Racial Turmoil in America," *Washington Post*, Jan. 5, 1970, p. 19.

22. King, "Schools Hire Own Guards as Violence Rises Sharply."

23. Gary Orfield, *Must We Bus? Segregated Schools and National Policy* (Washington, D.C.: Brookings Institution, 1978), p. 127, citing a letter from Assistant Attorney General Ben Holman to Senators Edward Brooke and Jacob Javits, June 10, 1976, and reprinted in *Congressional Record*, June 26, 1976, p. S10708–11.

24. Austin Scott, "11 Per Cent Seen Victims of Theft in High Schools," *Washington Post*, Jan. 6, 1978.

25. Franklin E. Zimring, *American Youth Violence* (New York: Oxford University Press, 1998), p. 32.

26. Mary Thornton, "News Leaks Are Hunted in Justice: 3 Employees Quizzed About Meese Stories," *Washington Post*, June 7, 1984.

27. K. Maguire and A. L. Pastore, eds., *Sourcebook of Criminal Justice Statistics—1995*, U.S. Department of Justice, Bureau of Justice Statistics (Washington, D.C.: U.S.

Government Printing Office, 1996), cited in "Violence in American Schools: An Overview," in Delbert S. Elliot, Beatrix A. Hamburg, and Kirk R. Williams, eds., *Violence in American Schools: A New Perspective* (New York: Cambridge University Press, 1998), p. 9.

28. Zimring, *American Youth Violence*, pp. 49–50.

29. Sam Dillion, "On the Barricades Against Violence in the Schools; As Fears Over Security Grow, New York's School Safety Force Struggles to Keep Up," *New York Times*, Dec. 24, 1993.

30. Kim Brooks, Vincent Schiraldi, and Jason Ziedenberg, "School House Hype: Two Years Later," Justice Policy Institute/Children's Law Center, 2000, p. 6.

31. U.S. Departments of Education and Justice, "Indicators of School Crime and Safety: 2002," p. 4; nonfatal violent crimes include assault, robbery, sexual assault, and rape.

32. Ibid., pp. 8, 34.

33. U.S. Departments of Education and Justice, "Indicators of School Crime and Safety: 2006," p. 6. The definition of school associated deaths includes students killed going to and from school or to a school-sponsored event, unintentional firearm deaths, such as a gun accidentally discharging, and students or school employees killed by a police officer at a school.

34. Brooks, Schiraldi, and Ziedenberg, "School House Hype," p. 4.

35. Lawrence W. Sherman, "The Safe and Drug-Free Schools Program," Brookings Papers on Educational Policy, 2000.

36. Ralph Frammolino, "Failing Grade for Safe Schools Plan," *Los Angeles Times*, Sept. 6, 1998.

CHAPTER TWO. WE ARE COLUMBINE

1. Pew Research Center for the People and the Press, "Columbine Shooting Biggest News Draw of 1999," Dec. 28, 1999.

2. Arlene Levinson, "Clinton Trial, Colorado Massacre Voted Top '99 Stories," *San Angelo Standard-Times*, Dec. 27, 1999, cited in Iris Hsiang Chyi and Maxwell McCombs, "Media Salience and the Process of Framing: Coverage of the Columbine School Shootings," *Journalism and Mass Communication Quarterly* 81 (1), Spring 2004, pp. 22–35.

3. Ethan Bronner, "The Columbine Killings Fuel a New Debate About Free Speech, Privacy—and the Right to be Safe in School: Are Schools Overreacting?" *New York Times*, Sept. 6, 1999.

4. Kim Brooks, Vincent Schiraldi, and Jason Zeidenberg, "School House Hype: Two Years Later," Justice Policy Institute/Children's Law Center, 2000, p. 7.

5. One highly publicized outlier was a Native American teen who shot and killed nine people at home and at his school on a reservation in Red Lake, Wisconsin, in 2005.

6. From Mike Males, *Framing Youth: 10 Myths About the Next Generation* (Maine: Common Courage Press, 1999), pp. 56–57.

7. Sara Rimer, "Good Grades, Good Teams and Some Bad Feelings," *New York Times*, April 22, 1999.

8. Mike Males, *Kids and Guns: How Politicians, Experts, and the Media Fabricate Fear of Youth*, rev. ed., Chapter 3: "The 'School Violence' and 'Kids and Guns' Hoaxes" (Maine: Common Courage Press, 2004).

9. United States Secret Service and the U.S. Department of Education, "Threat Assessment in Schools: A Guide to Managing Threatening Situations and to Creating Safe School Climates," May 2002, p. 5.

10. Steve Gutterman, Associated Press, "Gun Dealers Defensive at Show Where Columbine Weapons Were Sold," *Topeka Capital-Journal*, June 6, 1999.

11. "Source of Firearms Used by Students in School-Associated Violent Deaths—United States, 1992–1999," Centers for Disease Control, *Morbidity and Mortality Weekly Report* 52, no. 9, March 7, 2003.

12. Kaia Gallagher, *Suicide in Colorado* (Denver: The Colorado Trust, 2002).

13. "The Report of Governor Bill Owens' Columbine Review Commission," State of Colorado, May 2001, p. xviii.

14. "Columbine High School, School Accountability Report, 2005–2006 School Year," jeffco.k12.co.us/profiles/accountability/high/columbine.pdf, accessed April 15, 2008.

15. "The Report of Gov. Bill Owens' Columbine Review Commission," p. 98, n. 211.

CHAPTER THREE. CRIME AND PUNISHMENT: THE ZERO TOLERANCE EPIDEMIC

1. See Howard Witt, "To Some in Paris, Sinister Past Is Back," *Chicago Tribune*, March 12, 2007; "Girl in Prison for Shove Gets Early Release," *Chicago Tribune*, March 31, 2007; and "Freed Teen: I Feel Like I Have a Second Chance," *Chicago Tribune*, April 1, 2007.

2. Paris Schools Superintendent Paul Trull responded by e-mail on July 24, 2008, to requests for comment on the federal investigation into his district's disciplinary practices and allegations of racial discrimination: "The Paris

Independent School District has opened its records to the Office of Civil Rights, and in each and every completed investigation they have returned without finding discrimination. The school district is not permitted to open its student records to the media in order to combat false accusations. Moreover, the same individuals have repeatedly filed claims of discrimination which the Office of Civil Rights has determined were not supported by the objective evidence. If the parents that claim discrimination to the media were to sign an authorization form permitting the media to actually see the records rather than accepting as fact their allegations, PISD would relish the opportunity to share the actual evidence with the media and let the media objectively decide for themselves. It would be irresponsible for any credible media to presume that OCR and PISD are working together against these parents to discriminate against children, especially since it is the parents that are withholding the ability of both to release the documents that the parents claim support their allegations."

3. From "Opportunities Suspended: The Devastating Consequences of Zero Tolerance and School Discipline Policies," the Advancement Project and the Civil Rights Project, June 2000, p. 3.

4. Associated Press, "Wedgie Prank Earns Youths Community Service," Nov. 13, 1997, and "School Graffiti Nets 4-Months Suspension," July 7, 2007.

5. Augustina H. Reyes, *Discipline, Achievement, Race: Is Zero Tolerance the Answer?* (Lanham, Md.: Rowman & Littlefield, 2006), pp. 26–35.

6. Joy Mordica, "Analysis of Statewide Disciplinary Data: Executive Summary," Georgia Department of Education, Policy Division Report 2004–2005.

7. Russell J. Skiba et al., "Color of Discipline: Sources of Racial and Gender Disproportionality in School Punishment," Indiana Education Policy Center, June 2000, p. 2.

8. Skiba et al., "Color of Discipline," p. 17.

9. Deborah Fowler et al., Texas Appleseed, "Texas' School to Prison Pipeline: Drop Out to Incarceration, the Impact of School Discipline and Zero Tolerance," Oct. 2007.

10. Walter S. Gilliam, "Prekindergarteners Left Behind: Expulsion Rates in State Prekindergarten Programs," Foundation for Child Development, Policy Brief Series no. 3, May 2005.

11. Cited in Fowler et al., "Texas' School-to-Prison Pipeline," pp. 130–31.

12. Ibid., p. 64.

13. Ibid., pp. 2–5.

14. This section was originally published in *The Nation* as "Failing Students, Rising Profits," Sept. 19, 2005.

15. Russell Skiba et al., "Are Zero Tolerance Policies Effective in the Schools? An Evidentiary Review and Recommendations," a Report by the American Psychological Association Zero Tolerance Task Force, Aug. 9, 2006.

CHAPTER FOUR. SUPERMAX SCHOOLHOUSE

1. Rachel Dinkes et al., *Indicators of School Crime and Safety: 2006* (Washington, D.C.: National Center for Education Statistics, 2006), pp. 111–13.

2. *Security* magazine, Sept. 2006.

3. From Nicole A. Ozer, "Rights 'Chipped' Away: RFID and Identification Documents," *Stanford Technology Law Review*, 2008, stlr.stanford.edu/pdf/ ozer-rights-chipped-away.pdf, p. 6.

4. From SIAonline.org, accessed July 12, 2007.

5. "Report Card Narratives: Plumsted Twp," From the NJ DOE website, http:// www.state.nj.us/education/, accessed Aug. 12, 2007.

6. Angela Delli Santi, Associated Press, "Tiny New Jersey School District Testing Cutting Edge 'Eye Recognition' Security System," April 21, 2003.

7. Craig D. Uchida et al., "Safe Kids, Safe Schools: Evaluating the Use of Iris Recognition Technology in New Egypt, New Jersey," 21st Century Solutions, Aug. 2004.

8. Suzanne West, "New Caney ISD Computer Program Assists with Safety," *Houston Chronicle*, Oct. 2, 2003.

9. From "Penn Cambria School District: Demographic Information," retrieved from district's website, http://www.pcam.org/pcam/, on June 25, 2007.

10. From "Fingerprint Technology Speeds School Lunch Lines," *eSchool News*, Jan. 29, 2001.

CHAPTER FIVE. THE WAR ON DRUGS GOES TO SCHOOL

1. Dorianne Beyer, "School Safety and the Legal Rights of Students: Selected Issues," ERIC Clearinghouse on Urban Education, no. 121, May 1997.

2. Government Accounting Office, "Contractor's Evaluation Did Not Find That the Youth Anti-Drug Media Campaign Was Effective in Reducing Youth Drug Use," Aug. 2006 report to Congress, pp. 6–7.

3. Katie Ash, "Steroid-Testing Plans in Texas and Illinois Are Moving Forward," *Education Week*, Jan. 23, 2008.

4. Robert DuPont, Teresa G. Campbell, and Jacqueline J. Mazza, "Report of a Preliminary Study: Elements of a Successful School-Based Student Drug

Testing Program," U.S. Department of Education, 2002, p. 8; cited in Jennifer Kern et al., "Making Sense of Student Drug Testing: Why Educators Are Saying No," American Civil Liberties Union and Drug Policy Alliance, Jan. 2006, p. 11.

5. Ryoko Yamaguchi, Lloyd D. Johnston, and Patrick M. O'Malley, "Youth, Education and Society: Drug Testing in Schools: Policies, Practices and Association with Student Drug Use," Institute for Social Research, University of Michigan, Ann Arbor, 2003.

CHAPTER SIX. THE PROFITEERS OF LOCKDOWN HIGH

1. Linda Pohle, "An Education Market Primer," *SDM* magazine, June 1, 2007, www.sdmmag.com/CDA/Archives/BNP_GUID_9-5-2006_A_1000000 0000000115399; accessed Jan. 7, 2008.

2. Associated Press, "School Security Business Booming," April 28, 1999. Interesting to note is that Columbine H.S. chose not to install metal detectors after the infamous incident.

3. National School Safety Center, "Safeguarding Schools Against Terrorism," 2004.

4. Tom Breckenridge, "Anti-Gang Effort Caught in Officials' Crossfire," *Plain Dealer* (Cleveland), June 23, 1996.

5. Sherry Gavanditti, "Clevelander Locks in Role as Source on School Security," *Crain's Cleveland Business*, Nov. 13, 2006.

6. Amy Beth Graves, Associated Press, "ACLU Swamped with Complaints After Colorado Shootings," May 9, 1999.

7. Scott Stephens, "Budget Cuts, Other Pressures Sideline School Safety Plans," *Plain Dealer* (Cleveland), April 18, 2004.

8. In an e-mail message of Feb. 8, 2008, Tom Snyder, program director and a co-author of the NCES annual "Indicators of School Crime and Safety," responded to my queries about Kenneth Trump's criticisms of those reports and data showing a downward trend in school crime as being inaccurate:

> "There is evidence to believe that there is some under-reporting of school crime. On the other hand, there is no reason to suspect that this under-reporting has increased over time. If anything, there has been more pressure to fully account for crime. Since the statistical data show a decline over time, there is every reason to believe that an actual decline has occurred, even if there may be some under-accounting of the overall level. We also present data reported by both schools and individuals. The data reported by individuals show the longer time

trend where the decline has been noted. Presumably, there is less bias in under-reporting of crimes by individuals.

"The statistics we present are averages of the entire country. Some areas probably did have increases in crime, which were more than counter-balanced by areas with decreasing crime. It is logical that consultants assisting districts with school crime problems are going to be disproportionately contacted by districts experiencing difficult situations. We feel that we add strength to the report by drawing on a variety of sources. The various sources provide different perspectives and additional detail. Also, they allow us to better confirm findings from the different surveys.

"We feel confident in reporting that school crime has declined over a 10 year period. But, as noted in the report, there are still a large number of crimes in schools. Our role as a statistical agency is to present the most reliable data we can provide on this important topic. This information is intended to be used by policy makers, researchers, school officials, and the general public to help develop effective practices to reduce school crime."

9. Todd Ruger, "DUI Charge Dropped Against Former Deputy," *Sarasota Herald-Tribune*, Oct. 7, 2005.
10. Christie Taylor, "On the Right Track: Raptor Technologies Tracking Software Has Made the Grade with School Districts Around the Country," *Houston Business Journal*, May 23, 2005.
11. *Horton v. Goose Creek Independent School District* in *Great American Court Cases*, vol. 9, p. 13036; Bill Crider, Associated Press, "Sniffing of Cars and Lockers Is OK," June 1, 1982.
12. R. Dinkes et al., "Indicators of School Crime and Safety: 2006," U.S. Departments of Education and Justice (Washington, D.C.: U.S. Government Printing Office, 2006), pp. 111–12.
13. Marianne Costantinou, "The American Way," *San Francisco Chronicle*, Aug. 12, 2001.
14. Reynolds Holding, "Whatever Happened to Drug Testing?" *Time*, July 7, 2006; Holding cites statistics from the American Management Association on employer drug testing.
15. Anick Jesdanun, Associated Press, "House Republicans Propose Drug Testing in Schools," April 29, 1999.
16. "Colorado School Shooting Jumpstarts Federal Efforts for School Drug Testing," *Drug Detection Report*, May 6, 1999, p. 65.

17. Neil A. Lewis, "The Supreme Court: Student Rights; Court's Stance on Searches Evolves," *New York Times*, June 28, 2002.

18. Walter Shapiro, "Student Privacy Just a Specimen for Profit, Politics," *USA Today*, July 19, 2002.

19. "Market for Drug Testing in Schools Is Only 5 Percent Tapped Into," *Drug Detection Report*, Oct. 3, 2002.

20. See Wesley M. Fager, "A Study of the Involvement of the Drug Free America Foundation, Inc. (formerly Straight Foundation, Inc.) in American and International Drug Policy," Oakton Institute, 2002; and Maia Szalavitz, "Penis Pump Case Goes Limp, but Serious Issues Remain," *Huffington Post*, Dec. 29, 2006.

21. "The Feasibility of Per Se Drugged Driving Legislation: Consensus Report, 2002," funded by the Robert Wood Johnson Foundation's Substance Abuse Policy Research Program; and Paul Armentano, "Drug Test Nation," *Reason*, Feb. 9, 2005.

22. "Legal Crusader Predicts Universal Drug & Alcohol Testing in Schools (Datia Meeting)," *Drug Detection Report*, June 12, 2003.

CHAPTER SEVEN. POLICING THE SCHOOLS, ARRESTING DEVELOPMENT

1. NTanya Lee, "Report on Police Misconduct at Thurgood Marshall Academic High School on Oct. 11, 2002," Coleman Advocates for Children and Youth, Sept. 22, 2004, p. 2.

2. "COPS in Schools" factsheet, Office of Community Oriented Policing, Department of Justice website, http://www.cops.usdoj.gov/; accessed Aug. 21, 2008.

3. NCES, "Indicators of School Crime and Safety 2006," p. 58.

4. Jack McDevitt and Jenn Panniello, "National Assessment of School Resource Officer Programs: Survey of Students in Three Large New SRO Programs," National Institute of Justice, Washington, D.C., Feb. 28, 2005.

5. P. E. Leone and M. J. Mayer, "Safety, Diversity, and Disability: 'Goodness of Fit' and the Complexities of the School Environment," in M. J. Furlong, M. P. Bates, and P. Kingery, eds., *Best Practices in School-Based Threat Assessment* (Hauppauge, N.Y.: Nova Science Publishers, 2004), pp. 135–63.

6. Amy C. Eisert, "School Resource Officer Evaluation," Center for Schools and Communities and Mercyhurst Civic Institute, Sept. 2005, pp. 3–4.

7. Randall R. Beger, "Expansion of Police Power in Public Schools and the Vanishing Rights of Students," *Social Justice* 29, nos. 1–2 (2002), p. 122.

8. "Cop Suspended for 'Ghetto Handbook': Houston School Police Officer Distributed Offensive Ebonics Primer," *The Smoking Gun*, Aug. 31, 2007.

9. R. Dinkes, E. F. Cataldi, and W. Lin-Kelly, "Indicators of School Crime and Safety: 2007," National Center for Education Statistics, 2007, p. 6.

10. Interview with Chief Jim Kelly, July 25, 2007, in West Palm Beach, Florida.

11. While Latinos comprise 20 percent of the district's students, the arrest data was disaggregated only for black and white students, according to Judith Browne-Dianis.

12. Lee, "Report on Police Misconduct at Thurgood Marshall Academic High School on Oct. 11, 2002," p. 7.

13. Data provided on Sept. 25, 2008, by Community Assessment and Referral, a nonprofit juvenile justice service organization, which collects statistics on juvenile arrests from the SFPD.

CHAPTER EIGHT. BUSTING OUT OF LOCKDOWN HIGH: ALTERNATIVE PATHS TO SAFE SCHOOLS

1. Matthew J. Mayer and Peter E. Leone, "A Structural Analysis of School Violence and Disruption: Implications for Creating Safer Schools," *Education and Treatment of Children* 22, no. 3, Aug. 1999, pp. 333–56.

2. David Cantor and Mareena McKinley Wright, "School Crime Patterns: A National Profile of U.S. Public High Schools Using Rates of Crime Reported to Police: Report on the Study on School Violence and Prevention," U.S. Department of Education, Contract No. EA96055001, Aug. 2002.

3. P. E. Leone and M. J. Mayer, "Safety, Diversity, and Disability: 'Goodness of Fit' and the Complexities of the School Environment," in M. J. Furlong, M. P. Bates, and P. Kingery, eds., *Best Practices in School-Based Threat Assessment* (Hauppauge, N.Y.: Nova Science Publishers, 2004), pp. 135–63.

4. In 2007, Educators for Social Responsibility Metro changed its name to the Morningside Center for Teaching Social Responsibility, and Tom Roderick continues as executive director.

5. Joshua L. Brown et al., "The Resolving Conflict Creatively Program: A School-Based Social and Emotional Learning Program," in *Building Academic Success on Social and Emotional Learning: What Does the Research Say?* (New York: Teachers College, Columbia University, 2004).

6. Theo Emery, "The Big Easy's Next Test," *Time*, Aug. 17, 2006.

7. Downtown Neighborhood Improvement Association, "Send in the Specialists! Position Paper Supporting the Reduction of Security and the Increase of Social Workers, Interventionists and Counselors in Our Schools," Jan. 18, 2007.

8. Elizabeth Sullivan, "Deprived of Dignity: Degrading Treatment and Abusive Discipline in New York City & Los Angeles Public Schools," National Economic & Social Rights Initiative, New York, 2007.

ACKNOWLEDGMENTS

The seed for this book was planted more than ten years ago during a fellowship I had at Columbia University's Graduate School of Journalism to focus on reporting about children's issues. My great friend and long-time colleague LynNell Hancock, a professor at the school and director of the fellowship program, encouraged me to pursue my growing interest in the glaring inequities children and young people were facing in the juvenile justice system. The seed germinated and grew and led me to explore the way the juvenile justice system's crackdown on kids was spreading into public schools. Karen Rothmyer, then managing editor of *The Nation*, encouraged me to pursue my ideas, publishing three articles related to the topic that inspired me to begin thinking about a book. I thank them both for their early and continuing support.

My reporting, research, and writing for the book took place primarily from 2005 to 2007, although some material and interviews were obtained for my earlier reporting for *The Nation*. Judith Browne-Dianis of the Advancement Project in Washington, D.C., did groundbreaking work on zero tolerance and the school-to-prison track and encouraged my book project. In the course of reporting, two other sources became friends and great supporters of my work: Rod Skager, emeritus professor of education at UCLA, and Jennifer Kern, an organizer for the Drug Policy Alliance whose boundless youthful energy and enthusiasm was inspirational.

Thanks, too, to my family, for moral support and encouragement over the course of the project. And gratitude to Paul Young, my partner, who has been with me in the homestretch, cheering me on and, better yet, nudging me to look ahead to the next book!

INDEX

Manes, Mark, 39

Mann, Horace, 2, 11

Marshall, Larry, 74

Martzloff, Scott, 164

Maufas, Kim-Shree, 172–75

Mauser, Tom, 27–28, 30, 40–41, 43–44

Mayer, Matthew J., 45, 183, 185

Mayo, Reginald, 82

McCann, Richard, 10

McCrackin, George, 155–56

McDonald's, 87

McGivney, Terrence, 132–33

McInnes, Bill, 73

McKinney, Joseph, 120

McVeigh, Timothy, 134

Meadows, Larry, 98–99

Meadows, Yvonne, 97–99

Measom, Allan, 99, 139–43

media, 21–22, 24, 29, 34, 36, 82, 93, 117,
    119, 135, 140–41, 156–57, 163
  on black vs white violence, 36
  on guns, 41–42
  and security sales, 141
  and security spending, 134

Meese, Edwin, 17

Megan's Law, 140

Melus, Sigrid, 124

metal detectors, 19, 24, 26, 38, 45, 47,
    77, 81–84, 86–87, 89–90, 131,
    134, 164, 176, 179, 182–83, 186,
    193, 199
  Columbine rejects, 49
  sale of, 131–32
  for urban schools, 36

Mexican American Legal Defense and
    Education Fund (MALDEF),
    99–100

Meyers, Greg, 156

Mills, Cheryl, 76

Mitchell, Irving, 77–78

Mixon, Juhan, 74

Monitoring the Future, 111–12, 121

Morgan, Damekia, 194

Morningside Center, 186–87, 189
  peace corner, 187

Moses, Mike, 75

Moss, Bill, 76

MySpace, 82

NASRO, 32, 132, 138–39, 141, 145,
    155, 160–64, 169
  conference, 161–64, 169
  membership, 161

National Center for Education
    Statistics, 20, 58, 136, 158

National Institute on Drug Abuse,
    112–13, 150, 152

National Institute of Justice (NIJ), 81,
    84–87, 94, 141, 158
  school safety grant, 94–96, 142

National Rifle Association (NRA), 24,
    41, 43–45

National School Board Association
    (NSBA)
  security sales, 131–46*passim*
    Allan Measom, 139–43
    Curtis Lavarello, 137–39
    Fisher Labs, 131–32
    Inner Link, 132
    Interquest, 143–46
    Ken Trump, 135–37
    Scholar Chip, 132–33
    Stopware, 133

NBC News, 22